African Americanized

An African Man's Life and
Expedient Americanization

Omosa Julius Morara

iUniverse, Inc.
New York   Bloomington

iUniverse books may be ordered through booksellers or by contacting:

iUniverse
1663 Liberty Drive
Bloomington, IN 47403
www.iuniverse.com
1-800-Authors (1-800-288-4677)

ISBN: 978-1-4401-7849-8 (sc)
ISBN: 978-1-4401-7848-1 (ebook)

Printed in the United States of America

iUniverse rev. date: 02/02/2010

This book is humbly dedicated to our beloved sister:

Mary Bonareri Omosa

August 5, 1961—November 23, 2009

CONTENTS

INTRODUCTION

The journey through America has not been, was never intended to be, and will never be easy! The Bible alone states that human life must be full of struggles.

In this humorous American safari, I stand at the intersection of African values and heritage thus contrasting the African way of life with the American culture. It is a sincere, painful experience considering the initial dilemma in which African immigrants find themselves in upon arrival in America, the newness of the situation, a uniquely shocking culture, and subsequent orientation and expediency to Americanization.

To me, the safari and circumstances involved, on my arrival, appeared like a "second birth" without undergoing the early stages of childhood, growth and development. It was a new life started all over again.

When we develop from childhood into adulthood, we are nurtured, oriented into life-preparedness by our seniors while they provide us with all the necessary care and basic needs for our survival. Whereas in a new land like America, we are left free of care and yet faced with life challenges which require mandatory, immediate attention and guidance, and the strange difference is that we have to learn on our own—mostly the hard way!

In America, opportunities are many but choices are limited, more especially to immigrants, in respect to ignorance and the process of learning and adaptation from one form of culture into another which surely requires guidance, training and orientation. Inexperience and the many other burdens which one must fulfill in order to have those opportunities accessible within the highly standardized American way of life, is likewise an ingredient in the Americanization process.

Despite the many challenges, the land ultimately brings the best out of individuals. They stand alone, take pride in their personally and painfully acquired gains, and sometimes learn from their mistakes and failures. In most cases, when people fail, in America, it only becomes a chance to amend, to grow, or simply a set-up for a comeback. It becomes an opportunity to learn from their mistakes and advance to the next level. This is the step-by-step process which helps immigrants, especially those of African origin, to progress in their everyday endeavors toward greater heights.

Truly, life's struggles in America enable people to explore their greatest potential and, yet, extremely delicate pathways through which they tread. If mistakes are ignorantly made in the course of such explorations, the legal consequences usually become a painful teacher by which the majority of immigrants and American born citizens learn—by learning that the American justice system is equitable to all, and no one is above the law, and it does not discriminate on gender, race, religious beliefs, opulence, indigence and, or social status. But before one graduates into this sort of complete Americanization, they will have been through some form of agonizing tribulation, turmoil and countless episodes as well as some positive lessons and achievements. It, in the end, makes us better people as carefully analyzed in these pages of *African Americanized*.

This book is intended to provide an understanding and a clear picture, to those born in America, of some of the pros and cons of having been born within the American way of life in comparison with the many challenges which immigrants face before they fully get acquainted with the American lifestyle. On the other hand, I urge and encourage

Americans to diversify their understanding in regard to other cultures of the world since they will always live with immigrants. It is also helpful as a tool of survival and a wider, fruitful living and as a means of access to diverse knowledge and wisdom, as opposed to their own.

Conversely, Africans—whose American experiences are the focus and subject of interest in this book, mine being a good instance, undergo detriments while they are still novices in the land but most of them consequently claim heroism, positivity and success because they are able to survive anywhere. They also painfully learn from their experiences toward a better tomorrow so as to achieve their goals. Upon adequate and rightful orientation, they in the end fall within a position that facilitates appropriate use of their survival skills and diverse African reminiscences. These are derived from extensive social, interactive training and uplifting proverbs and story-telling opportunities in Africa, which in many cases solidly guide the *African Child*; as pictorially illustrated in this book.

By living in the United States of America, I strongly believe that I'm a better person and more awakened than when I first arrived in the land.

Interactions with people from various backgrounds and ethnicities, and subsequent exposure, is of value to all people in our historic times, Americans inclusive. This prepares us for audacity into greater thinking levels and desires in our lives because extraordinary minds dream extraordinary dreams and likewise face extraordinary challenges which require equal strength to overcome.

I strongly believe in destiny for each one of us in our lives. For this reason, I know that each one of us has their own paths of failure and success as a way of defining and living our prescribed destinies. Therefore, there is a reason, probably unseen, yet, why I found myself in America to live and share knowledge and life-experiences with some of the carefully sorted out strong minds of the world. There is no perfect person or place on earth. America, too, has its pros and cons but it is one place that brings the best out of those who are willing to know the true potential of their souls. It is a level ground where the best and the worst have equal opportunity to bring out the best in themselves in whichever way possible, thus living to the fullest.

There are so many people in the world who have been denied such freedoms as compared to those in America—to explore their potential to the fullest. There are great men and women out there still living under the chains and fetters of selfish transgressors. These oppressors have forgotten that when God's people are not left to live with the freedom that is rightfully entrusted to them by their Creator, they, themselves are slaves of prejudice, hatred and narrow-mindedness.

Apart from formal education, exposure to the larger world constitutes at least half of our information and knowledge. For instance, just as much as the majority of Americans need exposure to the outside world in order to enlighten themselves about other cultures as opposed to propaganda, hearsay and imagination, Africans too require the same informal experiences so as to eliminate fantasies and illusionary beliefs about the West.

Nevertheless, while formal education plays the initial role in information gathering concerning general world verities, a combination of both truly gives people the real perspective and definition of realities. Even those who offer initial formal education, to children, especially, should have first-hand information of the facts being put across because passing over the wrong information usually leads to untimely misconceptions and eventual ignorance.

For most Africans, they tend to have adequate general information concerning Western geographical, historical facts prior to their initial exposures to the outside world, which is attained through their formal education while in African academic institutions. Whereas, on the part of Americans, it's sad to witness the height of misinformation about other peoples of the world. This is mainly among the American youth!

The sorts of contemptuous notions they have developed, over time, as a result of imagination and hearsay from their propagandist predecessors, is the root cause of racist contentions which have modernly been broken down into a stereotypic chagrin between African Americans and Africans, for instance.

Considering that America is part of the developed world, it surely defeats logic when one learns of some of the weaknesses surrounding its youth population. Of course, as humans, we all have our shortcomings. Arguably, the strengths of American youths outweigh their weaknesses but this argument revolves around the fact that since they are blessed with technological advancement more than most other parts of the world, there is no sure reason for their deprivation of general knowledge about basic world truths and information, as opposed to exaggerated television shows and fiction!

In the course of my epic American sojourn, I have as well met African immigrants who have gracefully learned certain rather troubling things through interactions with some Americans. These people have asked them unbelievable, disturbing questions such as: "How do Africans manage to sleep in trees, and mysteriously avoid being eaten up by lions?"—"Why do Africans walk bare-foot?"—"What bus did they take from Africa to America?"—"Is there electricity in Africa?"—and so forth!

Such questions sound like they are directed toward the African population with the sole intention of insulting them but in the long run it is out of sheer ignorance.

I may not have achieved much material wealth, during my remarkable safari to the United States of America, but I have augmented considerable, substantial mental wealth and skill to what I already possessed prior to June 20, 1996.

Acknowledgements:

Since the very day of my arrival in the United States of America, on June 20, 1996, I have met great people, and others who were not so great but who contributed to my life desires, experiences and eventual destiny. Sometimes, when we come across people who hinder our progress and determination, it is not an implication that they are the wrong people. They may be contributors to what ultimately makes us meet our destinies or completeness in our lives. These are found wherever we go, just as much as those who positively augment to our desires and wishes.

At this point in my life, I highly hail, thankfully, all those whose existence has augmented to my life-achievements and given me encouragement of such a high magnitude that since the commencement of this challenging safari to America, I have been blessed to acquire so much mental wealth.

First, I thank my family members for their tireless efforts in aiding me in many ways as I traveled from Kenya to the United States, in fulfillment of my Godly destined journey through life.

Secondly, I concretely extend my gratitude to the benevolent people of Seattle, Washington, for their overwhelming hospitality and friendliness while I spent incredible moments there; as I contributed gracefully toward a better, enhanced environment, all the good people on the East Coast of the United States and everyone else wherever they may be—whom I have had the opportunity to interact with.

Thirdly, I pray for all those I have been blessed to meet in many American States in the course of our tireless, everyday challenges including the supportive team at *iUniverse* Publishers, USA, without whom this outstanding publication would not have been possible.

CHAPTER ONE

NAIROBI TO ROME

It came as a shock the day I received an invitation from Seattle, Washington's *Cascadia* Quest and the King County Government to attend a global environmental exchange program in the Summer of 1996. We were to carry out significant environmental restoration projects in King County, Washington State. The work included stream restoration, re-vegetation, tree-planting and wildlife habitat improvement projects.

The mission of Cascadia Quest and Seattle's King County Government was to foster among the young people of the world, an ethic of global service. The intention was to create, within King County, an effective, replicate model

1

of global service. One which groups could use to organize global service projects in their own countries so that someday, opportunities in global service would be available to millions of young people, worldwide.

It became a moment of excitement mixed with awe and worry, now that the gods had called me to start a life-time journey to a distant, foreign land which was only told and heard of in my neighborhood and beyond, as "the land of White people." I was in a dilemma but hoped that God, having elected me as an ambassador to represent and serve his people abroad, would show me the way to America and provide me with a foster mother and father since He was then separating me from the only parents I had known all my life.

At the American embassy, the female consul whom I faced for an interview asked me to name some of the tree species which I had researched while working as a Research Assistant for Nairobi University and The Forest Action Network. This was relevant since my mission in America was to share my environmental experiences with other exchange students.

My legs trembled, a cold chill shuddered through my spine and nightmarishly my mouth dropped open, murmuring: "*Croton Macro-carpus, Croton Megalo-carpus, Calliandra, Azadiracha Indica,*"

"Stop! That's enough," she said.

2

There I was on an *Alitalia* flight, on June 19, 1996, from Jomo Kenyatta International Airport, in Kenya, on my way to Seattle, Washington. This was my first time to board that unique vessel manufactured by men and women who were as well created in God's image and likeness. I wondered how the plane could lift itself from the ground with all its length, weight and gigantic size.

Within minutes, up we went in the air and in order to forget the hazards involved by being away from the earth's surface, where I always belonged, I chose to think about my family members whom I had left behind to voyage to a distant land filled with strangers. But this was not the right notion as I immediately felt lonely and disowned. It was as if my parents had gotten rid of me to unknown foster parents. So, in place, I recalled a story I had read in a local newspaper, in Kenya, about Chepchumba—a woman who chose to castrate her husband, and attributed her action to evil spirits.

The incident, which took place in *Silibwet* near *Bomet* Town at the height of December 1995 festivities, was still lingering in my mind. It therefore never made any logic to me, why I was leaving my own people whose history, tribulations and desperation I comprehended well, and now heading overseas to a strange and foreign land. However, I proceeded with my thought about Chepchumba.

As a man just like Chepchumba's husband, I knew that being a man has its undeniable advantages. Nevertheless, living in an era where nothing distinguishes men from women apart from the region below the belt, it appeared to me that men were eventually losing out on all fronts.

The tragic event originated at a party where new circumcision initiates were being feted after the end of their seclusion period. As it was and still is the custom, the traditional brew, *busaa*, which old men sipped through traditional giant straws and pipes, was in abundance. There was song and dance for the young initiates. The woman, Chepchumba, appeared even though she had not been invited.

Her demeanor changed instantly when she saw her husband dancing with another woman. After pulling him aside, the two engaged in a heated exchange of words before the husband went back to his dance partner.

Like any young wife, Chepchumba, who dropped out of school to tie the knot, had wanted to spend the evening with her new husband. Old men at the party poured scorn on her lack of respect and manners for dragging her husband aside.

"He is all over the place, kissing and dancing with other women while I'm alone at home. This is unacceptable," she yelled.

4

The old men were taken aback, but did not want anybody to interfere with their "honey"—as busaa was locally known.

"Ani amei nei chepyosok eng betusyechu, matinyei tegis agot kitigin. (What happened to the women nowadays, they have no sense of respect?) An elderly man was heard murmuring to another.

Unable to take the husband away, she left but not without a chilling warning:

"Take your sweet time with these women but I will castrate you once you come back home," she thundered.

As soon as the husband got home, he was received by an outraged woman wielding a short, knife-like machete.

"I hope you have had your fill of women because you are gonna lose your manhood today. You made me drop out of school because you claimed to love me but what are you proving to me now?" she asked him angrily.

"You can chop off my genitals if you wish, darling, but I will not take insults and disrespect from a woman. In fact, I can even drop my pants right now," the man cautioned. He proceeded to explain that the woman he was dancing with was a former classmate and there was no romantic relationship going on between them. All this while, he was busy pulling down his pants and did not see his wife go for the offending organ. It happened in a flash, such that it lasted

5

moments for the reality to sink into them both. Like one in a trance, his wife stood at the scene with glazed eyes.

Abruptly, she screamed that demons had invaded their home, a revelation her husband freely accepted, confessing that his wife had been possessed by evil spirits.

When I woke up, I was in Rome, the capital city of Italy, and the home of the epic Vatican City. Chepchumba's story diminished from my mind, now that I was moving away from her territory into the Western hemisphere.

At the airport in Italy, the connecting flight almost left me there because I had gone to locate my luggage only to be assured by an airport official that I had not arrived in America yet. I felt bitterly embarrassed. I ran, and was the last person to enter the connecting flight to Heath row Airport—London.

Chapter Two

Rome to London

On the flight to London, I would not understand what was happening to me but it was all good, I thought. At least my forefathers were brought to a distant land in chains and shackles and forcefully loaded onto slave ships. And here I was in an aircraft delivering myself voluntarily—upon seeking strict permission.

I was again being hounded by occurrences of human history, so I chose to recall another ancient East African story which had been told to me when I was only ten years old by my maternal grand-mother, Elizabeth Kemunto Nyarigoti. It was about a girl who shockingly became chief, in the old days; times when such a reality was unheard of in the African society just as much as Obama, the man from *Kogelo*, *Syaya* District, who raised international eyebrows by marching into the American White House.

So to evade psychological agony about where I was headed, I recalled *Mazembe*—a man eating monster which lived in a cave surrounded by bushes, trees and anthills in *Moshi*, adjacent to Mt. Kilimanjaro in Tanzania.

Mount Kilimanjaro

In her village, was a well with clean, cold water and there was no other place where water would be found in her neighborhood.

People met here and drew water, talked and laughed, since the water was used for domestic purposes but were all terrified and dismayed by Mazembe because he had many mouths, fire-like eyes and extraordinarily powerful. Whenever he stamped his foot on the ground, the earth shook. He was also very eloquent. His body was solid rock and there was no fur on him.

One strange thing about this monster, was that he had power to enlarge himself. Sometimes he grew as big as a mountain, and this happened when he faced an adversary. He also had power to change from animal-like to a human being. Whenever he saw a man ahead of him, he would drastically change himself into a gorgeous woman. Those men who moved close to her, so as to seduce her, were kidnapped into the cave.

Sometimes Mazembe would go to the well balancing a pot on his head like the women in the neighborhood did. While at the well, he would pretend fetching water and none of the women ever doubted him, but the moment any of them moved closer to him, he would suddenly change into an animal, grab the woman and carry her to the cave.

Mazembe never killed right away, he kept the captured person alive in the cave for a number of days, later killed and ate them up.

Renown hunters in the village, with sharp weapons, tried to kill him, but in vain. He instead continued to kill people in the neighborhood, and this brought about confusion and terror. The villagers were afraid to walk at night and people hardly grazed their animals during the day, as a result of the monster. So their animals fed themselves and returned home on their own.

The peoples' security was now threatened, so they approached the chief for help. The chief, himself, was defeated and in the eventuality when he spoke about the issue, he promised his people that he would find ways and means of protecting them.

When they left, he was disturbed about Mazembe's threat to his people and had no solution to the problem. In two days, he invited two elders. The elders advised him to build an enormous house near the well. Strong men of the society would stay there to protect the people. The elected men worked vigorously and trained their hunting dogs around the new house, close to the well, in which they lived.

One morning, Mazembe changed into a beautiful woman and went to the well. She put aside her carrying pad and began washing the pot. Shortly, the local chief's daughter arrived to fetch water. They both shook hands, and suddenly, Mazembe turned into an animal, seized the girl and dragged her into the cave. She cried and shouted for help. When the hunters heard her cries, they carried their bows and arrows, spears and clubs—dogs ahead of them.

The brave men of the village went after the beast, their dogs scenting its whereabouts. Suddenly, the dogs returned with their tails tucked in between their legs. The beast approached them, enlarging moment by moment.

The hunters left the scene and explained the situation to the chief, requesting more help of additional warriors. The chief agreed to send more hunters to rescue his daughter but they too were sent away running—by the beast. They returned, assuring the chief that Mazembe was beyond human power. The chief immediately called the clan elders to find out ways in which they could rescue his daughter and his people altogether.

The elders came up with an idea that if the chief offered a reward, a person in the village who owned the strongest weapon would present it to kill Mazembe. He accepted. He vowed to step down and make anyone that killed Mazembe the village chief.

A ten-year-old named Fanta had the same ambition as Hillary Rodham Clinton: to become the first woman president of the United States of America. When she heard the news, she gathered her natural strength and wisdom.

Fanta had in the past secretly studied Mazembe's strengths and weaknesses, and daily movements.

She knew that his body was made up of solid rock and had a soft neck, and her mother once told her that Mazembe was a heavy alcoholic. In fact, whenever he drank, he swallowed the beer and the pot —together. He would later be intoxicated.

Fanta then, convincing her mother and vowing to kill Mazembe, declaring that children of today are wiser than those of yesterday, she set out to find the beast. She also told her mother that, "when you use your brains, you don't have to fight or struggle. Men try and fail because they use their weapons."

"Life is precious and a blessing that nothing can buy, be cautious!" her mother advised her.

"I want to be chief, I don't want to become anything else but a chief, so I can have people consult me when they are in trouble. When they have suggestions, I shall listen to them carefully. Together, we shall make this place the best to live and work in," vowed Fanta.

For a moment I paused my mind, and thought of a man with similar plans and wishes as those that Fanta had. Perhaps he knew Moshi Village, and in any case Mt. Kilimanjaro is not far from Kogelo Village. If he sticks to his dreams, he might end up killing Mazembe and become the first African Americanized president. Time will tell, I thought and continued meditating my story.

Fanta chose to use three weapons on Mazembe: beer, a rope and a sharp knife. She visited the chief, who was sitting outside his hut and heart-broken. She looked at him and said, "Sir, I want to help you."

"With what my child?" asked the chief.

"Please allow me to go to the cave and rescue your daughter from the beast," she requested, steadily gazing at him.

15

"The beast has defied all the brave warriors and greatest hunters in the village, who are you, little girl, to defeat Mazembe?" asked the chief.

"I know people have tried and failed, many have asked you to lose hope on your daughter, but let me also try. I'm a child, but it is true that a child—like King David—can kill a humongous beast," declared Fanta. She then told him that she had three simple but extremely dangerous weapons to kill Mazembe.

The chief was hesitant but only wished her good luck because he wanted his daughter back, and promised her the reward of her dreams—the first female chief in the village's history.

Fanta wanted to be chief so she would govern and help her people instead of fetching water, collecting firewood and milking cows.

"May God bless you and guide you in the cave. May He be kind and gracious to you in your risky mission and make you successful. Let Him cause wonder, something to be remembered for a long, long time in human history." Her mother Ann Dunham, grandmother, Habiba Akumu Nyanjoga, and grandfather, Onyango Obama, prayed to God and blessed her with all the wisdom and might they had ever gathered in their many years as parents.

After the blessing, her mother handed a pot of beer to Fanta, a rope and a sharp knife.

"My daughter, go in peace and be guided by our spirit and wisdom. Cast away fear and discouragement, and remember, there is no person or force greater than faith and hope itself—the audacity of hope."

Fanta, upon arrival at the cave, met the adversary eye to eye. Mazembe did not enlarge this time, nor did he change into human form. He was amused to see her. He thought she would soon make a delicacy.

In the cave, was a stream and small lake of scarlet water, in which fishes swum, fishes that had no eyes and scales. At the far end of the cave, was a large flame of fire, with every sort of meats sitting next to the fire place. The chief's daughter sat at one of the corners.

Fanta advanced towards the beast and placed a pot of cold beer before him. "Thank you my daughter, I will drink the beer but you are not returning home because I will eat you both when this meat is over," Mazembe said, his laughter echoing all over the cave.

Fanta sat next to the chief's daughter while the monster drank the beer greedily, and swallowed the pot as well. The beer was bitter and strong. In a short while, Mazembe was intoxicated, he fell down on the ground and blacked out. The two girls quickly bound him with a rope and killed him.

The chief prepared a feast and a huge bull was slaughtered to mark the return of his daughter and honor Fanta's heroic action. Drums were beaten and men and women formed a circle, singing overwhelmingly. Young women of Moshi

19

hopped forward into the circle in ululation, and backwards when they were exhausted, so that a new group took their place, all night long. Fanta was ultimately crowned chief.

Fanta becomes chief of Moshi Village

Chapter Three

London to Chicago

These make good stories to narrate to my new American friends, especially the youth, I said to myself.

When I peeped out the plane window, I was amazed to see tall buildings becoming larger and larger. A man next to me called the area, England. He distracted me from my thoughts about the home I was gracefully leaving behind.

My way of thinking was now changing from African into Western, perhaps American.

A White man at Heath row Airport directed me to the American Airlines entrance, asking me what mission I had in America. I explained that I was on a mission to work with others to find new ways in which we can solve environmental problems facing our earth, in a place called Seattle, Washington. For a moment, he stopped and tried to convince me to stay in the United Kingdom. He then whispered to me, upon learning that I was of Kenyan descent, a people who have all along stood by peace, love and unity, that Great Britain, and not America, was the most ideal destination for me. I promised to return to Great Britain, and proceeded to American Airlines.

A team of unruly Black teenagers stood by the airline entrance, throwing obscenities all over place: "Where the *fuck-n'* airline? Fuck, man! These *niggas* are gonna delay us. Shit! I should be in Chicago in the next *mother-fuck-n'* six hours and catch a damn cab to Milwaukee. Fuck!"

When men are given too much freedom, they often abuse it, I thought. But on the other hand, it appeared to me that these fellows had escaped from a prison of some sort because I had never witnessed a related dress-code and the kind of hair-styles they displayed.

I had all along known that hind-ends were private parts that should not be advertised in public. But again, was this a spell they were casting on me so that the flight could crash? I wondered.

For heaven's sake, they were pretty and attractive. I chose to advance towards them to solicit ethos love. But they spoke in a deep male voice. They are boys, but why are they hanging ear-rings on their ears. I was getting confused. I should probably try phi las love because they are males.

If, for instance, a lion appeared from nowhere into this airport, how would they take to their heels with pants almost dropping, exposing their posteriors? Did they live with their parents? How could they walk in front of their mothers exposing their buttocks in the open in the name of modernization? I wondered.

Before I boarded the airline, I approached one of the boys and asked him if he knew where the male toilets were located. *"Wha- a' fuck ya'll talkin' bout, you mean bathrooms? Who dis nigga man! Get ya ass off my face,"* he cursed. I remembered that familiarity breeds contempt and so I left the brat alone. I also recalled a secret I had been told that if you want to hide some information from an African American, put it down in writing! Then thought of a book I had read in high school by Earl Ofari Hutchinson.

The black poor and the new black bourgeoisie are inseparably bound by race, and agonizingly divided by class. The black schism cannot be cavalierly dismissed or ignored with simple pleas about "black unity." The problem goes much deeper and so must possible strategies for change. It was so much simpler when the crisis was in black and white.

23

The crisis in black and black is not a doom and gloom. While class divisions have been hidden and denied by generations of academics and political leaders, they are a fact of life among Americans.

When I lived in Kenya, racism, contempt, prejudice or apartheid-like fidgets and rhetorical bubbles were abstract concepts that were comedic mockery in movies or music videos. People only worried about their skin if it related to a dermatological problem.

Just as much as many people argue, today, that it seems better to have been a slavery victim, back in the old days, than to be a modern slave, since in the old days it was much easier to identify the person enslaving you as opposed to now, when you cannot tell your tormentor—such as those Black boys who were psychologically enslaving me but I could not identify them.

It is true it was so much easier when the crisis was in black and white. But it has never been specified in any book that mutual action by Africans cannot be instituted against African Americans to resolve these stereotypes and brain-washed notions, now that the problem seems to be between black and black.

The American Airlines flight headed to O'hare Airport, in Chicago, took off at four o'clock, that evening, and then I was worried about where I was going after a brief orientation of the kind of youth I was going to live and work with. First, I had to practice understanding the kind of English they spoke, and secondly learn to utter similar words. Therefore, during the trip, and to avoid embarrassments of pardoning people whenever they spoke, I pretended I was asleep. I also wanted to avoid being asked by the flight attendants what kind of refreshments or food I preferred because the only meals I was familiar with were: *ugali,* corn, beans, various sorts of meats, and all other heavy, filling foods which I knew were unavailable on the flight.

Pretending to be asleep, I actually fell asleep and dreamed about a derisive middle aged woman named Mama Michael whose guests were deeply shocked when, for their entertainment, she played a pornographic movie in place of gospel music, in her home.

The church is a convenient place where all manner of characters congregate, some in pursuit of a higher spiritual calling, and others to camouflage their dark ways and mannerisms. What makes the church an especially attractive place for people with something to hide is the fact that it operates on the basis of faith, respect and trust. One's image counts a lot. Thus, as long as one projects the "right" image, their pronouncements and actions are to be believed even by those who do not go to church. It is this moral high ground that gives the church the authority to pass judgment on society.

Mama Michael was highly regarded in the area where she chaired the local women's Church organization. She had just chaired a meeting before she invited a group of members to her house for refreshments. At home, she switched on the television while she prepared drinks for her guests. They were, however, unhappy with the on-going program being aired because of its obscene Western lyrics.

Mama Michael, for that reason, chose to play for them a gospel DVD that her teenage son had entertained a male friend with the previous night. This, she believed, would improve her status in the visitors' eyes as a woman of God.

Unknown to her, her son had replaced the gospel DVD late in the night with a pornographic movie and since it had no cover, the mother couldn't tell the difference.

"Let's have some gospel music and forget the Western trash we have just watched," she suggested to her guests.

Everyone concurred and beamed with anticipation. Then the unexpected happened. Pornographic images appeared on the screen accompanied by the usual erotic whines and screams. Mama Michael's mouth dropped open in shock.

Some of her guests shot up screaming as if possessed by ancestral spirits.

"Mother of Michael, what is this you are putting on for us? May the devil be defeated, totally defeated!" the women prayed.

26

The poor woman was too shaken to move or speak. She rushed and pressed the "Stop" button on the machine. Her embarrassment knew no bounds as she tried to stop the women from running out.

Although some sympathized with her, others thought that she was a sinister and immoral woman. The ruckus attracted many neighbors who sought to know what had taken place. Things only softened when Mama Michael apologized and invited a local pastor to pray for the entire household, so that the devil could be cast away into the forests.

CHAPTER FOUR

CHICAGO TO SEATTLE

When my eyes opened I was in O'hare Airport, Chicago. One of the feminine boys gleefully glanced at me and clicked contemptuously. *"I don't think dis mother-fucker know where he going,"* he reported to his companion. Another one, who was dread-locked, shot up from his seat, pulled up his jeans which had slipped down, close to his knees, and majestically swung his posterior toward the plane exit. I trailed him, steadily gazing onto the floor so as to avoid undermining, premature blindness. These early signals made me realize elements of racial contentions and stereotypes earlier rumored to me about America. I felt emotionally suppressed and deceived because I was poor.

28

I then strolled about the airport corridors in search of my next flight to Sea-Tac Airport, in Seattle, Washington.

While on the flight to Seattle, I compared morality and ethics in contrast to the American transgender boys I had traveled together with from Britain to the United States. The equation and development from earlier forms with ethical and moral deterioration seemed to define them as nothing more than the sum-total of unforeseen creations functioning within an intolerantly uncaring world without ethical standards. It surely occurred to me that the moral sense in them and moral principles in their "culture" constituted laws of nature, forces of their culture, and the extraordinary pathways of history. Then I thought of the dilemma faced by Africans, not only in the West, but as well in Africa, that they have been historically attacked, destroyed and torn into shreds by slave masters and colonialism and are now standing in the midst of life-events, assuming that God created and exhausted natural laws and culture to create within us morality and a set of moral principles.

Sentiments in us, in the sense of morality and principles develop through the lens of choice functioning on us and subsequently through communal judgment of events and values functioning on people. We are faced with numerous laws of nature and, or culture and history that shape our thoughts and conduct, but we are still free of choice for our actions because none of us can explain the cause of certain behavior such as exposure of posteriors. Those of socially considered appropriate conduct may face adversities and the ones of behaviors that are considered unacceptable may face fortunes. But since morality is provisionally acceptable in most human societies and circumstantially, it happens that personal blame or pummel exists within our societies which provide complacence, guilt or justification.

Since I'm a staunch believer in freedom of choice and conduct, I did not condemn or criticize my feminine "friends" for their disregard of relativism—flexible set of rules for virtue and wrong behaviors derived from how the situation is defined by society; by piercing their ears and exposing their hind-ends in public.

At Sea-Tac, I didn't know my next step or who was to meet me, now that I was officially in the United States of America.

Then I saw a middle aged woman approach me in the company of a little girl and a teenage boy. First, I felt like my circulatory system had come to a standstill because I'm the kind of person who takes a while to fully understand strangers before I freely socialize with them.

"Are you Mr. Julius Morara Omosa from Kenya?" she benevolently asked.

"Yes, mom," I quickly remembered the initial training I had been given by my eldest sister, Professor. Mary Bonareri Omosa, that all American women are referred to as "moms."

"Well, we are delighted to meet you. We will be your host family for as long as you work under the King County Government and Cascadia Quest. This is my daughter, Sukie, and her brother, Zen, and I'm Heidi Jefferson. Welcome to Seattle," she said as she introduced her family.

Seattle Space Needle – Washington State

Seattle Skyline – Washington State

I said to myself; what a wonderful family I will be staying with. My attitude and misconception about White Americans started changing into a positive one now that I had began the long journey of getting to know and comprehend them, spiritually as opposed to imagination or hearsay.

On our way from the airport, Heidi asked me what kind of foods we ate in Kenya. I didn't quite know how to answer her question because to me, human beings eat similar foods but in different forms and textures—depending on their styles of preparation. However, I announced to them that we mostly preferred common sorts of meats, potatoes, bananas, cabbage, and maize.

"What is maize, mom?" Sukie asked.

"Corn," her mother answered.

When we got into their house, they were all excited and anxious to learn more or new facts about Africa, more especially Zen and Sukie who requested a story about animals—a characteristic of Seattle's residents which truly makes them distinct from most fellow Americans, besides their traditional summer-time pot-lucks, hospitalities, unity, environmental awareness, codes of conduct and cultural affiliations I later witnessed in Washington state.

This truly became the beginning-point of our close association, and subsequently with their half-brother, Robin, who had just visited from England in that particular year's summer.

Heidi, Sukie and Robin   Robin and Sukie

So I decided to put aside my past pains, including those that were inflicted on me by the five feminine boys on the flight because I knew that if I was unable to access the energy of the present, each emotional difficulty that I encountered left a mark of tribulation in my soul. But if I viewed my past grief as non-existent and an opportunity to grow, then the closer I was to reality and prosperity. This is one barrier to success among many Africans and African Americans because they carry their past pain into a new day.

Because I was ready for a new perspective and beginning, I chose positivity rather than pain because if it took me over, I would want additional pain, and if happiness overcame me then I would want more happiness. This I knew, so I became part of the American family and envisioned the day God would open my door of fortune and prosperity because that is why he appointed me as one of the chosen few representatives of a generation marked by epic truths and arbitrary judgment.

Upon my arrival in America, I was in search of my wholeness rather than a deep-seated mentality of incompleteness. So I created a belief in me that nothing really occurred in the past; it happened in the present which meant that from my past experiences, I was in a position to determine my future by acting now, and acting accordingly. If my ego was right, when I arrived in the United States, it must have inevitably followed that all our planetary journeys to nowhere ultimately delivered us to our destinies, then, today and tomorrow. This means that wherever you find yourself, if only you keep walking, you will find your planned destiny.

Zen and Sukie had a glimpse of how they could transform their perceptions, and being as spiritual as children are, what they knew and wanted was a permanent shift in consciousness. They avoided being judgmental, like most American children, of my foreign accent, but observed my soul and the kind of message I had to deliver to them.

So since Sukie was 9 and Zen 13 years old, at the time, I chose to narrate to them a story about "Why the Cat Lives with People" because they owned two cats in their home. Besides this story, I henceforth played a game named *Mancalla* with Sukie; at least everyday, for the rest of my stay in their home.

34

Zen   Sukie

Many, many years ago, somewhere in Masai *Mara*, in Kenya, in the wild, lived *Kimbo*, the kitten and her mother *Blue-Band*. I commenced.

Kimbo was a lovely and healthy kitten. Her fur was white with brown stripes running horizontally on her body which made fellow animals admire and envy her a lot.

One day, Kimbo's mother became very ill. She anticipated her own death but did not want Kimbo to know and only wondered how long she had to live, and the repercussions of her death upon Kimbo.

As days passed by, Kimbo's mother stayed in bed night and day. Kimbo really got worried and wondered where she would go in case the worst happened to her mother—Blue-Band. She wept silently.

Blue-Band's condition deteriorated day after day. On one chilly night, she groaned with pain throughout the night,

35

terrifying Kimbo, who sat by her mother comforting her. Blue-Band revealed to her young one, "I'm about to die."

"Mother," called Kimbo, tears rolling down her cheeks.

"Yes my little one," answered Blue-Band in a hoarse, faint voice.

"What shall I do without you, Mother?" Kimbo burst out loud, sobbing. "I don't even know how to hunt and catch mice for myself yet. Oh, I shall perish of hunger!"

"Don't worry my child," said Blue-Band. "Do you know Lion?"

Kimbo nodded and said, "Oh yes I do, the one who implies to be king of the jungle?"

Blue-Band was groaning in pain. She did not hear what Kimbo had said. She again asked, "My little one, do you know Lion?"

"Yes mother, I know Lion, the king of the beasts," answered Kimbo.

"Yes my child, Lion is my cousin. We both belong to the Cat family, I think he can care for you when I'm dead. As soon as I die, you must run to him before somebody kills you. Do you comprehend?"

"Yes mother," answered Kimbo. Blue-Band died a day later.

Kimbo went straight to look for her uncle, Lion, upon the demise of her mother—and it was not tedious since everyone in the jungle was familiar with Lion.

"Excuse me, Great King," Kimbo commenced.

"Well, little one, what can I do for you?" asked Lion in a deep, loud voice.

"My mother is dead. She was your cousin. She told me before her death that you can look after me. Can I please stay with you?" asked Kimbo, benevolently.

"You are welcome to stay with me," said Lion. "But you must learn to hunt on your own. For the first few days, I will teach you how to hunt."

"Thank you very much King, I will learn to catch mice."

But because Lion chased and caught animals for their meals, Kimbo became extremely lazy and never even

38

learned to catch mice. But Lion loved Kimbo's company because she was a good story teller. She told such humorous stories to Lion that he would laugh until tears rolled down his bushy cheeks.

But the two friends did not stay together for long. After a few weeks of mutual friendship, a hunter shot Lion. He did not, however die immediately. He therefore crawled to his den.

Kimbo was worried that she would be left without Lion's foster care so she asked Lion: "Do you think I can live with the "straight-one" if the worst happens to you?" she asked her dying uncle, referring to human beings, as straight-ones, which was the name given to us by animals retrospectively.

39

"Oh yes, that is a great idea niece," said Lion, painfully. "The straight-one is strong and more intelligent than any beast you can think of. If you build friendship and a lasting relationship with him, nothing will happen to you." Lion instantly dropped dead as soon as he croaked these words of wisdom and goodwill to his niece—Kimbo.

Kimbo wondered if the straight-one would be pleased to see her in his house. "Can he love my stories as Lion did? Maybe I will be of help to him."

She went back to the place where the straight-one stood the moment he shot Lion, and from that point, she followed his footsteps which led her to his house.

Kimbo followed this path for some time, and then she saw the straight-one's house.

Soon she was in the hunter's compound. She went quietly around the house and saw an open window. She then jumped into the house through this window.

When she got in the hunter's yard, she went around his house and then jumped inside through the window and hid behind a large pot where the hunter kept his food. There she saw a big rat attempting to climb up the food-pot. *This is a golden opportunity, I must kill this rat and prove to the straight-one and his wife that I can kill rats,* Kimbo thought.

She puffed. The rat took off and Kimbo went after the rat at top speed, past the hunter and his spouse. Soon, she caught and killed the rodent. Seeing this, the man and his wife were overjoyed. His wife went up in cheerful adulation. "We have found something better than a trap and poison, this is incredible!" They both agreed concurrently.

Because Kimbo was hungry, she ate the rat. The man immediately called her. "Please stay with us so that you can help us kill rats and as a remuneration, we shall give you milk, every morning."

Kimbo was so delighted too. So she said, "Meow, meow, meow, thank you very much!"

She killed all rats in her sight within the home and, henceforth, she lived with people, sometimes walked with the hunter and sat by the fire with human families. This relationship lasted forever.

This friendship lasted forever after.

Chapter Five

King County World Conservation Corps

The following morning, a man appeared at my new residence and identified himself as Mr. Tom Don lea. He put it to me that he was an official at Cascadia Quest, then managed by the King County Government, and had been appointed to work with me and other International Corp Members. He further gave me the official schedule for the program. Later we headed to Cascadia Quest for introduction of ourselves and orientation to the State of Washington.

The King County World Conservation Corps had provided over 15,000 hours of work in the King County community in 1996. The scope and complexity of work performed by KCWCC had increased significantly in the 1996 field season. Corp Members had planned entire community planting events and invasive plant removal days, conducted field surveys to develop restoration sites, and significantly improved both the quality and technical abilities of their crews.

Therefore, we were expected to give a preview and histories of our work related activities both in the agencies and countries that we represented. I represented Kenya, and before my introduction, Chie Osawa, from Japan, sang to us a Japanese folk song to bind and unionize us all—called *Sakura.*

Sakura   Sakura

Yayoi no sora wa

Miwatasu kagiri

Kasumi ka kumo ka

Kasuka ni niou

Sakura Sakura

Hanazakari

"Weave, Weave"

Weave, weave, weave us together,
Weave us together in unity and love,
Weave, weave, weave us together,
Weave us together, together in love.

We are many textures,
We are many colors,
Each one different from the other,
But we are entwined with one another
In one great tapestry.

We are different instruments playing,
Our melodies,
Each one tuning to a different key,
But we are all playing in harmony,
In one great symphony.

Then my round came about to introduce myself and give a brief speech about the Forest Action Network—for which I worked in Nairobi, Kenya, and Kenya, as a country which I represented in the United States of America.

I then nervously climbed up the dais and began:

"My name is Julius Morara Omosa, representing Forest Action Network, based in Kenya," I commenced in a poetic voice—soft cadence and erudition.

"Although Kenya may have provided the setting for the earliest development of the human species, the ancestors of the modern nation's African population began making their appearance in the region less than 1,000 years ago, and in the immigration of some ethnic aggregations continued into the twentieth century. Culturally and linguistically, heterogeneous groups of agriculturists and nomadic *pastoralists* settled in the physically varied environment of the country's interior, where as many as 40 distinct ethnic categories have been recognized. Among these, the Bantu-speaking Kikuyu emerged as the dominant group in Kenya's fertile heartland. The coastal region experienced a distinct history, coming under Islamic influence as early as the tenth century. Arab and Persian merchants founded towns there whose ports became part of a commercial network linked to the Middle East. Intimate contacts between the Arab and indigenous Bantu cultures on the coast produced over a long period of time the Swahili culture, in which the characteristics of both were assimilated.

The history of Kenya as a political entity began with the nation's inclusion in the British sphere of influence in the late 19th. Century and the subsequent establishment of a British protectorate and colony in the country. The British brought together the country's diverse elements under a unified administration and bestowed on it the name Kenya after the 5,200-meter peak in the central highlands that the Kikuyu called *Kere' nyaga*—the "mountain of whiteness."

The aim of British colonialism in Kenya was to integrate the country into an imperial system and to develop its economic potential, while providing the security of the indigenous population and improving their general well-being, as defined according to the prevailing mentality of colonial authorities. The political, economic and social changes brought about by the British were not effected smoothly, however, nor from An African perspective were they uniformly advantageous. An early realization that the climate and fertility of the Kenya Highlands made the region ideal for European settlement encouraged the reservation there of large tracts of the country's best land for the White minority and corresponding restrictions on African and Asian land use. Social pressures engendered by these restrictions and the inability of limited African reserves to meet the land needs of an expanding population-together with growing African resentment of the inferior status accorded them, provoked unrest that contributed to the formation of political action groups, organized on the basis of ethnic affiliation, in the 1920's.

Improvement in the lot of the average African was limited until after World War II when political movements, like that among the Kikuyu led by Jomo Kenyatta, demanded a role by the Black majority in Kenya's government. The determination of the European community to retain exclusive control in a "White Man's Country" and the continued denial of African rights set off a violent reaction during the *Mau Mau* (*Mzungu Arudi Ulaya, Mwafrika Apate Uhuru*) emergency in the 1950s. The Kikuyu-led insurrection was suppressed, and the lengthy imprisonment of Kenyatta and other African leaders suspected of complicity in it caused a hiatus in organized African political activity until 1960, when the campaign for majority rule within the framework of the colonial regime succeeded in submerging ethnic differences among Africans and in winning the recognition of British authorities.

In 1961 the British government set Kenya on a course that led to majority rule and, at the end of 1963, to complete emancipation within the Commonwealth of Nations. The following year Kenya became a republic under a unitary form of government headed by Jomo Kenyatta as its first president, and the principle political parties voluntarily merged under his leadership in the Kenya African National Union (KANU). Radical dissidents and ethnic interest groups fearful of Kikuyu domination followed

Oginga Odinga out of KANU during an interlude in the

late 1960s, but the rival political movement that they

formed was banned in 1969, and Kenya reverted in

practice to being a one-party state.

Ethnic antagonisms remained the principal stumbling

block to national unity, but Kenyatta's firm, paternalistic

rule nonetheless provided the country with a substantial

degree of stability during the first decade and half of

Kenya's independent existence. Although the *Mzee*—

the "Old Man," as Kenyatta was familiarly known, held

tightly to the reigns of power, Kenya maintained basically

democratic institutions. Parliamentary debate was

controversial and apt questioned government policies,

elections were vigorously contested by rival candidates,

and the press was relatively free in its reporting and

commentary. A program of "Kenyanization" of

government and the economy was instituted, nevertheless,

gradually forcing the departure of most of the country's

European and Asian populations. Operated by an African

entrepreneurial elite with close ties to the political elite,

the Kenyan economy developed along capital lines,

emphasizing rapid growth and modern production

methods. The favorable orientation of the economy and stable political conditions inspired a confidence in the country's future that encouraged investment. Political opposition, however, focused on substantial inequities in distribution, particularly in farmland, environment and official corruption.

People of three distinct language groups—Bantu, *Cushitic*, and *Nilotic*—are found in present-day Kenya. The interior of the country extending to Lake Victoria, is populated by intermingled groups of Bantu-speaking and Nilotic peoples, whose ancestors migrated to Kenya after the beginning of the second millennium A.D. The early Cushitic people who inhabited western Kenya and parts of the highlands area were absorbed or driven out during these movements. Elements of the present Cushitic-speaking population, which occupies the northern and northeastern parts of the country, began arriving sometime before the sixteenth century. Somali clans eventually ranged over most of northeastern Kenya.

In their oral histories, the Kikuyu, the nation's largest ethnic group, claim that their ancestors came originally from northeast of Mount Kenya in a migration that

52

was probably under-way in the fifteenth century. Archaeological discoveries in central Kenya, related to the presumed Bantu-speaking people who entered southern Kenya during the first millennium, indicate that these people preceded the Kikuyu in the region. Linguistic studies further suggest that they may have been the ancestors of several subsequent Bantu groups in the area, including the Kikuyu.

During the three to four centuries after their migration began, the pronto-Kikuyu moved slowly southwestward, splitting into new groups that by the late 19th. Century occupied a broad area in the central part of the highlands. In the course of their movement they absorbed other groups already in place. Such ethnic elements included the short-statured *Gumba* and the *Athi* both hunting and gathering peoples.

The Gumba, believed to have been Cushitic speakers, were primarily hunters in the open grasslands. Oral traditions state that they were skilled at iron working and pottery making, knowledge of which they imparted to the Kikuyu. The two ethnic groups seem to have lived in a symbiotic relationship, exchanging meat and skins for agricultural products, and considerable assimilation of the Gumba by the Kikuyu groups occurred. The expansion of the Kikuyu, nevertheless, resulted in friction and eventually war, as land used for hunting was cleared for cultivation. Little is known about the Gumba after hostilities with the Kikuyu in the mid-nineteenth century.

Bantu speaking peoples had began arriving in the Lake Victoria region of western Kenya by about the eleventh century. Sometime during the next few centuries, separate agricultural groups that later came to constitute the *Luhya*, occupied the lake shore. During the sixteenth century, the pastoral Nilotic *Luo* pushed into the area north of Win am Bay from present-day Uganda, displacing the Luhya eastward. Settled agricultural practices appear to have been adopted by at least some Luo, but by the middle of the next century, others were on the move southward along the shore of the lake, conquering new territory as they moved. There they came against the Bantu Kisii (*Gusii*), who were also expanding into this part of Kenya. Territorial adjustments between these three peoples, as well as with Nilotic groups on their eastern fringes, often involved warfare and continued until the imposition of

54

British control early in the twentieth century effectively
brought an end to the forcible occupation of land by rival
ethnic groups.

The time of entry and dispersion of the ancestors of various
other Nilotic peoples in modern Kenya is uncertain. The
first groups must have began their in-migration from
the general area of southwestern Ethiopia in the early
centuries of the second millennium, for the ancestors
of the *Kalenjin* peoples, among them the *Nandi*, appear
to have reached the Mount *Elgon* region before 1500.
By the early seventeenth century, Masai pastoralists
were pushing southward through the Rift Valley and are
known, from oral records, to have been at the southern
end of the Kenya section of the rift in the eighteenth
century, becoming the dominant force in southwestern
Kenya. Although weakened by internal warfare, the
Masai warriors were so feared by neighboring groups that
few dared challenge their control of the southern valley,
plains area, and surrounding plateaus. Among the latest
major Nilotic arrivals were the *Turkana* pastoralists, who
entered northwestern Kenya in the eighteenth century.

Both casual observation and land use inventories provide strong testimony that trees have an essential role as one of the many small-holder land use options in many high potential agricultural zones in Kenya. In most cases, farmers grow trees to meet the demand for construction poles, charcoal and fuel wood and in response to other market forces. Trees are also cultivated to demarcate boundaries or to shade other crops such as tea or coffee.

Still, more so in Kenya, there remains the question of why farmers maintain trees on land that could be used for the cultivation of other crops which could potentially generate a substantially higher income. Central to this question of tree planting in Kenya is the inter-linkage of issues such as land tenure, capital accumulation and labor use. Several of the most common tree cultivation and management practices are the long-term outcome of these closely related issues. Others have been adopted either as a result of relatively recent interventions or due to the evolution of traditional tree management practices.

Simple observation in many high potential agricultural areas of Kenya would inform the casual observer that trees, protected, cultivated and well managed, have assumed an essential place as one of many small-holder land use options. The observation poses some interesting problems for our conventional view of peasant agriculture. It is not that farmers have nothing else to do with their land. Population pressures in many parts of Kenya have become extreme. It is precisely in those areas, where pressures on agricultural land are greatest, that the proportionate area of land used for growing trees increases so substantially. In the face of these types of pressures, and because returns from trees are relatively low, it is evident that there are strong reasons why farmers grow trees rather than other potentially more profitable crops.

According to my own observation, the likely reasons are that since Kenya is a developing nation, most of its nationals depend on tree products for their construction, firewood and charcoal, and fodder for their animals.

Although planted tree species are predominantly exotic, such as *Grivillea robust a*, Eucalyptus, Acacia, and many others, a number of indigenous species such as *Markhamia lute a*, *croton* species and *Sesbania*

57

sesban, also feature in farmers' range of choices. The dominant species vary from district to district in Kenya. For instance, in *Kakamega* District, in Western Kenya bordering the famous Lake Victoria, wood lots are almost always dominated by Eucalyptus, while *Murang'a* District in Central Kenya is dominated by Acacia and Kisii District in *Nyanza* Province is highly dominated by Croton megalo-carpus, Cypress and Markhamia lute a.

Traditional law in many areas of Kenya is generally controlled by the needs of individual members of a community. For instance, the center of Kikuyu country is traditionally associated with the area around the town of *Gakuyu* in Murang'a District. Gakuyu is some form of the name for the *Mukuyu* tree—from which the name Kikuyu is as well derived. Another site, *Mukurwe wa Gathanga* is named after another tree; *Albizia*, as is where we are told, God appeared to the man, *Gikuyu*, and allotted him all the land south and west of Mount Kenya, to the edge of the forest.

Trees in high potential agricultural areas of Kenya occupy a significant land area. Land use inventories have suggested that planted and managed trees usually cover between five and ten percent of agricultural land. Even when other forms of land use could generate substantially higher levels of household income, the planting and management of trees has remained an important form of land use.

Last but not least, labor constraints could be somewhat alleviated if capital were available so that farmers could hire higher wage laborers to help cultivate other crops. Nevertheless, capital for this specific purpose is seldom available through formal lending mechanisms, though it can sometimes be generated through informal mechanisms such as kinship lending, mutual savings societies or the redeemable sale of crops or capital assets.

These few remarks about the history and social and economic incentives for small-holder tree growing in Kenya, a country I nobly represent here today will, hopefully, give you an insight into some of the political, economic, and more so, environmental challenges which the country may be facing as a result of unplanned inhabitation, ignorance of its occupants and modern practices of deforestation as a result of population increases demanding more land for agriculture.

We gather here in the State of Washington, on this day, to learn, and in return share, new alternatives on how we can overcome global environmental challenges for a sustainable, viable environment." I concluded the brief historical background of Kenya.

Next, I climbed down from the dais and this round accompanied fellow Internationals in briefly announcing our personal environmental reminiscences. Again, I was the first one on schedule:

"I have participated in community service projects and I'm still engaged in the same since June, 1993. After high school in 1991, I enrolled for computer lessons with the intention of developing a career in computing. I successfully went through the basic training in DOS, word processing and spreadsheets. Two months later, I got a job as a Research Assistant on a project focusing on the market potential of fresh and processed sweet potato products. For purposes of undertaking this study, I received a briefing on the art of interviewing and how to make an entry and be accepted into a community where one may even be unknown. While on this job, I learned about creating a report; a skill I enjoy applying.

Although my assignment as a Research Assistant required that I only ask questions and record answers

60

received, this never came easy. Hence, I learned how to talk to farmers and environmentalists. In addition to previous experience, my knowledge of the study area earned me another community based assignment.

This time I worked on a voluntary basis, collecting indigenous tree seeds. This activity soon expanded and transformed into a local tree nursery where various seedlings were raised. We were only a handful of us at the beginning. Each of us performed all the duties in the tree nursery, including seed-bed preparation, watering seedlings and reaching out to the community. Involving the community in tree planting practices was not easy. It required that we establish some form of campaign, aimed at creating awareness about the essentialness of the *agro* forestry species that we were promoting at the tree nursery. I was subsequently recruited into the expansion department on a full-time basis and made in-charge of the youth outreach program.

I worked with neighboring schools and churches. Here I talked to my fellow youth about the importance of tree planting and proper management. This was necessary because the area had for a long time favored exotic trees which however took too much land. I have also since developed interest in lobbying as an outreach approach.

My basic interest was in community based work. I was also keen on current affairs. My activities included

61

encouraging and demonstrating how to use and utilize home nurseries as a source of seedlings, and this later earned me a position at the Forest Action Network (FAN) based in Nairobi, Kenya."

The multitude abruptly shot up from their respective chairs in unison, amid thunderous appraisals and mixed adulation from an audience which was comprised of people from all walks of life —men, women and children of host-families, Cascadia Quest and the King County Government officials. It appeared like they had never before witnessed an event of that nature, considering my origin and foreign accent in which I made my pronouncements. All that I cared about was emphasis on the message I had to deliver to them so that they all understood my Kenyan-molded intellect, wit and ability, and not the commonplace low expectancy and disregard most people have about the African continent.

At the conclusion of our orientation to Western ways of life, we stood up in song and dance. Praveen Kumar Prithvi and Deepa Anandakrishnan from Madras, India, led the dance, shifting from one point to another, and, inaccurately, slow-motioned round and round in a manner suggesting awareness and total devotion to Hinduism. The song was called *Thillana Thillana*, a song of the Tamil people in southern India and northern Sri Lanka who constitute a portion of the Dravidian.

Thillana Thillana Ni Thithi Kindra Thena
Thiku Thiku Nenjil Thillana

Thillana Thillana Ni Thithi Kindra Thena
Thiku Thiku Nenjil Thillana

Oh Manja Kattu Mina Ni Ena Konji Konji Pona
Thiku Thiku Nenjil Thillana

Ah Ah Ah Ah Ah Ah Ah

Kanuum Vechidhum Ni Da Na
Adi Kani Vechidhum Ni Da Na

Kattil Pottu Kapam Katta Kaman Sonana

Thillana Thillana Ni Thithi Kindra Thena
Thiku Thiku Nenjil Thillana

Thillana Thillana Ni Thithi Kindra Thena
Thiku Thiku Nenjil Thillana

Corp Members, host families and KCWCC officials
dancing to "Thillana Thillana."

The following week, we commenced our imaginary
journey to a place beyond—but hopeful, predictable and
foreseen. For the first week of Cascadia Quest program,
we were engaged in an orientation training where we
learned from experienced facilitators skills in cross-cultural
communication, environmental education, and conflict
resolution. We learned to break down our stereotypes and
prejudices while exploring various cultural value systems,
as well as trained about the surrounding environment. Then
we divided into groups of six and went to respective work-
sites within King County.

My crew which comprised of Pieter Straub, as the
crew leader, Deepa Anandakrishnan, Shoshana h Landau,

Carla Bowditch, Allan Bradley and myself, and nicknamed *Kukumanga* crew, (Kukumanga is a powdery substance given to cattle to enhance their sexual libido), joined the other crews and visited co-operating agencies in Redmond, Tacoma, West Seattle, Renton, Mountains to Sound Green way and the Cascades.

(Left) Pieter Straub, Julius Omosa and Allan Bradley.
(Right) Shoshana h Landau, Julius Omosa and Carla
Bowditch.

Corp Members: Nanise Talakai, Glenn Kuhn, Pieter
Straub, Julius Omosa and Edan Zabooloon.

Carla Bowditch performing the "Trust Test,"—meant to
enhance our faith toward fellow Corp Members.

Kukumanga Crew, Sody's and Murphy's crews

Within the Metro area, these included the Beach Stewards, a Water Pollution Control Division, assisted by the KCWCC in annual monitoring of nine Puget Sound beaches. The agency assessed the inter tidal invertebrate and plant species diversity and density which was conducted on random plots within an established grid. Clam populations were assessed for weight and length, and tested for toxicity levels. Data was compared with bench-mark data from the mid 1970s and is nowadays used to establish an animal health index for inter tidal marine life adjacent to sewage treatment plant outflows.

KCWCC assisted Mountains to Sound Green way in their second year program to catalyze the re greening process of recently cut forest lands. We installed water bars and access trails, seeded, hayed and planted on then recently decommissioned logging roads. KCWCC also assisted the University of Washington with experimental techniques of using composted bio-solids to re green logging road scars and log landings. Experimental terraces were built on steep, scarred slopes to retain composted bio-solids until planted grass could take root.

The Redmond Nursery Program assisted the Water Pollution Control Division in the further development and maintenance of the Wetland Plant Nursery in Redmond. The nursery propagates native wetland plants for use in riparian and estuarine wetland restoration projects. The nursery program conducted by the corps included bed construction, native seed collection, transplanting and plant care. In addition, the nursery experimented with composted bio-solids and other growing media for herbaceous wetland plants. We, as the Corp Members, were responsible for the set-up, maintenance, data collection, and interpretation of these experiments.

KCWCC planned a community-wide planting event on October 19, 1996, to plant 1300 conifers and woody shrubs in *Sammamish* State Park. Working in conjunction with the Public Involvement section, we were responsible for all elements of project planning including ordering plants, surveying sites and developing a planting scheme, educating and coordinating volunteers, soliciting food donations for volunteers, and staffing the event with the entire corps and staff.

We as well worked with the Engineering and Environmental Services section to develop a conifer under planting project which aimed to plant 6,000 conifers in the Spring of 1997.

Planting preparation work included invasive removal, plant labeling and sorting, transplanting, willow and dogwood stake harvesting, preparation of willow bundles, post event quality control, and post event planting of remaining trees, woody shrubs and herbaceous native plants. We worked at the site after a large community planting event to complete planting. We planted close to 4,000 native trees and shrubs at this site which included species such as: *Sitka Spruce, Douglas Fir, Western Hemlock, Big-leaf Maple, Oregon Ash, Western Red Cedar, Black Hawthorn, Pacific Crabapple, Cascara, Bitter Cherry* and *Black Cottonwood*.

Subsequently, we participated in a community loose strife removal at Lake Desire in *Renton*. This included contacting and gaining support of landowners, applying for and obtaining necessary removal and transportation permits, organizing and facilitating the community event, staffing the event, and proper disposal of removed loose strife.

Next, we were to steward at least 20 priority sites along the Sammamish Slough. We established survey methodology for assessing the entire nine miles of the slough for vegetation characteristics, slope, access, and significant natural features. A database was drafted using this information to select priority sites for removal of non-native shrubs and replanting with native trees and woody shrubs. Community group "packets" were developed for all sites including maps, permit information, site design and planting methodology.

The Engineering and Environmental Services section maintained 13 restoration sites, of which throughout the summer of 1996, we visited biweekly to water, weed and otherwise maintain all trees and woody shrubs.

During the 1996 field season, the King County World Conservation Corps had corp member internships that allowed some Corp Members to work on special interest research or projects they wanted to take up. It was modified to be more tied to actual field projects that needed more planning, coordination and logistical support. Each Corp Member was given a Project Assistantship to work on in a team of Corp Members from their crew. Over all, ultimately, this was a success for both the Corp Members who were able to take on many more onuses in project coordination, planning and community organizing. This as well benefited the agencies in relieving them of a lot of administration and coordination time. From our understanding, several of the projects we took on under this aspect of the program, actually wouldn't have gotten done otherwise.

Our project was to plan, implement and share ultimate responsibility and success for the Sammamish river project.

As the connector between Lake Washington and Lake Sammamish, the Sammamish River has historically served as a travel corridor and staging area for upstream *salmonid* spawning habitat. However, the river was channelized in the 1960s and much habitat diversity was lost. Then, the river had very little shade or structural differentiation, both of which are essential elements of salmonid habitat. The banks of the Sammamish River were predominantly covered with invasive weeds such as the *Reed Canary* grass, Purple Loose strife and Himalayan blackberry. These weeds crowded out the native plants and trees and did not serve as a source of food or shelter for salmonids.

We, as the Project Assistants, were briefly educated on the history of the Sammamish River and its importance to the livelihood of the Pacific North-West salmonid. Training was also given in plant identification, mostly to foreigners because their tree species are different from the native and non-native that grew along the river.

Once the goal was ascertained, an essential visit to the river was made to establish the assessment parameters. The parameters were determined as follows: slope, existing vegetation, existing trees, access points, adjacent tributaries, and adjacent land use. We then divided the river into 18 stretches.

We analyzed the collected data to determine priority sites. The sites were prioritized by parameters, in descending order, to determine whether they were adjacent to a tributary, the accessibility of each site, the steepness of the slope and the existing vegetation.

The Sammamish River project was generally successful. Although we were unable to completely finish it in the time allocated, we did accomplish quite a substantial bit. We surveyed the entire Sammamish River and determined 6 sites, which were in immediate need of restoration and were feasible work areas.

In reflection of all the time and planning that went into the project, some aspects were satisfactorily and complacently accomplished and others which we would maybe rethink.

At this point of unfolding events, and from my own observation, a judgmental feeling captured my soul about the many American friends I had come across. I developed an impression that each American seemed to know more than the other. I was also more than half-way Americanized now that I was able to understand their slang and dialects, and could catch up with the lightening speed at which they uttered English words.

Angelito "Ags" Geverola, from the Philippines, will apply stabilizing straw to slopes along creek beds to reduce erosion.

Volunteer crew members working on Rattlesnake Mountain.

"The work was tough but it has brought me closer to my community and environment. This is one of the most rewarding things I've ever done."
--**Hughes Lee, World Conservation Corps Crew Member from Des Moines, Washington**

"This is an exciting opportunity for DNR, the World Conservation Corps, and the University of Washington and Mountains to Sound Greenway to work together and share expertise. We're pleased with the road-to-trail project completed on the Rattlesnake Mountain Scenic Area, and look forward to being an ongoing partner in future efforts." --**Doug McClelland, Department of Natural Resources**

World Conservation Corps Crew

Doug Schindler, Program Supervisor for the Greenway Trust, points out new grass, which was planted on this rocky roadbed only days before. Schindler coordinated the 1995 summer projects.

This abandoned road near Hansen Creek is covered with a layer of compost to be tilled into the soil. It will soon sprout a cover of new vegetation.

Crews apply GroCo provided by Sawdust Supply using a truck equipped with a compost blower hose.

Before -- This road in the Hansen Creek drainage was an unstable logging road, highly visible from I-90.

After -- 1.2 miles of this road are now stabilized and supporting new vegetation.

Volunteer work crews applying compost in the Hansen Creek drainage near Snoqualmie Pass

Bill Mckee and Julius Omosa along the Puget Sound

Corp Members upon completion of the restoration
projects.

CHAPTER SIX

COGITATION:

Now that I'm African Americanized, I totally comprehend that service to others is based on mercy and benevolence even toward those who have obliterated virtue. I must not dispute the fact that kindness and generosity, compassion and forgiveness are vital in any human society.

Hatred and vengeance are never true responses to life itself. Such feelings may tempt us when we find ourselves in situations of personal betrayal, but it is wise to wrestle with the great ethical, moral and spiritual powers we possess.

In the absence of awkward anxiety and social tolerance of actual concern, there is unprecedented law and order and gratitude by being of our very core significance whenever we find ourselves, today. That is what God has created and designed us to be and do on our earthly existence. When we choose this sort of path or devotion, it is not an assurance that vices will not happen upon us, it is simply that we can no longer lean toward discouragement or resentment in our torment. Fear, itself, signifies lack of defense, protection and confidence and resentment is an implication that if a tragedy occurred, it shouldn't have taken place like it did. These two conditions are wrong and insignificant to those of us who have a strong belief in ourselves toward success and achievement.

Remember that so many great achievers including: Martin Luther King, born in 1929 and assassinated in 1968, in Memphis, Tennessee, whose nonviolent demonstrations against racial inequality led to civil rights legislation; Abraham Lincoln, born in 1809 and assassinated in 1865, the 16th. president of the United States, who led the Union to victory in the Civil War and abolished slavery; Bob Marley, born in 1945 and died in 1981, a Jamaican musician, whose music, much of which he wrote himself, established reggae internationally as an essential part of pop music. Nelson Mandela, the South African statesman, born in 1918, who, after a long incarceration as a political prisoner (1964 to 1990), became the first Black president of the Republic of South Africa; Thomas Alva Edison (1847 – 1931), who invented the light bulb, the microphone, and phonograph, in

1877; Karamchand Mohandas Gandhi, the Indian national leader, born in 1869 and died in 1948, whose nonviolent civil resistance to British rule led to India's independence in 1947, among many others, were not wealthy or rich in a material sense, but were successful in their endeavors, desires and goals. One can die poor, materially, but succeed in achieving personal goals which culminate into a rich soul full of complacence and foregoing benefits.

We are all on this planetary journey, together, and my implication is that since we are all special beings created by a special God, in His image and likeness, we can not be defeated by anything. But this is determined by how we approach life and the kind of understanding we develop about daily occurrences whether positive or detrimental to us. The extent of faith and self-judgment we develop in ourselves determines the outcome and its impact on our lives.

One problem that people face in their lives is self-comparison to others and selfish desires to greedily gather all good aspects of life without regard to the welfare of their companions or fellow humans. If only individuals can learn to, first, know themselves, what their desires are and the desires and needs of others, and ultimately have faith in themselves, and believe that whoever they are is what God intended them to be and are for that purpose of unique creation and purpose, then it may be easier to curb many difficulties that the world faces in our times.

God has a path and purpose for each one of us. This is one sure lesson I have learned by taking the long journey that delivered me in America and know that the journey is still not even half-way but only a path toward my destiny, where my ultimate significance lies so as to serve God's purpose and His people in numerous ways.

If we magnify everything in our perspective to a broader context, it is much easier to cast away anything that might deter us from reaching higher heights and sure happiness. This is simply to comprehend what change—as my change from living in Kenya to America, can bring about. Some may call it luck, but luck is when good planning meets opportunity, and without either aspect, more so good planning on the individual's part, there is no constitution of luck itself. Then we can determine what change, collaboration and hard work can and cannot accomplish if only people left others free of care and judgment.

The story below was narrated to me, in 1981, when I was a third grader in Kisii Primary School, of the significance of determination, hard work, team work, and the magic of independence.

Sometimes, we harbor ill will against those we believe have misguided us or who have offended us. We hope that one day we shall find an opportunity to get free blessings

82

or get even with those who have worked harder, on their part, in order to attain positive results. However, harboring a grudge because of positions in which we find ourselves due to laziness or shortcomings of our own making can be counterproductive and detrimental. Such actions may poison our lives with bitterness and resentment as we seethe in anger. On the other hand, laziness or unwillingness to collaborate with others can lead us into self-made slaves. Thus, we become a burden and a threat to others and ourselves. People have ravaged themselves physically, psychologically and emotionally as they yearn for vengeance.

And yet, they could have taken the easiest route to achieving peace of mind and complacence. It is imperative to forgive and build bridges with those who have upset us or insubordinately undermined their responsibilities, regardless of the magnitude of their mistakes.

Many, many years ago, Hare, Hen, Cat and Rat lived together under one roof in a distant, small farm of their own along river *Sondu*, a river flowing into the famous Lake Victoria, a few miles away from Kogelo Village. Their friendship had a long history, dating back to the ages when crocodiles lived on land, times when hippos had hair on their skins and hyenas never laughed like human beings.

The four therefore had phi las love for each other and everyday, shared a lot in common, including daily meals.

One day, Hare, who was so hard-working that whenever she placed her tools down, she fell sick, came across some corn seeds which she presented to the other three friends on the farm so that they could plant them for the forthcoming hunger season. This way, Hare knew that they would have abundant food in their granary for a happy living.

"Who will give me a hand in planting these corn seeds?" asked Hare.

"I have never learned how to plant," said Cat. Rat claimed she was sick.

"I like corn, let me eat the seeds," declared Hen.

"If that is the case, I will plant the corn alone because you are not hard-working and do not know what team-work can help us achieve." Hare announced and chose to carry out the planting by herself.

Two weeks later, corn seedlings had germinated and this really made Hare overjoyed. A month later, the young seedlings had been infested by weeds in their fertile farm.

She, for this reason, asked her three friends for assistance in weeding the garden; but Cat regretted that she had a flu. "Rain is about to fall," argued Rat. "Just let the weeds grow where they belong. In any case the soil is fertile enough to support all plants including those interfering with your selfish interests," said Hen.

So, Hare had no option but to perform the duty herself and was in the end amused by the good work she had done on her own. Eventually, the corn grew into maturity and strong—producing cobs.

Since the corn was now fully grown, it was the right time for harvest. Hare once again asked for help from her friends: This time Cat said that she was going on a safari (journey or adventure) and Hen complained that she was tired. "I do not like corn that much," declared Rat.

Ultimately, Hare did all the work by herself, including the harvesting, piling and storage, locked up the granary and hid the key. Since there was still enough food in their little house for consumption, the other three animals did not mind.

When the food in the house ran out, they were ready to work. "Who will go and bring the food from the granary?" asked Hare.

"It is me, it is me," shouted all the three friends. "But you gave all sorts of discouraging answers when it was planting season."

"I never thought I could be this hungry," said Rat.

"I thought the food in our kitchen would never get finished," said Hen.

"I wish I had helped you, dear Hare," said Cat.

87

"The corn in the store is all mine, I worked so hard, by myself, requested assistance from each of you but you all turned me down with all sorts of stupid responses. You lacked focus, determination, fore-thought, team-work, and thought I had no goal to achieve when I was wearing off my little hands in the farm. If you live in this hut with me, insure your own food security. If you feel neglected, you can find a better place elsewhere," Hare announced.

Cat decided to go out in search of food. At the end of her first day, she had not been successful in looking for food. She yawned so badly that tears rolled down her face. But she was fortunate the moment a woman from the nearby village, on her way from the local *Oyugis* Market, saw Cat shading tears and bestowed some food to her, who upon her return home whispered to Hen and Rat about the kind and generous woman. As they slept, that night, all they contemplated was the humble, heart-rending woman.

The following morning, the three starving little animals dressed up and arranged to pay the woman a visit. Because Cat was familiar with her, she approached the woman, first, and revealed to her that if she let her stay in her house, in exchange for food and protection, she would in return chase all the mice and roaches away from the house.

The woman hated the presence of mice and roaches in her house, so she let Cat live with her.

Then Hen appeared next. "If you let me stay in your residence, I will lay eggs for you," she vowed, and since the woman's children liked eggs so much, and had only been eating bird eggs, they persuaded their mother to let Hen be their guest as long as she delivered her promise to the family.

Finally, Rat appeared and promised to sing lullabies to her children late in the night so they could fall into deep, peaceful sleep. "Let's hear you sing a little bit," they asked Rat. Her songs were so disgusting as she opened her tiny mouth in an endeavor to sing. The family members disliked her hisses so bad.

"If you don't allow me to live with you, I shall be stealing food from your kitchen," promised Rat.

When the woman heard Rat's remarks and had had terrible experiences from mice, Rat's cousins, she asked Cat to chase the rodent away from the home. Both, since then became great foes, and Rat still remains a thief, stealing food from human kitchens.

Hare remained in the wild and is still there working so hard, daily, to feed herself and has continued laughing at Hen, Rat and Cat, as she watches them in their daily struggles to survive in the human home, where they do not have as much freedom and independence to eat whatever and whenever they like.

Hare, for this reason, wrote a song:

91

Sweet, sweet banana!
Cat and Hen are slaves

Rat is a thief

Sweet, sweet banana!
Cat and Hen are slaves

Rat is a thief

I'm free and on my own

Ha! ha! Ha!

Ha! ha! Ha!

La! la! La! La-lah!

In the same tone of being African Americanized, I'm able to look at life from both perspectives. The story above is not just meant to entice children into humorous moods, but it is a clear revelation of what history has turned peoples' lives into, more especially the lives of Americanized Africans.

This is not to suggest that Africans are lazy or the West is at fault for its welcoming hand, of hidden purpose, but they find themselves in such a situation that they are forced to live as slaves to the West—just like Hen, Cat and Rat.

Here we are, maybe due to unawareness, ignorance or undetermined laziness, modern slaves who have to dance to every tune and blackmail of the West so as to be fed when there is abundant food out there in the wild (Africa) just left to Hare.

A professor of Economics at Nairobi University, in Kenya, named Mwabwa, once declared that: "Africa has now jumped out of the frying pan of British colonialism into the raging fire of American neocolonialism."

When in the course of human events, it becomes essential for one people to dissolve the political, social, cultural and economic forces which have interwoven us together, and to ignore earthly, Godly, truths which we found already in existence on this earth, the distinct, yet similar finishing point to which the Ten Commandments and Common Laws, a modern respect to our distinct thoughts dictate and require us to announce, to all, the very reasons why we cannot live in togetherness. In harmony, love and dignity, as well as cast away tribalism, racism and human differences which will not only create bloodshed and death, but will not deliver us to the promised land, and plain reality and truth.

The progress of a people is not only defined by economic growth statistics. To deliver holistic advancement, progress vision must be founded on a well-articulated guiding philosophy.

The absence of this essential ingredient has been worsened by the lack of political and moral will by successive regimes since the abolition of slavery and the end of scramble and partition of the African continent. That is the only reason why the founders of existing regimes formed them after thorough unification, and their initial goal has worked so successfully even after four centuries; still working to divide the African people further while we strive to settle in the West, at our own accord, to fulfill the slave-masters' will as Africa remains abandoned and discarded by its own people, although the continent is the wealthiest in natural resources.

"African socialism and its application to planning in Kenya," for instance, had excellent ingredients from which to fashion a holistic development vision.

The manifesto pointed out that political equality, social justice and human dignity were key elements for the country's vision. But politics of opportunism and imposed development blueprints crafted in Washington and London, culminated in the total disregard of the values; which were intended to create opportunities in Africa and to its people, so as to discourage or stop modern slavery.

Upon attaining self-rule for most African nations, if Africans had sought answers to the disturbing question: How do we attain human dignity, equality and justice through a national progress vision and proceed to craft a vision based on the answers, we would have evolved into the most socially adjusted and empowered societies on the face of the earth.

Answering that question would have forced Africans to formulate core values and guiding principles upon which our development philosophy, plans and programs would have been anchored.

We conversely rushed into unforeseen adoption of foreign growth models. The result is a doubtful reputation and blinded philosophies without humanizing values that will give birth to a model to ensure and secure shared prosperity, respect for human dignity and equal access to opportunities for sustainability and social advancement, so that we reverse from colonial trends and mentalities that Africans will always be beggars to the West.

With immense social and economic challenges, we cannot afford to pursue a blind development course by merely running away from the problem—deep into the West, instead of confronting it and securing a just and stronger economic society for the good of our children and grand-children.

This is crucial, especially when we are living witnesses to the turmoil caused to the so-called leading economies by the unforeseen and blind pursuit of nude capitalism and material accumulation in disregard of equal progress for all.

With equal and just development for all nations, then there would be world-peace and respect for all races and cast away discriminations even among people of the same race, like the feminine idiots whom I met in London, who were acting more sophisticated as a result of political, historical, economic and social imbalances, created by the so-called economic powers which forces people to act with contempt and hatred towards others because they are of African origin which, to them, graduates them from more blackness.

This as well brings about stereotypes that have ravaged humanity in America, just like the ethnicity monster that is consuming Africa daily. The concept of preference to be branded "Black" rather than African American because Black people in America have been brain-washed by their media and other scrupulous sources, to believe that Africa, which is their mother-land, is the worst place on earth. Then, here is where exposure, self-education and diversity play such a vital role in shaping up human societies by taking time to imbue and digest hearsay and rumor, intended for selfish, political agendas in order to sustain the foundations and ideals on which painful human societies were founded.

Stereotyping is a very common American culture especially when it runs along race, and surely as biased and baseless as these stereotypes are, even interestingly agitating, yet they are let to dictate alliances with people rather than internal sinister self-contradictions.

But the difference is that racism in America does not necessarily affect the peoples' ability to produce positive economic results or work together in unity as opposed to tribalism in Africa which divides people at the grass-root level.

"Despair is typical of those who do not comprehend the causes of evil, see no solution, and are incapable of struggle," declared Vladimir Lenin.

Whereas it is true that historical human differences are in a perilous condition, and impunity is the norm, Africans must resolutely decline to accept the notion of stereotypes, racial contentions by African-Americans—now between black and black—peddled by those dismayed of Black peoples' unity and emancipation, that our salvation and the true reforms of the African continent will emanate from abroad through the World Bank or the International Monetary Fund.

We are however, at the tipping point to a chaotic situation and with little or no chance of redemption unless we make an emergency turn away from racism in America and tribalism in Africa.

Lasting emancipation can only be acquired by permanent institutions, and eradication of ignorance to be replaced by expanded academic facts, invested, manned by Africans and African-Americans and addressing all the facets of our historical ills. Redemption, like independence, will only come with the efforts of the victims in question.

The prognosis is not very promising. It is factual that human beings are complex and somewhat unpredictable. Their conduct and actions recur with such metronomic regularity that you could use them to set your watch.

It is hardly astonishing that people are not any different from cows. They both follow a leader blindly. They at times take cues from a vocal few even if by doing so they undermine their own interests and dignity.

If Africa's political landscape, for instance, were the setting of a movie, it would be difficult to name it. It would probably be titled: The Apocalypse Forever, Tragic Political Skull-duggery or The People as Cannon Fodder.

People have been treated to a deluge of features, with the most significant feature being the contest of wits between those who form governments of the day and the opposing side. It comprises of an ordinary re-run named theft from the people who appointed chiefs of governments of the day, lies about performance, and insurance of lawlessness, ignorance, poverty and illiteracy, so as to suppress those who are supposed to question their performance and credibility, in executing their day to day government duties in false indignation.

Whenever the peoples' voices pounce and pursue the gluttons involved in state governance with the sort of zeal portrayed, some inner questions arise because it is imperative, for the peoples' survival that African governments should not just work, but be seen to be working.

I'm trying to show the link between leadership and consequences of the status quo because each and every activity and element in our existence is inter-linked and webbed up in a manner that gives today's results. America's history, for instance, is determined by Africa, Asia, Australia, Blacks, Whites, Asians, our virtues and vices and all that gives this earth its definition and its significance.

Therefore if we question ourselves why we are at peace or rising against one another, the answers we develop for either the good or bad solution is a result of who we were and our actions five hundred years ago, a decade ago, last year, yesterday, today or now.

If we expect supernatural times, increases and abundance in our earthly existence, then we better let all humans be optimistic that they will be satisfied even in times of catastrophe. It should be within our remembrance and awareness that there will never be peace to particular individuals if their neighbor is not at peace. For peace to prevail on earth, there will have to be the presence and assurance of equity, harmony and mutual respect. A time when no brother or sister will envy or be envied by fellow brother or sister when it comes to social justice and universal fairness. Not necessarily envying your partner because of any possession acquired through means of fairness, hard work and blessing, but equity in the sense that what belongs to many or all, is shared among all.

But again, these social imbalances refer us back to history; which dictates that the lines have already been drawn, unless one side of the entire argument backs down which seems unlikely, considering human greed and egoistic, selfish desires.

I have time and again emphasized to those I have had the opportunity to be free with that the happiest persons seem to be the poorest men and women in society, for they have no greed and selfish ambitions like most us do, or rather the desire to acquire all at the expense of others irrespective of surrounding consequences.

Apart from the three basic human needs—food, shelter and clothing—there is no disturbing notion before the poor. Poverty is as well not the best life experience but what about simple but comfortable living? Because in opulence, there doesn't seem to be a standard measure of how much is required by the greedy human soul in order to give in to want and selfish desires.

Such arguments may seem trivial and or senseless, but they are the resultant causes of our behaviors at the moment and the world histories, which range from the eras of creation to this very minute when we are rising against one another without the wisdom that we did not invent these detrimental facts and ideals which we stand for or are against, in our history.

If only people would realize that their brothers and sisters are not to blame for their bitterness in life, then there would be reconciliation and acceptance of each other's position of existence rather than point fingers at one another while claiming to know better than others.

This brings about many questions and answers about the many challenges and dilemmas our brothers and sisters are faced with in America, for example, and without concrete knowledge and wisdom, point fingers at those who look strange to them, or who are at times branded nicknames such as "immigrants," or "aliens." No wonder America is orbiting in parallel universes, which provides us with answers as to why other human beings are viewed as "aliens." Being a distinct universe, it gives them enough reason to blame innocent people who are trying to make ends meet, for failures of their own crafting.

People have since time in living memory faced adversities, tribulations and challenges of unimaginable magnitude. My own story being a perfect one. Mine is a clear testimony that we all live our earthly lives because we have been destined by Godly powers; that no human can dictate another's destiny because it has already been crafted and stored in a holy place.

As far as my memories can take me, it was when I was eight years old that I knew to love and respect those I have been blessed to share a life with. It was a period when I witnessed the first solar eclipse and countrywide hunger of unprecedented magnitude in Kenya, when the country's citizens were forced to consume yellow corn flour. It was also the year of my graduation as a young initiate in my family so that I gained status and responsibility, upon circumcision, as an acceptable member of my society.

In that specific year, 1980, because of the hunger experienced in the country, some men devised creative domestic austerity measures to counter the difficult economic times that had cropped up. Some sounded crazy, seemingly borrowed from the devil's personal container of deception.

Whenever their wives prepared meals, more especially ugali, men, who were the bread winners of their respective families, personally poured the corn flour for them, in the cooking process, and subsequently marked with the palm of their hands, the balance so that they knew where the next meal preparation commenced. In those difficult times of the eighties, it was the only way the family head would know if an intruder interfered with the flour while he was gone.

Whenever ugali was prepared, they left handprints to prevent their wives from cooking in their absence and knowledge.

To maintain the kitchen expenditure at their homes in proper check, they devised a strange method to ensure that no meal, especially ugali, was prepared while their presence was not felt in the villages.

Those who reared chickens got hold of the fowls and made marks on the corn flour with their claws. Only known to them, was which fowl made the marks. Woe unto their wives should the marks be different from the ones they left after the last meal.

For others, the challenge had been ensuring that the same quantity of ugali was prepared each day. To ensure this happened, they made holes on the sides of the cooking pots so that any attempts to add water in order to increase the size of the dish beyond the standard level would not succeed.

I vividly recollect an incident of Maria Angoi Gisese, a housewife in my village, who was among the women that bore the brunt of the machinations of their husbands in that period of hunger in Kenya. Her sister at some point paid them a visit and brought them some sugar, curdled milk and some traditional vegetables.

Her sister received her ceremoniously in the absence of her husband, Ongiri, who had left the homestead at cock-crow to market a sheep at the local *Nyakongo* Animal Market.

Since Maria could not go after a free-ranged chicken, in the home, a choice delicacy for guests of nobility, she chose to prepare ugali and eggs instead.

As fate had it, the day never turned out prosperous for her husband, Ongiri. He didn't sell the sheep as he had anticipated, and his hope for getting the money he needed lay in the egg-laying fowl. That morning he had left three eggs, and on his way home he was silently counting his chicks even before they hatched.

He went straight to the spot where the chickens laid their eggs but to his astonishment, found no eggs.

"Who took the eggs that were here?" he thundered. The wife explained that she had fried the eggs for her sister who had visited earlier and left.

"You mean you ate three chickens?" he exclaimed, as he proceeded to swing hard kicks and punches on her.

The issue was only settled when elders intervened and forced him to apologize to his in-laws.

Thrifty men, I discovered as I matured, were bound to be found in every society and still some who seemed blessed with abundance, portrayed some form of shabbiness.

I recall the case of a couple who devised a peculiar formula of telling whose pieces of meat cooking in the pot belonged to whom. They tied together the meat pieces so that it was easier to identify which belonged to whom once the sensitive moment of feeding themselves came about.

As a result of that year's unexpected hunger period, some people posted signs on their doors reading: "we have moved;" to ward off unwanted guests whenever they cooked a delicacy. To such people, uninvited guests constituted intrusion which led to woes and unplanned expenditure.

In the neighborhood, there was as well rumored of a man who had been enjoying a whole roast chicken and a mountain of ugali, when he heard an unexpected knock on his door. Dreading the prospect of unwillingly sharing his rare viand, he slipped the dish under his bed.

All went according to plan and selfish wish, until he heard a cat munching away under the bed, to the amusement of his guest.

This also brings about memories of the ancient life-styles of the villages when some children went to school without shoes, and it mostly seemed like those who wore shoes were irrelevant because they were only just a handful, special individuals.

Ideally, every village boy owned a hut where he enjoyed his privacy. However, not every parent in the village had the means to build even a simple hut for their boys. As such, many of the unlucky boys, who thought that spending nights in the kitchen or old grain store was unmanly, were forced to seek alternative accommodation from that fortunate comrade who owned a hut, or what the people of my tribe call *esaiga.*

In the nights, it was common to meet boys with old, battered blankets hanging over their shoulders, walking along the village footpaths headed to a friend's home.

For privacy, esaiga was always located some distance from the parents' house and always hidden behind over some grown shrubs; disguised as flowers. The mud-plastered walls of the grass-thatched cubicles were normally

106

decorated with newspaper or magazine pages, especially those with splashy pictures of pretty women. And to make the walls brighter, the cubicle owners usually added their own unflattering photographs in strategic places where there was a chance that it would attract the eyes of neighborhood girls whenever they visited..

The cubicles were hardly swept and if they were, the dirt was left in a heap behind the door. Under the beds, were battered shoes and one could even spot a rat as big as a cat dart from one end to another.

But when a girl was expected, the dusty floor was sprinkled with water, swept and the bed, which usually remained unmade for days or even months, was made and kept neat.

The huts were always shared among two or three boys. And when one of them had a date with a village girl, it mostly turned out to be an inconvenience. The roommates would unexpectedly seek alternative accommodations.

Since few village girls had the courage to visit boys' cubicle, they were usually fetched by the boyfriend, armed with a club, machete or another crude weapon, at a pre-arranged place and often under the cover of darkness.

As the other boys gave room to the two, they could hardly wait for the next day to be regaled with the accounts of the escapades of the lucky roommate. And since no one would want to sleep on the floor, it would not be a shock to

107

find more than four boys squeezed in one bed. To maximize space, some slept facing upwards and others downwards despite the fact that some may have had stinking toes from athletes foot.

During the rainy season, the boys were lazy to find firewood but since in one way or another they had to keep warm, they in the cover of darkness uprooted a neighbor's fence poles and sneaked them into the cubicle as firewood. These became many of the days villagers were heard swearing by the names of their mothers or tribal gods that one day they would burst the brains of anyone interfering with their fences.

"I did not erect my fence for rascals to harvest it for firewood. The day I will catch someone messing with my fence I will fry their genitals," they would warn. However, witty boys managed to vandalize the fences.

Once caught, the hefty monetary fines and other punishments imposed by the no-nonsense tough talking chief and village elders, quickly cooled down the fence owner's temper.

The situation got worse when it was the rainy season and maize had matured. The boys invaded the neighbors' farms to collect corn to secretly roast in their huts. But the worst came when the fire became uncontrollable and razed the hut. Only then did they reveal the socially unacceptable activities that had been going on in the esaiga.

Chapter Seven

Kisii Primary School

1981 was also a year of remarkable events as it marked my first bold step toward exposure and civilization. It was the year of my first visit to Kisii Town. I might have been to the town in the course of the preceding years, but not to my knowledge and attention—as I was too young.

So, on the material day, the first time I was privileged to see a three-story building on my way to the hospital in the town, was a day I shall never forget, not because my brother, Donysius, caused this fortune by striking my right eye with a stone catapulted, but because it marked the beginning of the journey which I'm still traveling into my Godly-commanded destiny.

Since my mother wanted me to have a quality education, which was never the ultimate case, she later, that year, secured me a vacancy in *Sakawa* School, a privately owned institution. But tuition fee was too high here (10 dollars per semester) so my father chose to relocate me to Kisii Primary School, where I paid about two quarters per semester.

Kisii Primary School was basically my childhood foundation and this became a testing period of my social abilities. In this school, we remained under the free care of Mr. Oyugi Orora, as the headmaster, and his deputy— Oriku. It was a time when I freely inter-mingled with early-childhood friendships in the company of Muigai Muhia, who was my first desk-mate in the institution, as a third grader, and henceforth remained a desk-mate in St. Mary's Mosocho into subsequent years in Cardinal *Otunga* High School, in 1989. Other peers included Omuria Robert, Onyambu Nicholas, Otachi Felix, Masese Seth, Gerald Keraro, Nayan V. Shah, Anwar Ahmed, Johakim Ondieki, Kiwango Simon, Eddy Kasumba and *Tin tin.*

Since we never had modern toys to play with, our versatility at Kisii Primary School enabled us come up with crafty innovations like the toy cars we drove—made up of wire, and bounded up with black rubber bands.

But on the other hand, exposure or rather the so-called civilization constituted nothing short of troubled times both with family members and the world. My family members complained that I was getting too exposed, perhaps turning criminal, by merely learning to cope with activities of the day and my common interaction with children of the earth. It surely occurred that I had no place on this earth— perhaps too open to people, irrespective of their social status. It was not my wish and intention to discriminate and choose what God's children I was destined to interact with; but those that were blessed to share a life-time with me. This was surely the commencement of name-branding, which culminated year after year, into this very minute when others have tenaciously assumed that what they portend me to be in their own minds is what I ought to be. This is the unseen war that most of us fight every given day without determination. That, simply by living your God-destined life, others are obstinately in resistance so that we may live a life of their own liking and belief. Otherwise; you will be branded definitions and considered an outcast or social misfit.

I have in the past been called a family reject just because I'm trying to play my role of creation; be the one and only Julius of my sort that ever existed and serve God's interests and purpose. Perhaps people are and are expected to be so sinister that when you happen to be the peoples' person, benevolent and loving, then you turn out irrelevant and therefore an outcast living among the evil- possessed majority.

111

Although I never excelled in school like most did and, as I was expected and required to do by family and society, my level of imbecility proved that I was pursuing an illegal profession by attending academic institutions which time and again explained concocted theories that I was already aware of— but in a distinct formula. I, everyday, believed that not merely a single experiment could be used to define us, and our potentials in achieving ultimate goals. I therefore adhered to the man-made rules which I was born with, since society would be defined as sordid without order and conformity.

The only two days of the week of which I enjoyed myself in 1981 were Saturdays and Sundays, when we either went to Cardinal Otunga High School or invited Brother Patrick, one of the missionaries in the school, to put into permanent record, pictorially, our images, so that no one would dispute in the subsequent future that gone days are the best compared to the unknown, unseen forthcoming days.

As little and fragile as we were, we posed in all *old-school* postures that the Brother asked us to take including, myself, wearing a wrist-watch which I had borrowed from one of my sisters, Florence Nyasuguta, around my long-sleeved shirt.

Julius

Susan, Josephine, Donysius, Mary and Julius Omosa;
dancing to "Elusion"

113

Julius and Timmy

Mr. Evans Gesicho, Julius and Donysius Omosa

Little did I know about the many obstacles ahead of me, more especially those that were brought about by human differences in opinion, character, and selfish desire to acquire power so as to build a society which serves their personal interests and material gains in order to weaken me insidiously.

In my tribal, Kisii society, just like all other African communities, we are guided by proverbs—for instance the one which is non-racist, that sees no skin color but justifies all human beings as of one origin, and therefore brothers and sisters, the only difference is our unknown differences in souls.

So, in that particular year, I chose to accompany my age-mates and age-sets on Saturdays to a local church in Mosocho where a man named "Kiage the evangelist" preached and taught about the origin of man, his actions on earth and its projected consequence. I wanted to know where I belonged, as a young man and member of the larger human society, and for the same reason to recognize my need.

This was called the Mosocho Community Religious Day Program, and Mr. Kiage, in 1981, told us that in the beginning, Man was endowed with noble powers and a well-balanced mind. He was perfect in his being, and in harmony with God. His thoughts were pure, his ambitions holy. But through disobedience, his powers were perverted,

115

and selfishness took the place of love. His nature became so weakened through transgression that it was impossible for him, in his own strength, to resist the power of evil. He was made captive by the devil and he would have remained so forever had not God specially interposed. It was the supreme sinner's purpose to thwart the divine plot in man's creation, and litter the world with woe and desolation; so he would point to all this evil as the result of God's work in creating man.

Mr. Kiage also reminded us that men may have flattered themselves that their lives have been upright, that their moral character is correct, and imagine that we need not humble the heart before God, like the common sinner, but when our souls are cleansed, we shall see how impure we are; we shall discern the selfishness of motive, the enmity against all that is good, that has defiled every act of life. Then we shall know that our own righteousness is in fact filthy Christ alone can cleanse us from the defilement of sin, and renew our hearts in his own likeness.

One ray of the glory of God, one gleam of the purity of His son, penetrating the soul, makes every spot of defilement painfully distinct, and lays bare the deformity and defects of the human character. It makes apparent the unhallowed desires, the infidelity of the heart, the impurity of the lips. The sinner's acts of disloyalty in making void the supreme law, are exposed to his sight, and his spirit is stricken and afflicted under the searching influence of God's spirit. He loathes himself as he views the pure, spotless character of Christ.

Many are quieting a troubled conscience with the thought that they can change a course of evil when they choose, that they can trifle with the invitations of mercy, and yet be again and again impressed. They think that after behaving contrary to the spirit of grace, after casting their influence on the devil's side, in a moment of terrible extremity they can alter their course. But this is not as easy as fore-casted. The experience, the education of a life time, has so thoroughly molded the character that few then desire and wish to receive the image of our savior; Jesus Christ.

Even a single trait of conduct, one sinful wish and desire, persistently cherished, will ultimately neutralize all the religious power. Every sinful indulgence strengthens the soul's aversion. The man who manifests an infidel hardihood, or a stolid indifference to divine reality, is but harvesting the result of that which he has himself sown.

In the entire Biblical teachings, there is not a more scary, fearful caution against trifling with sinister realities than the words of the wise man, that the unwise and transgressor is caught in the cords of the socially unacceptable.

After the Saturday religious programs, we usually crossed over the fence into Cardinal Otunga High School

117

to witness sporting activities there which were held every Saturday—because the institution had some of the best extracurricular equipment in Nyanza Province, back then.

Kenya Army helicopters also triggered many people from the local community to cluster in the institution so as to witness the rare, and sometimes a one time in a lifetime opportunity, so that they could closely see the true appearance of the wonder vessel. Those who laid claims to bravery actually touched the helicopters or posed for pictures near them.

On these Saturdays, once Brother Anthony triggered the marathon gun, myriad uniformed Kenya Army and Air Force recruits raced uphill toward *Soko* Primary School, and downhill toward *Nyakoe*. They negotiated onto *Marani* Road, through *Bomeroga*, by Mama *Cherosia's* hut, *Kula Jasho Lako* grocery shop, and finally back into the institution.

Cardinal Otunga High School was always a remarkable and unique institution. When it was under the management of the White Brothers from the Netherlands, in that era, the Diocese of Kisii which managed Catholic Schools in the district was much more effective.

Contrasting leadership eras in Africa, when African governments and various public and private institutions were under the management of the White minority, then, leadership obligations, such as transparency and accountability, should have been adopted by subsequent regimes—for public commitment and prosperity within the African continent.

When freedom of self-rule was attained, not only in government, but in many other institutions such as schools like Cardinal Otunga High School, Africans took over from where the White man had stopped. Some White people remained to ensure a smooth transition of power, orientation and co-ordination.

Without going into detail of occurrences in between the period of transition and self-rule, the outcome of African independence has led to more complications and tribulation to the continent's people, so that those who did not get a chance to flee the failed state of leadership now wish the White people should have continued with their initial involvement. Besides, there is the question as to how to define a failed state. Is it one that has a government, or rather authority, for smaller institutions, that is present and ready for inspection, or perhaps, one that is steadily focused on its survival that the people in whose name it exists cease to matter or exist?

Could it be one that is permanently at war with itself, with those in leadership and arms of the same government pulling in different directions, where mutual suspicion and disagreement seems to lead every mission?

Without going to higher levels of African governance, I would like to stick to that of Cardinal Otunga High School, since it is a clear reflection of the Kenyan government and all other African governments in general, because I would like to believe that Brother Innocent Dekok and the interests he represented, in the 1950s when the school was founded, feel the local generic men and women in Mosocho. But those people, including Magori, who donated the piece of land where Cardinal Otunga High School stands today, have all along lived on the edge of indigence for as long as we can recall, that we would have to shockingly ask: "why solve their problems now?"

Besides, they are poor and voiceless and no one really considers their concerns to be of any value.

Those in power and governance feed themselves by snatching to the last penny from the poor and suffering, rather than do the right thing which would in return only give them the correct remuneration that they deserve for the services rendered to the community. To their belief, if they honestly serve their people, like *Morimbocho* and all the White Brothers did, then they will be subjecting themselves to voluntary self-enslavement.

It is one thing for the people to disagree on how their institutions or government should be run but for those differences to result in a life and death situation is totally satanic.

120

Those in authority in Cardinal Otunga and Kenya have a duty to positively govern. They waste no time in ascendancy to power, even if it requires that human sacrifices are made for fulfillment of their selfish intentions, and should therefore know that those they are oppressing are about to stand firmly for what they most hold dear.

All these institutions; schools, hospitals, and governmental entities, including central governments, are in a failed state due to personal greed and lack of good planning. These are negative traits that must be acknowledged and overcome.

We customarily break the law without flinching, with a self-crafted culture and corruption which are deeply ingrained. People should learn to rely on public institutions to deliver and distribute their wants and needs, instead of embracing a culture of corruption, nepotism and favoritism.

When individuals are caught in corruption scandals, shame is foreign. Africans have been known to cherish free things and shared national wealth, without taking part in the production and generation of the same. They rightfully insist on their fundamental rights and freedoms but ignorant of their fundamental responsibilities, and fail to honor and appreciate each other's rights.

Kenyans, for instance, are excellent at doublespeak and promises. They will tell you of one thing, while they believe, think and execute the exact opposite. They abhor criticism, disrespect one another, and their memories seem to be short. Past evils are drastically forgotten, even by their courts, and then routinely repeated so that a space and opportunity is created to point fingers at each other and permanently ever-complain disrespectfully without regard to the initial cause of the debilitating problem. They expect the government to solve all their problems, with disregard that the Kenyan government is the problem, and not the solution, even when they intentionally inflict harm on themselves.

But there is hope and positive characteristics for Kenya's troubles too. Her people are hard-working, given opportunity, considering the bad governance which has drawn the country back from its ever-forward moving ambition and will. Although the *Harambee* spirit has over the years been adulterated, Kenyans are benevolent and love to volunteer and bestow all the help they can. Almost every adult has membership in a neighborhood group or project through which social capital is mobilized.

Kenyans also love education, religion and most of them are Christians, Muslims and practitioners of African Traditional Religion and as well subscribe to ancient, positive values.

They must come up with an authentic dialogue process, both localized and national to decently argue ways in which they can construct a nation of prosperity and foregoing benefits to its people. Even with strong institutions and constitutional stability, fundamental national goals cannot be reached unless a culture of inclusive democracy, human rights and the rule of law is developed and adhered to accordingly, with recognition and awareness that no Kenyan citizen, irrespective of their political and or material influence, is above the law of the land; when delivering justice.

In order for African nations to stabilize, deliver to their people and encounter their numerous problems, the first and only drastic step toward achievement of the above mentioned is enforcement and respect of the rule of law. The police force, being a powerful agent of government and the only tool that ensures that the rule of law is respected and enforced, must be well trained, equipped and be well remunerated so as to deter members of the force from becoming public beggars—by soliciting bribes from common citizens in exchange for illegal favors. Police officers in Africa, should be among the highest paid government workers, for effectiveness in execution of their fundamental duties because without enforcement of the rule of law, no other government business is possible.

Secondly, the political class has to commit itself to the national interests rather than self-interests and secular civil society must stay away from fragmentation. Nationals abroad, the academia and creative artists must help unveil a workable vision. The media must also educate on positive values in society and the youth must recognize that it is the largest stakeholder in unity and direction of any nation.

For the case of Kenya, it would be a much better place if "political responsibility" looked as right in deed as it sounds good in word. Excessive mouth-work without corresponding action is insignificant as Kenyans are no longer a timid mass of illiterate humanity but citizens who can assert and demand what they believe and concretely know to be part of their fundamental rights.

Discipline is not the enemy of enthusiasm, and leaders must bear in mind that by driving the country into a point where it is reeling from skewed distribution of national resources, inequalities in opportunities for generation of wealth, failed prosecutions and fortified impunity, it signifies nothing short of a state of emergency and consequent collapse of a nation.

We live in a society that is becoming more and more polarized and should therefore be in the transition to re-order and reform our institutions so as to reduce disparities. Perhaps, devolution of power should be adopted, in countries like Kenya, to reduce ethnic politics by eradicating some divisive aspects from the central government's jurisdiction, and insulating the center from parochial issues. On the other hand, federalism has its demerits too, because if unchecked, it can buttress parochial loyalties and catalyze regional or ethnic groups to demand excessive autonomy from the center.

Without a doubt, Kenya has graduated from the stage of those African democracies that are susceptible to mass riots, political assassinations and insurrections. The flip side, however, is that the country is headed in a direction where the State will in the near future commence to lose its legitimacy.

In early 1980s, although public servants were not highly remunerated, by the government, the safety net was in the fact that they could still survive in government houses located in prestigious neighborhoods.

All these came to an end when the country adopted the Washington Consensus; shrinking State in rhythm with the dogma of limited and market friendly government.

In irony it resulted that the State never decreased in size, considering *ceteris paribus*, it has in reality expanded, resulting in a larger State that provides insufficient services to the people.

The centralized State has had negative results on the pattern of urbanization with the majority of the people jostling to the capital city for employment opportunities, while the initial plot to adopt the so-called subordinate cities to cut down the pressure from the center failed, leading to slum development.

The country's slum dwellers are people with better rural homes than the embarrassing structures they live in, and are growing faster than formal settlements.

My argument concerning this crisis is that the government should register all those slum dwellers and immediately evict them so that they return to their rural homes, and subsequently establish government housing projects on the slum land, in order to re-settle its former occupants at a reasonable rental payment while their efforts are closely monitored to ensure that they secure themselves well paying and sustainable jobs.

The state of Africa, today, as a continent, is a clear testimony of failure. Firstly, its failure to gainfully govern itself without dependency on the West for bailouts from continuous, conspicuous problems which are easily solvable as they are not foreign or new to the continent and its people. Corrupt practices, malice, selfishness, brutal treatments by those in power and possessing self-imposed impunity, and selfishness of politicians and their weak minds, are an endless obstacle on the path of Africa's prosperity and stability.

Secondly, it is a failure of the West in its well-intended interventions in solving Africa's self-manufactured problems, that even after several decades of endeavors, the West has failed to wipe away the tribulations and death on the African continent.

Poverty is not the unavailability of money, it is the lack of opportunity, and the West's focus and interest seems to be attention on treating the symptoms and not as much on confronting the more difficult and intractable ailment beneath. They impose tariffs, manipulate the value of their currencies, discourage imports—more especially imports from African countries—and are governed by a strong arm, the sort of conduct that would give the International Monetary Fund apoplexy.

Now that Africa is the issue of the loins of cultural diplomacy, the best alternative is to not remain a darling of the opulent and a stain on their conscience by sweating a facsimile formula that has failed the African continent for decades but, like China, discard the IMF regulatory brochure into their most appropriate rivers and lakes and threshold take off independently.

1981 was also the year I was requested by my eldest sister, Mary Bonareri, to invite three of my friends who were then A-Level students in the neighboring Cardinal

Otunga High School to come to our home and tell her some of the animal stories which they had also been told by their grandmothers—for her first-year University thesis.

So on that Monday evening, Christopher Onuonga, John Omuya and Geoffrey Keronchi honored their invitation and commenced, in turns, narrating humorous tales about the "Hare's Medicine Bag," "The Cunning Tortoise," and "The Blind Man and the Lion."

Onuong'a started his side of the story by stating that about ten thousand years ago, Hare and Baboon were neighbors. Hare had a son named *Kiwi* but Baboon had no children.

One day, Baboon suggested to Hare that he intended to visit his relatives in Sondu, so, since this would be a long journey, he wished to have someone to chat with on the way. "Would you please let your son come with me," he requested.

"Very well," said Hare.

"I shall provide the food we will need for the journey, so do not interrupt your wife from her busy schedule to prepare any for us," Baboon announced.

"That is agreed upon," said Hare.

The following morning Baboon and Kiwi started out very early in the morning on their remarkable journey. Baboon, however, was not carrying his provisions as he had promised to do, and since Kiwi was tenderly young and due to excitement of this visitation, he did not recognize that Baboon had no food for their lunch.

"Uncle Baboon, I'm thirsty," said Kiwi.

"Wait until we get to the Nyakoe River," answered Baboon. "It is only a few minutes from where we are."

Upon arrival at the river, Kiwi stooped down to quench his overdue thirst with a cold drink, when Baboon intervened, "Don't drink!"

In shock, Kiwi turned his short neck and asked; "Why uncle Baboon, is it a mistake if I drink from the river?"

"Yes, I had forgotten that if children of your age drink from this very river, they will cease to live," explained Baboon.

"Why?"

"That is just the way it has been ever since in living memory, and stop asking too many questions as that may provoke the spirits of the Nyakoe River."

This came as a shock to Kiwi, but as it was customary in the African social setting children were not required to ask too many questions, as it was always known that only elders had answers to the many disturbing mysteries in existence—like why certain meats were only meant for the older people, among others. So Kiwi was dismayed to question further, but he grew even thirstier when he saw Baboon drinking from the very river. Once Baboon was through with his drinking, he splashed his face with some cold water; in order to cool himself down from the hot sun above them. Then they proceeded with their journey toward Sondu where his relatives lived.

"Uncle Baboon, can we sit down and relax ourselves a little since my feet are sore?" asked Kiwi

"Sit down and rest! Do you know what you are really talking about? Ho ho ho! I'm sorry, I forgot that you are still very young. Do you know what they call this jungle? This is the notorious "Eat Me or Eat You" jungle. No one can dare sit down and rest in this jungle, not even Honorable Lion."

Kiwi silenced himself, and the unending journey was resumed. They had now gone past Mosocho Market and were negotiating the last corner before Riverside Tourist Resort, up the hill onto an area in Luoland named *Ruga*.

Once they completed climbing the steep hill leading to Ruga Market, Kiwi was exhausted and dizzy, so he complained of hunger, with tears rolling down his streamlined cheeks. "I can't proceed, I'm hungry. Why don't you let me pluck a few *omenta* leaves from that farmer's land where his goats are grazing?"

"Look, across that hill, is Mr. Omamo's farm. He might have sweet potato leaves ready on the farm."

"Let's go and confirm," answered Baboon.

When they got into the farm, they witnessed that the sweet potato leaves had gotten so healthy, that they had started to turn dark-greenish-purple. Kiwi's mouth watered as he crossed the barbed wire fence to pluck a leaf at the stem.

"Don't eat!" said Baboon.

"Why, Uncle? Did I make any mistake? I'm hungry."

"I forgot to remind you that in this area, whenever you see healthy green leaves and ripe fruits, children are expected to shout, "Mine are the young, unhealthy, unripe ones," and the elders shout; " the mature, healthy ripe ones are meant for me!"

"Don't ask me any questions as to why it is like it is, unless you want to die. I suppose I told you the name of the jungle surrounding us."

"Eat Me or Eat You," whispered Kiwi, a big, round tear rolling down his right cheek because he couldn't take the hunger any more.

"Yes, remember that name but don't recite it too often or else we won't leave this area alive," Baboon whispered, as if he too, was dismayed of something beyond his sight.

Kiwi promised himself to find out from his father, soon upon their return, if he too knew about the dangers of the jungle, that is, he thought, if he didn't meet his demise on the way because he had become dismayed, terribly hungry and his tiny feet were sore.

They proceeded once again, in the direction of Oyugis Market but Kiwi was now a little overjoyed and confident because they both walked at a very slow pace, the reason being that Baboon had feasted on too many leaves and berries that his belly almost dragged on the ground.

A little before sunset, they emerged out of the jungle, on to a grass plain with a few scattered green shrubs. They had walked a little way when Baboon aroused Kiwi's attention. "Look," pointing to a small bush that grew a little way from their path.

"What is it?" asked Kiwi, anticipating that it was something edible; and which children were allowed to eat.

"That shrub's leaves are very good for burns, blisters and flu. Should you ever hear me cry, "I'm burning! I'm burning!" You must run to this particular shrub, called *omoroka*, and deliver its leaves. Don't forget."

"No, I won't forget."

A little later, just as the sun was setting into the horizons of Lake Victoria, toward the distant Kisumu City, they both reached their destination. The home of Baboon relatives who were overjoyed to see them. They gave Baboon and Kiwi some water to drink, and while they rested, they prepared them some potato *hash-browns* and coleslaw salad. When Kiwi saw the coleslaw and the huge pot of steaming potato hash browns, his mouth was filled with saliva. He said to himself that it was good that he had not eaten all day. Then he could fill up his belly without fear that he had eaten excessively because he did not expect his uncle, Baboon,

132

to eat so much since his belly was still filled with the wild sweet potato leaves and berries he engulfed down on their way to Sondu.

They both washed their hands, and because Baboon was the eldest, he was the first one to eat. Then as Kiwi was about to put a morsel of hash-brown into his tiny mouth, Baboon jumped up and, spitting what was already in his mouth, cried out as if he were in pain; "I'm burning! I'm burning!" Without hesitation, Kiwi stood up and made for the little shrub which Baboon had told him was called omoroka.

Upon Kiwi's return, Baboon had eaten up all the food. Just a few remnants of hash-browns remained dispersed in the bowl. Kiwi ate these, a few bones which baboon had discarded on the floor and some countable pieces of coleslaw that stood on the tray. He tried to complain, but there was no attention because Baboon was busy chatting with his relatives about the invasion of their corn on the farm, a few months earlier, by foreign, black worms.

That particular night, Kiwi found it rather impossible to fall into deep sleep; as he hallucinated huge pots of potato hash-browns and countless trays of coleslaw standing before him but could not reach them as this was a mere dream.

The following morning, his uncle woke him up at 5 a.m. to commence their journey back home. *Daraja Mbili* was quite a distance away, the very reason they got up this early

133

in order to avoid risking darkness through the jungle—Eat Me or Eat You.

On their way home, Kiwi once more ate the bitter, unripe fruits while his greedy uncle ate the ripe ones.

Hare was glad to see them back home, although he did not like the looks of his son, Kiwi, who looked worn out and exhausted.

"Are you ill!" Hare exclaimed.

"No, it has been a long journey," Baboon intervened drastically, before Kiwi could reveal the ordeals he went through along the way to Sondu. "Your son is still young and weak for a journey like that one," Baboon continued, and after some little conversations between Hare and himself, he left the home and headed to his own house.

After he had left their homestead, Kiwi narrated to his father, in detail, about everything that had taken place and about the Eat Me or Eat You jungle.

"There is no such a jungle in existence, why did Baboon take you along to subject you into all these painful experiences? This is totally unacceptable, you better run fast to your mother and get yourself some sustenance before you collapse in my presence. I will talk to your uncle about it."

Hare never asked Baboon about it, and six months later Baboon again asked Hare to let his son accompany him to visit his relatives. Because Hare had not talked about the last journey, Baboon thought Kiwi had not mentioned anything to his father.

"I'm sorry, friend, I sent Kiwi to visit my mother who is very ill; but if you don't mind I can come along with you since I have some issues to sort out with your brother in-law—Monkey."

Baboon was reluctant but because he was afraid to walk alone through the jungle, he accepted Hare's offer.

"Don't worry about our food on the way," said Hare, "I will provide the food myself."

"That's right. I was a little worried about how I was to carry two baskets because I always have to carry my medicine with me, as I have an illness which has to be given immediate attention three times daily."

"What happens if you forget the medicine?" asked Baboon.

"I will meet my death," said Hare.

The following morning, they both began their long journey, and as they traveled, Hare occasionally sipped from his bag. Baboon grew hungry and very thirsty, as he anticipated they would reach Nyakoe River before the mid-day direct sun but this was not the case because Hare had suggested an alternative route, which he claimed was much shorter than the famous *Nyabururu-Embassy-Geteri* main route. They instead cut through *Getare*, across *Nyamataro*, onto *Nyaore* Tea Factory.

The sun was now directly above their heads and they were not any closer to the river yet. Hare was increasing his pace while Baboon was gradually getting weaker each time he saw Hare sip from his bag. With time, Hare started to run. He would run ahead, and then sit down and sip from his bag while he awaited Baboon to reach him.

"I think we are lost," said Baboon, after he had caught up with Hare for the fifth round.

"No, I don't think so," said Hare.

"We should have gotten by the Nyakoe River by this time," argued Baboon.

"Not along this route, if we had taken your way, yes. But now the river is in the opposite direction and we are almost approaching *Nyasore* High School. What is wrong with you? Do you want to turn back?" asked Hare.

"Oh, no, no, no, it just crossed my mind," said Baboon, afraid of being branded a coward if he explained his troubles.

"Are you hungry?" asked Hare. Baboon thought of saying no, but felt like he would die of starvation and replied vaguely, "just a little."

"Let me give you some of this medicine, it is sort of filling," suggested Hare.

"Do you think it is medically wise for me to have some?" questioned Baboon, anxiously.

136

"Yes, except you must not eat or drink anything else after you sip this medicine, all day today."

"I will take the medicine," said Baboon, complacently, convincing himself that if Hare could survive the whole day after sipping the medicine, then he too could.

"Well, don't say I didn't warn you in advance," Hare said, handing his bag to Baboon.

Baboon sipped a little of the medicine and then greedily galloped down five gulps. He seemed as if he was not stopping, when Hare shouted, "Hey! Stop! That's my medicine, remember!"

Baboon removed the bag from his mouth, and said, "It tastes like honey," wiping his lips. "It is mixed with honey," said Hare.

They then proceeded and a little later, they arrived at the Nyakoe River.

As Hare raised his arm, ready to take a drink from the river, Baboon interrupted him warning that that was Baboon country and if he drunk the water, he would die as he was not totemic to the Baboon classification. Although Hare was not of a credulous character, he stood up, reluctantly, unslinging his bag from the shoulder.

As he clicked and gazed at Baboon snobbishly, Baboon in turn bent forward in attempt to quench his long overdue thirst which had been excessively caused by the direct hot sun and honey.

"What are you about to do?" asked Hare. "I'm excessively thirsty," said Baboon. "Well, what did I tell you before you greedily drunk almost all my medicine? Didn't I emphasize that you should never claim that I never told you that you cannot eat anything else after taking the medicine, all day?"

Baboon confessed that he thought Hare meant only food, but Hare clarified that, "I said anything." He further warned that if Baboon drunk the water, swearing surely as his mother's name was *Nyaituga*, his people would say their last prayers for him and ask the god of the animal kingdom to cast his unrepentant soul into the sinister location of Eat Me or Eat You jungle. Hare's voice held such a spiritual threat and authority that Baboon saw his open grave and hallucinated that he was being lowered into the earth by fellow apes.

Baboon regretfully ejected himself up and apologized to Hare, but instead, Hare comforted him that he shouldn't have felt sorry, anyway, and conversely Hare apologized to him because he was the one who gave him the medicine.

Baboon felt threatened at the area where he almost committed unintentional suicide, so he kindly asked Hare to continue. They both proceeded but Baboon was not aware that Hare had left his medicine bag by the river bank.

After a few strides ahead, Hare exclaimed, "Oh! My dead mother—Nyaituga!""What the hell is happening?" asked Baboon.

"Have you lost your vigilance too? Can't you realize that I forgot my medicine bag at the river?" asked Hare.

"You go and collect it, I will wait for you here. I don't feel like seeing that nice cold, clear water again; which has almost caused me untimely death."

So, Hare returned to the river and had a cold, prolonged cold drink of water and later, with his bag, joined Baboon and their journey resumed.

"Got it?" Baboon asked, exhaustively, as Hare approached him. Hare raised the bag up in the air.

In Baboon's mind, as they kowtowed, was the healthy berries and wild fruits in the jungle ahead. He looked at Hare briefly, and half-heartedly begged for another sip of the medicine; since he was growing so thirsty. Hare in return gave him a bare, pensive look and called him stupid, asking him if, at his age and mental status, knew what an overdose of medicine signified. "Next time," warned Hare, "if you value your dear life, take caution. This is medicine, not food!"

Hare was energetic as they advanced, but on the other hand Baboon, who had grown thirsty and hungry, could not keep up with Hare's fast pace. He felt fire light in his chest and he felt as if rocks were tied to his feet. He thought of retribution to Hare if a chance came his way. When Hare realized these developing differences, he went up in dance, song and adulation, an action which got Baboon even more intimidated and vexed. Baboon reactively stared at him in a manner suggesting that he was going to cook Hare for dinner on that material day.

"Remember this is a Baboon territory," cautioned Baboon when he saw Hare pluck a berry when they arrived at the jungle, "I told you that not only water you cannot drink, but food too. Don't both of them drop down into your little belly anyway?"

"Yes, they do," answered Hare as Baboon continued to pluck berries from another branch with both hands.

Hare stretched his arm and pulled his hands down reminding him, as if it was a universally acceptable philosophy. "The Medicine! Do you want your people to kill me? How many times do you want me to keep reminding you that life is dear and precious, and that if you kill yourself, there will never be another Baboon who looks exactly like you, eats like you, with identical characteristics and reasoning abilities."

They both for a reasonable moment stared at each other; that when they, in surrender of no contest, resumed their journey out of the jungle, Baboon, who was in disbelief, did not witness Hare unslung his medicine bag once again, which he left at the spot where they stood.

After moving for about one hundred yards, Hare said, "Oh my God, your lack of understanding and senility has caused me to forget my bag for the second time."

"Not again," complained Baboon, "are you playing with my mind? Next time you leave your bag behind I won't wait for you." But he waited as he was tired and hungry, and needed some rest. As he lay leaning against a shrub, he fell asleep.

At the jungle, Hare gathered several handfuls of berries and sorted out varieties of ripe wild fruits he could find and ate them all to his complacence.

"Okay buddy, there you go," Hare bellowed and suddenly woke Baboon up, when he reached close to where he was rested.

On and on they traveled until they came to the omoroka shrub. "This particular shrub is very good for burns and blisters, so if you hear me shout. "I'm burning, I'm burning, I'm burning, you must deliver to me its leaves."

"That's good, but let me have a closer look of the shrub because it is now getting dark." While Baboon was destructed by a bee that buzzed across his face, Hare plucked a number of the omoroka leaves, and in lightning speed, stashed them into his medicine bag.

Eventually, they reached the home of Baboon relatives. They first shook hands and were then given some water in a calabash to wash down the dust and mud on their feet and legs; acquired as a result of the long journey. Then Baboon girls took up their responsibilities in the kitchen and boiled them broccoli, fried shrimp, oyster and scallops and *Moo Goo Gai Pan* Chicken *Chow Mein*; since unlike Kiwi, his father was an adult and a respected farmer in Nyanza Province whose popularity had been announced on National Television News, of which Baboons and Monkeys in the neighborhood had witnessed with their eyes.

While the dinner was underway, the guests were treated by their hosts to sumptuous refreshments including appetizers such as Egg Drop Soup and *Won ton* Soup, while they entertained themselves to that day's evening Black Entertainment Television (BET) music shows by *TI, Snoop Doggy Dog, JZ, Lil' Wayne, Lil' Bow Wow, Dr. Dre, Ne yo, 2 Pac, Akon,* Chris Brown, among many others.

Later, the Baboon girls delivered the long awaited meal. Baboon abruptly dipped his fingers into the Moo Goo Gai Pan Chicken Chow Mein, and instantly jumped up wailing, "I'm burning! please, I'm burning!" Hare immediately produced the omoroka leaves from his bag and nobly handed them over to him.

In disbelief, Baboon gazed at Hare in pain, and took the leaves, squeezed them and applied the chlorophyll on his finger. While he did this, Hare was almost in the middle of the delicacy. Baboon almost told Hare that that was a

142

Baboon territory, but he was terrified since his people would disapprove and expose his open lie, and since Hare was a unique renown guest, they couldn't let him sleep hungry. He somewhat never wanted to share the meal with Hare from the same pot but when he witnessed him burst into a chicken Chow Mein bone, dressed up by mustard, ketchup and onion relish, he put aside his pride and reached for a chicken wing.

Hare grabbed Baboon's hand, pointing at his medicine bag. The other apes saw this and wondered what was taking place. Hare sneezed twice—*achio! achiiio!* Then he remarked:

"Well, it is extremely complicated to explain but I shall try my best possible. You see, we took a rather longer route than we should have because I had to deliver a borrowed machete back to the rightful owner, who is also one of my best friends, across Nyakoe River, and it occurred that my comrade had not equipped himself prudently before we began the journey and so he was hungry on our way here. The bag you see resting at the far end of this living-room belongs to me, it is my medicine bag. I suffer from a foreign ailment which requires me to carry along with me the very medicine which I sip every now and then depending on circumstances and my health conditions. Baboon felt extremely hungry that he was almost unable to walk, and since it is mixed with honey, I chose to give him some to avoid unexpected death or emergency response due to starvation. I however forgot to warn him that after taking the medicine he was not supposed to eat. I just couldn't watch him starve to death." Hare then cleared his throat and proceeded with the meal from where he had stopped.

"What about you?" asked an elderly Baboon who wondered why Hare was eating when he had obviously taken the same medication.

Hare swallowed a chunk of broccoli and answered, "It is not that easy to explain, as I said earlier. After you have used the medicine as long as I have, you can eat and drink anything of your choice and desire. However, when I first took the medicine, the *omo-arobaini*, it sent me wildly impractical, only to find myself tied up around a tree because I could have easily injured or killed either myself or others around me. The first time, it gives you severe hallucinations resulting in physical violence or death."

Baboon could not believe and understand why Hare was telling all these lies when he was close to death from starvation, and had filled his shirt with saliva from his mouth as a result of watching Hare munch away all the shrimp and seasoned chicken, which he loved most.

He abruptly went wild yelling: "He is the biggest liar I have ever seen, he's lying, Kill him! Kill him! Kill him! He pounced on Hare, aiming at his throat, but missed, hit his

144

head on the big pot which contained ripening bananas, and went into unconsciousness, briefly.

"You think I was imagining the risks involved? I was fearing for such a reaction the entire day because instead of the normal one sip within several hours, Baboon galloped down five sips without my realization, at first. This is surely a strong living thing, no one could have survived such a dose but I suppose he will be psychologically and physically sound if he does not eat or drink for three days.

By the way, if I were you, I would tie him up. It is almost impossible to predict or guess what damage he could do if you let him loose. I regret this occurrence, I couldn't let him die of hunger on our way here." Hare began to apologize sobbingly.

"No, no, no, Mr. Hare, it isn't your error at all, not at all our great friend," confessed the elderly Baboon. Baboon, Hare's companion, had commenced recuperation from his head bang and when he heard this, he intervened, "No, he is a liar for sure, he advised me against drinking water at the river."

"Do not waste any more time in tying him up, boys," ordered the elderly Baboon, to a group of young Baboon men who had been invited into the guest house to entertain the two guests.

In a struggle of trying to explain himself, Baboon was air-lifted, by the young men, outside, and tied to a tree, next to another little hut.

"There is a medicine-man nearby, don't you think there is a remedy for such craziness?" questioned one teenage female Baboon.

"No dear," interjected Hare, "this is the first time he took and overdosed on the medicine, and so if he eats or drinks anything in the next three days, his people will have to bury him that material day."

"One mind-boggling thing I don't understand, is why he didn't carry any food when he very well knew he was traveling here," wondered the elderly Baboon.

Hare nodded his head, in exasperation, and then commented, "I urged him to do the same thing. Maybe he can answer you better if you ask him yourself."

"I will, at my own liberty," confirmed the older Baboon.

"However," Hare raised his index finger in warning, "after three entire days, or else you won't get an aesthetic response from him. Worse still, his condition may not enhance."

"Of course we will abide by your instructions since the medicine was initially prescribed to you," concluded the older Baboon with a wisdom-filled, wrinkled forehead.

"Girls," he then shot up, "here you are listening to wise people sharing wisdom-filled agreements, and yet the food is cold. Remember that the guest has a family, too, to care for. You should have warmed up the food by now!"

"No, no, I can't eat while my friend is in such a state," cried Hare.

"No, my dear friend, if we cannot thank you enough by word of mouth, then we should at least ensure that you remain in outstanding health for saving our idiotic relative. This is practical evidence of where selfishness, little brain and limitless greed can land you. In fact you deserve freshly cooked food," remarked the elderly Baboon, half-decidedly, as he clicked with contemptuous regret.

"Some people look like adults, physically, and yet they are still childish, and others, still, grow in bodily size while their minds decrease in size; like our dear friend, who is recuperating in front of us. He is even very lucky that the overdose symptoms caught up with him here at your residence as opposed to elsewhere." Hare summed up the conversation as he covered his tiny face with a green bowl filled with mushroomed scallops, this time, freshly prepared with chopped carrots and dark-gray mushroom roots.

Hare ate so much, so that both his bowels conspicuously exposed themselves any time he took a stride. At this juncture, traditional beer and colorless liquor blinded the hosts and guest into the wee morning hours of the following day. Throughout, they could hear poor Baboon groggily chuckling and whining in his imprisonment.

Shortly before sunrise, Hare commenced his long journey home. Augmenting to his medicine bag, he also loaded his back with a large calabash of stewed chicken Chow Mein, broccoli and shrimp, and some more millet beer named *toivo*—to clear the dust off his throat as he headed back home.

"Thank you all for your hospitality, and I, in the same spirit, invite you to my home for a similar experience, but, remember! "Three days.""

Then Onuong'a, who had just completed his story raised himself from a three-legged stool to grab a cob of roasted maize which I had aligned on a tray, as if they were on display for sale.

One leg of the stool stood for peace, the other, the people, and the last one signified the environment including land, vegetation and the animal kingdom which he had just finished articulating and its human-like ordeals.

Omuya did not, on his part, waste any time in explaining his own treasured side of what his grandmother had revealed to him about "The Cunning Tortoise."

He explained that, a long, long time ago, there was a record drought which dried up all ponds, pools and rivers, a catastrophe which disturbed all the animals in the wild because they would have no water available to drink.

On a Friday evening, the lion called a meeting of all the forest animals. They took their respective sitting positions and listened to the king of the jungle, who announced that: "I have called you together at this venue because we have run out of water in Serengeti National Park. We shall all perish if we don't find a drastic solution to this immediate life-threatening situation. Can any of you, more especially those who are naturally gifted with prudence, intelligence and extra skill in thoughtful analysis and wisdom, think of a way in which we can find some water?"

149

The animals scratched their heads and then their sides—along their ribs. Looking up at Elephant, Lion only augmented his dismay as he observed him shake his head in defeat.

"No, I cannot think of a place where we can find water," lamented Elephant.

A little hare, who had been thinking pensively, climbed up a mango tree as everyone was caught in suspense as he began to speak: "I know what can be done to overcome this crisis. Last year, there was a spring over there, the water has only sunk down into the ground. Let us dig where the spring was and the water will once more come up."

"Eureka! Eureka! Yes!" cheered all the animals.

"I will begin digging the first thing in the morning with my trunk," vowed Elephant. "You can as well use your little nose to dig, my little friend," Elephant urged Hare.

"I think my small tail can dig as perfectly as your little nose," suggested the tortoise.

One after another, the remaining beasts, in turns, offered to give a helping hand to avoid alienation among themselves because of the water shortage in their neighborhood.

The following morning, they began to dig and eventually water came up the spring but Elephant vowed to keep watch, together with the other animals because not all the animals helped to find the water. "Those that did not assist us in digging up the water will not drink," warned Elephant, who had used his trunk to break the hard ground.

"Hyena may come and steal the water at night while we are asleep. Have you considered that risk of concern?" Asked the tortoise.

"Then one of us must stay awake all night or at least every time others are asleep." Suggested the lion.

"I shall be the first," announced the hare.

So all the other animals left to take care of their daily obligations including nurturing their young ones while the hare attended to the newly founded spring.

That particular night, when all was quiet and peaceful, the hyena showed up and was inquisitively concerned why the hare was all alone by the spring.

"I'm watching the spring," answered the hare. "Remember, you never helped us to dig up the water so you cannot share this water with us."

"I don't want your water, but I can give you company if you want me to, and perhaps dance our old traditional dance that we were used to back in the days if you don't mind." said the hyena.

The hare accepted the hyena's notion.

While the hare dressed himself up, under a paw-paw tree, by tying himself up with a traditional skirt for his occasional dances made up of banana leaves and sisal, the hyena escaped to a nearby bush and secretly rolled up a cigar-sized marijuana smoke.

When the hare returned, the two animals started dancing. They danced and danced, and in the middle of their dance, the hyena "fired up his joint" which the hare shared with him amid prolonged periods of laughter, weakness and resultant deep sleep underneath the paw-paw tree. When the hyena saw him intoxicated and asleep, he called all his brothers, sisters and relatives including the jackal and wolf, who drank as much water as they could and absconded into the deep forest before the hare was relieved from his security duties by another animal.

152

The following morning, all the animals that had taken part in digging up water on the spring showed up to find out how the hare's night had been. They realized that he looked very exhausted and fairly intoxicated, and the spring water level had gone down, almost half-way. So, the hare guilt-consciously narrated to them how the hyena had come and tried to drink the water.

In protest, one giraffe, named *Ochi-Krazy*, and the zebra, walked away vowing to find drinking water in Masai Mara National Park; since fellow animals honored their scheduled duties so that they could treat themselves to illicit drugs instead of guarding the spring!

Then three other giraffes followed Ochi-Krazy because the zebra returned to the spring and asked them to accompany their brother to Masai Mara—as it had then become evident that there were no glimmers of collaboration within the animal kingdom.

"This is unfair, a symbol of laziness and a parasitic, contemptuous act. It will not work as long as my heavy legs keep treading the soil of this great land where we were all born and will inevitably be buried. I swear in the name of my great-grandfather—*Tusker*—whose tusks he lost to selfish human poachers; hailing from the snow-filled Mt. Kilimanjaro. More than just the greedy, opportunistic hyena alone must have been here last night drinking our hard-earned water. Look at the footmarks, I think tonight is my night. I'm prepared to trade my own life with death if those gluttons appear tonight!" The elephant vowed, and immediately trumpeted into the clear sky, enabling his echoing trumpets to diminish into horizons beyond Kogelo Village, where President Obama's father, and grandfather, had denounced hyenas for killing the community's donkeys.

155

The hyenas were rumored to have been expelled because they had becaome a menace by killing the villagers' donkeys, which were the only animals in the area used to ferry goods to and from the various markets within Kogelo Village, Nyanza Province.

President Obama in Kogelo Village

President Obama's father, an economist in Kenya's treasury in the late 1960s, rubbed officials of Jomo Kenyatta's government the wrong way when he angrily demanded an explanation to Tom Mboya's death, moments after the Minister for Economic Planning and Development was assassinated.

"I was with Tom only last week. Can Kenyatta's government identify his whereabouts," a distraught Obama fulminated as he abandoned work in protest.

Mr. Obama was emotionally attached to Mboya who made it possible for him to further his intelligence in the United States of America. It was courtesy of Tom Mboya's famous airlifts that Obama landed at the University of Hawaii.

President Obama's father

President Obama's grandfather, Onyango Obama, was a native of *Kanyadhiang* area near *Kendu* Bay, *Rachuonyo* District.

Although, upon his demise, President Obama's father was buried in *Alego*, Kogelo Village, following his sudden death in a car crash in Nairobi, he was not born there.

The president's grandfather, Onyango Obama, who was also buried in Kogelo, moved with his family to this village in Alego, Syaya District, when the president's father was a young boy after he was persuaded to do so by his brothers.

Onyango Obama was the second born son of Obama Opiyo's eight sons. He happened to be the only one from the family to be recruited to fight in the Second World War. After the war participation, he returned a Muslim— Onyango Hussein Obama—after having married his first wife, Helima, during his service in Zanzibar.

Explaining the Obama family link to Kogelo Village, that today is associated with President Obama's Kenyan roots, the president's great-grandfather, Obama Opiyo, was born and raised in the sleepy village in Syaya District.

Opiyo, the president's great-great-grandfather, grew up in Alego Kogelo. He had a twin sister called Jalang'o. She, in her turn, got married to a man in *Karachuonyo*, Kanyadhiang, near Kendu Bay, and due to her love for her twin brother, she invited Opiyo to join her there because land was plenty at the time.

Opiyo got married to a woman from Kendu Bay and among his sons was Obama Opiyo, the great-grandfather to President Obama.

As fate would have it, Obama Opiyo's second born son, Onyango Obama, was exposed to the world by his reminiscences in the Second World War, and returned a controversial figure who did not agree with the highly respected Chief and Chairman of the Luo Council of Elders at the time—Paul Mbuya Akoko.

To save Onyango from trouble with the chief, his brothers advised him to migrate to their ancestral land in Alego Kogelo, in then Central Nyanza District, and secure it for posterity.

At this juncture, Onyango Obama had already lost his wife, Habiba Akumu Nyanjoga, the biological mother of the president's father and married Sarah Ogwel.

Whenever in social places, the president's father was fond of invoking the names of his two mothers, in the presence of his peers, reminding them that he was the proud son of two mothers — Akumu Nyanjoga and Sarah Ogwel. "*An wuod* Akumu Nyanjoga *kod* Sarah Ogwel (I'm the son of Akumu Nyanjoga and Sarah Ogwel); was his characteristic vaunt in social places and many a time reminisced times of his youth when they expelled all the hyenas from Kogelo Village, and how a group leopards forcefully migrated to the neighboring Kisiiland, and in the

159

eventuality, were speared to death by a newly circumcised group of age-sets in Kisii, that particular year.

The president's father had his early education at *Gendia* Primary School near Kendu Bay and later joined *Ng'iya* Intermediate School when the family moved to Alego Kogelo, before proceeding to *Maseno* High School.

Before President Obama's father airlifted to the United States of America, to further his studies, he was already married to his elder wife—Keziah. Ann Dunham, the biological mother of President Obama, whom he met while at college in Hawaii, was his second wife.

The president's father returned to Kenya after his Ph.D. at Harvard University without Ann Dunham, but with another White woman, Ruth, with whom he did not live with for long either. Ruth remarried and still lives in Kenya.

President Obama's father was a remarkably brilliant scholar, immensely proud of his academic achievements, and never hesitated to point out that very few people of his academic era beat him in academics. He fondly talked of his son in the United States of America, was an immensely proud and ambitious man who had little respect for non-achievers and opportunists, such as the former hyenas in Kogelo Village who only benefited from the hard work of others.

President Obama with some of his Kenyan relatives in 1987

That material night, while the elephant was executing his security duties, the hyena came and played the same trick on him. The elephant was even more intoxicated than the hare was because he inhaled larger amounts of ganja smoke than the hare did. He slept, snoring so loud, that he attracted even insects and rodents such as mice, rats and moles from nearby ant-hills so that even the laziest porcupine got a golden opportunity to drink the cool water of the spring.

Realizing the seriousness of the situation, after Tusker's great-grandson's trumpets into horizons beyond Kogelo, all the other elephants shamefully left the scene because they had all been betrayed by their partner notwithstanding their gigantic bodies.

"This is totally unacceptable. Does it imply that some of us have gigantic bodies for no apparent reason. I saw a group of crickets and a harbinger of locusts fly away this morning upon our arrival here. Mr. Elephant, does it mean that with your heavy breath alone you were unable to scare away those insects?" argued the disgusted gray crowned crane—named *Radical*.

Radical subsequently flew away to Lake Nakuru to find himself some drinking water, and, upon his arrival, announced to his cousins, the flamingos, about the hare's and elephant's insubordination. The flamingos stretched their long necks and laughed, giggled, hugged and smooched each other.

The tortoise had spent so much time and vigor digging up the water, so he offered to provide his security complaining that it was unjust to enslave themselves to the merriment of others, who were factually lazy opportunists.

"No," interjected the cheetah, "this guy is incredibly slow. How can he guard our spring? He cannot go after the slowest intruder or thief in this neighborhood. Unless you don't, for sure, care about his safety and earthly presence, I don't understand why you want the poor tortoise to get killed, prematurely, and yet you know his wife delivered two little sons the other day who require their father's presence and wisdom for their future survival."

"Let him guard, do you think those of us who have risked our only lives are idiots? He is benefiting from the water as much as we are all benefiting. It is the most ideal way to prove to you all that the hare and I have not fooled you, are not cowards, and we did not shut our eyes the entire time we desperately sat here as you shared your beds with your wives," lamented the elephant.

"Tortoise, what are you doing here at this late hours of the night? You know I walk in the nights, searching out leftovers after the lions and leopards have exhausted themselves hunting down their food. That is the only way I can keep witnessing the dawn of another day. I don't work that much but benefit from others' sweat. Since I have already fed on remnants of a wilder beast whose life was incidentally cut short by three leopards, this afternoon, due to the crocodiles down at the Mara River who had injured his leg while he crossed the river, before the drought, I'm now looking for a dance partner," announced the hyena upon his arrival that particular night.

Shockingly, the tortoise did not move, nor did he speak.

"I will kill you if you don't talk to me," warned the hyena, and instantly pounced on the tortoise's back.

Tortoise only pulled his head in and produced long giggles of laughter. The hyena, time and again jumped on his back as the tortoise continued with his laughter. Whenever the hyena paused his repeated attacks on the tortoise back, the tortoise ejected his head out of his shell and proceeded with prolonged periods of laughter.

In the end, the hyena feared for his life as it was almost morning, and chose to leave the tortoise alone.

When the other animals visited the spring, they were very pleased with the tortoise's courage and bravery; as he explained his heroic encounters with nocturnal beasts whom he had defeated in defense of their precious source of water. He since became the first one to drink from the spring before all the other animals drunk.

While it was Omuya's turn to grab a piece of the roasted maize, it automatically became Keronchi's turn to speak into the one-speaker, black *Phillips* tape recorder into which their tales were being recorded, the same one into which my brother, Donysius, and I recorded a poem named *The Oracle.* It was also part of my sister's first self-earned fixed assets that she owned after her first remuneration, as a teacher at Marani High School.

Keronchi then told a story of an old blind man named Akai; who together with a young boy, Ivo, lived in a little hut in the middle of a jungle. They both had been left behind when the people of their village escaped from a pride of marauding lions that had gone wild in the area.

"Please take me with you," cried the old man when the villagers were in the middle of running away from the lions.

"You will only put us in further danger," they said. How could an old blind man help them, anyway, they asked themselves, and in the end left him there in the forest.

"I may be of value and essence to you some day," the man pleaded to them as they left, but they still left him behind.

After the people had left, the old man wandered alone in the abandoned village. He went from hut to hut and collected food which he packed into a sack which he carried on his back. As he entered one of the deserted huts, he heard a voice of a little child whining.

"What is wrong, little one?" he asked when he heard the child crying.

"My parents have left me alone. They said they couldn't carry me because they were carrying my brothers and sisters."

"Stop crying and come with me," Akai said.

"Thank you," said the little boy.

"You can thank me once we have abjured the lions," the old man said.

"Do you see any hills around? Because I don't know if we can evade the beasts or not."

"I can only see a big forest to the east," Ivo said.

"Let's head there, but isn't that where the lions live? However, they won't look for us because they know that people live in the villages." Suggested Akai.

So, the two started their journey to the forest. There, the young boy helped Akai to build a hut in the topmost branches of a huge Eucalyptus tree.

The two lived in their hut for many years and ultimately the boy grew up to be a strong young man. During the day, they would climb down from the tree hut and set for the jungle to search out food and water and subsequently return at night to sleep. They were safe from wild animals, and during this period, Akai taught the young man some ingenious tricks and tactics he knew about his people's ways and traditions and how to hunt for honey and little animals such as hares, antelopes, and gazelles.

One day, the old man sounded worried as he revealed to Ivo that he would soon make emancipation from disturbing thoughts and emotions with life, and fly away home to his heavenly recompense.

Ivo only laughed and comforted Akai that he was still fit and evidently strong.

169

Still, the old man wondered what Ivo would do when he rested from this practically painful theater of competition, hatred and apartheid-like life, where men and women have been knocked off their foundations of faith, love and lost agape love resulting in altruistic, anomie and egoistic suicides.

"I know you may not want me to reason this way but death is inevitable, more so, at my age. I shall die very soon, maybe even before the next unknown solar eclipse, right here in the *Kerugoya* area!" declared Akai.

"I wish there was a way of bribing death, so that I can buy your soul to be physically available in such a manner that we can both live and die together because death never seems to realize how much pain and the size of gap it leaves on those who are left behind, only not to witness their own death anniversary. And then, if you die, I will also perish," Ivo lamented.

"Son, remember that we all have destinies to fulfill and specific paths to follow through our earthly existence. There is a sure reason why your parents left you behind when they abjured the lions so that I could find you destitute in the abandoned village. In addition, there is as well a reason why I have spent all the time with you here in the forest, just as much as God created me blind so that I could find a little child to guide me through this final journey of ours in the forest, which gives us the reason why I'm older than you, although we have shared a life-time together. You also

170

have a duty and obligation to fulfill to others before your inevitable moment nears," the wise Akai advised Ivo.

"What do you think I should do?" asked Ivo.

"We shall make an effort to find you a wife," suggested Akai.

"We are all alone in this jungle, where do you think you can find me a wife?" asked Ivo.

"We will search for her," said Akai.

"Where?" wondered the young man.

"Just do as I say and don't bubble words full of pessimism and doubt," Akai cautioned with wisdom expressed in his wrinkled forehead.

The following morning, the two ravaged their little hut and set out deep into the jungle to search out a wife. For several days, they treaded on bushes and climbed ridges through the jungle as they spent nights on trees and fed on wild fruits and captured hares, birds and mice of the forest.

One day, Akai stepped on something that felt like a stone and yet he was assured it wasn't a stone.

"What is it I have stepped on?" he asked the young man.

"A tortoise," Ivo answered.

"Pick it up," the old man ordered.

On another occasion, the old man stepped on something that felt like a long stick, yet he knew it wasn't a stick.

"What is it that I have stepped on?" he asked.

"It is a gun," Ivo told him.

"Pick it up," Akai advised the young man.

Ivo picked up the weapon and they both proceeded, and after their movements in the jungle for several days, they came to an open plain.

"Look!" Ivo shouted humorously.

"What is it!?" exclaimed Akai.

"It looks like a village," said Ivo.

"Is it a big village?" asked Akai, curiously.

"That is what it appears to be," said Ivo.

"Okay, let's keep moving toward that direction."

As they approached the village, they came across a well where they met two women filling up their water-pots. After exchanging greetings with the two older ladies, Akai asked for some water to quench his thirst with. Afterwards, he told the two women that they were seeking help.

Then one of the women was curious to know what kind
of help they wanted.

Akai answered by asking them whose village they had
come to.

"It is called the Women's Village."

"The Women's Village? What a foreign name. Why
the funny name?" asked the old man.

"Because it is only occupied by women," answered one
of the women.

So, the old man asked why there were no men in the
village. One woman, in return told them that there was
formerly men in the village but they were all eaten up by
the lions of the village.

They continued that, the men were in the village before
the lions but when the beasts arrived, they fed on each of the
men—one by one.

"Why didn't the men fight back?" asked Akai.

The two women looked at each other as if the old man
had immediately turned childish. Neither of them answered
him and instead diverted from the question into asking what
kind of assistance they were looking for, at first.

"Yes, we are looking for a wife for my "nephew," who
is here with me," the old man revealed sternly. The women
laughed shyly; as if the man was seducing them indirectly.

"We just told you that there are no men in our village,"
one of the women said.

"What does that have to do with him? He has never told me, at any given time, that he wants to marry a man," Akai said.

"The lion in our village will not allow any man to live there," the women said, emphasizing that strong, circumcised men of the land had been eaten up by the beasts and had no reason to spare Ivo, under any circumstance.

Akai then asked if they could see the lion. The women laughed, contemptuously, and told Akai that the men who were eaten up by the lions were stronger than him, had guns just like he had one but were not old and blind as he was.

In the end, they stopped the arguments and instead requested the women to find them a safe place to spend the night. The women, however, were not confident enough to let them spend the night because they feared that if the lion came at night and ate the two men up, then their spirits would come back to haunt them.

Still Akai was not satisfied with their claims and so he asked if there was a headsman in the village. The older woman answered that she was the heads person in that particular village, and warned them to leave before it was too late; at least before the lion returned from his daily hunting routine.

Sympathetically, they decided to let them spend the night and therefore led them into the village, and while in the village they felt embarrassed as all the women there

174

belittled them and asked weird questions including why they chose to intermingle with people of opposite sex—in large numbers, when they only possessed two testicles each. But because the old man wanted Ivo to find himself a wife, they held on to their shame. Ivo, however, wondered of what essence the woman would be when he was dead.

The old man told Ivo that he had never seen the sun all his life but was not dead yet, and so he should not think that he wouldn't see the following morning due to the alleged lion.

That material night, they were well fed by the women and comforted that at least it is not hunger that they were likely to die from but the lion. They were shown and directed to the hut where they would spend their night.

"Did you bring the tortoise with us?" asked Akai.

"Yes. Together with the gun too," said Ivo.

Minutes later, Akai was in deep sleep, snoring but on the other hand Ivo could not catch any sleep because he was busy saying his final prayers before the ruler of the jungle appeared.

Toward the early morning hours, Ivo heard loud footsteps and within seconds a male lion roared outside the hut. He immediately tapped Akai and briefed him that they were living in their last minutes. Then the lion asked, "What fool has the audacity to sleep in my hut?"

"And what fool has the courage and strength to ask such a foolish question?   And don't think anyone is scared of you—idiot!" Akai answered back fearlessly.

"Do you wanna see my beard?" the lion asked as he pulled out some long hairs, infested with ticks, from his cheeks and inserted them into the hut through a tiny opening. Akai, in return, cautioned the lion that if he showed him his beard, he would perhaps run into his grandmother's niece. "Let me show you one of the ticks that have made a home in my beard."

The old man then pushed the tortoise through an opening in the door. The lion stepped back a little at the sight of the humongous "tick" and silenced himself for a while. Akai proceeded, "Are you still there, or you have fled into your mother's groin?"

176

"Fuck you! Do you want to hear me roar?" The lion responded to the challenge and roared like he had never done in his entire life-time. The women of the village trembled although they were safe in their huts while Ivo was half-way dead, silently reciting the most common prayer he could recall from the rosary.

"Did I hear a rat speak?" Akai asked. "I didn't hear any sound when you claimed to have roared. Move closer to the door and put your mouth straight onto the hole and roar louder than you did a couple of minutes ago so that I can hear you. I have my ear ready around the hole on the door to hear you."

The king of the jungle then put his mouth to the hole on the door and opened it wide to release the loudest roar ever heard in the Women's Village. Akai instantly pulled the trigger on his gun.

The following morning the women found the lion dead with all his four legs pointing toward the clear sky, outside the little hut in which Akai and Ivo spent their night.

The old man was elected Chief of the Women's Village and Ivo acquired himself a beautiful wife and subsequently sired several sons who became the first men in the Women's Village and were never terrified of lions.

Once Keronchi was through with his story about "The Lion and the Blind Man," a local woman, in my home area,

177

named Bonareri, who had as well been attentively listening to the tales, stood up from where she had been resting herself and began to sing and dance. My mother was also busy preparing dinner for the three guests, who had done a wonderful job!

Sindigisa omwana bwo-Omuoyo!

Esiri yo-mogaka, moe etaro; eee bananga,

Eee sindigisa!

Sindigisa omwana bwo-Omuoyo!

Esiri yo-omogaka, moe etaro; eee bananga,

Eee sindigisa!

Bonareri Mochoge

CHAPTER EIGHT

1982 ATTEMPTED COUP

Being ten years old then, the only major event I remember in 1982 is the attempted coup organized by the Kenyan Air Force and announced by Leonard Mambo Mbotela on National Radio Broadcast.

An enduring mystery in Kenya's history is how rebel junior officers of the Kenyan Air Force planned and executed the failed takeover of President Moi's government on August 1, 1982.

The failed coup of 1982 was a catastrophe for the Kenyan people. It should have never been allowed to proceed for the sake of testing political loyalties. Having allowed it to go ahead in order to settle scores was wrong and poor judgment, because the coup organizers were underestimated. The coup almost succeeded. Many people suffered after the attempt because people only needed to point a finger at someone and add his or her name to those who were involved in one way or another with the planning of the coup. Many politicians, academicians and even maintenance people had their lives turned upside down the moment they were picked on as suspects, whether they knew of the coup plot or not. It was enough to belong to some groups considered to be rowdy or be a brand unwilling to dance to expected tune of the day.

How the soldiers made their move despite the presence of the much touted intelligence network headed by Mr. James Kanyotu still baffles Kenyans.

It is however reported that the Kenya Police Special Branch—the precursor of today's National Security Intelligence Service (NSIS), and the Military intelligence had gotten wind of the plotted coup three months in advance.

While it remains a matter of speculation as to what exactly transpired a few days before the coup attempt, what is in no doubt is that Moi significantly changed tact after the event. The failed coup changed him into a dictator and heralded crackdowns over the subsequent few years on all forms of dissent.

Kanyotu's intelligence network was central to the arrests, detentions, tortures and disappearances that marked the dark days. Yet looked at in hindsight, the coup was not an event out of the blue—it seemed like part of a process.

Not long before the coup attempt, the Government had rammed through the infamous Section 2A of the Kenyan Constitution that made Kenya a one-party state. Detention without trial had also made a comeback as Kanyotu's intelligence network went in pursuit of radical university lecturers and the lawyers who dared to defend them.

After the failed coup it was open season. Other than the military plotters led by Sr. Private Hezekiah Ochuka, who were sentenced to death or to lengthy jail terms, prominent victims included Mr. Raila Odinga, the then Deputy Director of the Kenya Bureau of Standards and son of the opposition pioneer Jaramogi Oginga Odinga.

Raila was one of the four civilians charged with treason before the charges were withdrawn and substituted with detention without trial.

However, that was not all. Once Moi was through with dissidents, he turned viciously on presumed disloyal elements in his own Government. The most dramatic was the sudden fall from grace of his once all-powerful Attorney-General, Mr. Charles Mugane Njonjo.

The impressive political and security network assembled by Njonjo was swiftly dismantled. He was taken through show trial in the form of a Judicial Commission of Inquiry where among the raft of allegations, was evidence brought in that the Air Force coup was mounted to pre-empt another key takeover by forces loyal to Njonjo.

Two days before the failed coup, machinery had been set in motion to apprehend the ring-leaders, but the operation was mysteriously called off at the last minute.

Much earlier, at the beginning of May, the intelligence team had learned that junior Air Force officers stationed in Nanyuki were planning to overthrow the Government before the end of the year.

Mr. Kanyotu immediately assigned one of his senior officers to monitor progress and report to him on a daily basis. The officer quickly infiltrated the coup plotters by planting his moles among them.

Towards the end of June, August 3 was agreed on as the actual date for the execution of the coup, the day when Moi was to travel to Libya for a summit of the African Heads of State.

All this time, the Commander-in-Chief was kept abreast of the developments and four days before August 3, Mr. Kanyotu started to plan his counter-move on the rebel soldiers.

He instructed his main investigator and four other senior Intelligence officers to proceed to Nanyuki Air Base where they would be joined by Military Intelligence officers from the Department of Defense headquarters to execute the arrests.

However, while at Nanyuki, the acting base commander told the Intelligence team that he had no instructions on any impending arrests and asked them to await as he consulted his superiors.

A rather hostile base commander returned and advised the Intelligence officers that there was no arrests to be made and asked them to leave.

The senior officer immediately consulted his boss, Mr. Kanyotu, who confirmed that the mission had been canceled.

The following day, on August 1, the coup attempt took place two days ahead of schedule because news of the impending arrests was deliberately leaked to the plotters, throwing them into panic, hence the rush.

Former Minister for Internal Security, G. G. Kariuki, cited subsequent events as pointers that the coup attempt may have been used as an excuse to wage political battles within the Government.

Hardly a week after the failed coup, he received a directive from the Head of Public Service; Jeremiah Kiereini, to the effect that visits to State House, even for Cabinet Ministers, would be strictly by appointment. A week later, his security detail was withdrawn, leaving him with just one police officer.

184

The Air Force commander, P.M. Kariuki, was also put on trial; who told the Court Martial that the head of Military Intelligence had personally told him not to worry as everything was under control. And Mr. John Keen, the then Internal Security assistant minister, claimed to have suspected at the time that Kanyotu knew everything that went wrong before the failed coup took place.

But Intelligence sources privy to the goings-on at the time hinted that whoever wanted the coup attempt to proceed may have underestimated the extent of damage it would cause the country.

Subsequently, in 1987, Intelligence officers picked up a prominent figure in motor rallying circles from his Limuru home for interrogation at the dreaded Nyayo House offices of the Special Branch, and Mr. Stephen Mbaraka Karanja was never to be seen again—dead or alive.

When his family could not trace his whereabouts, they applied for a writ of *habeas corpus*.

High Court judge; Derek Schofield ordered the police to produce him in court, but was told that the police could not comply because Mr. Karanja had died in police custody— that he was shot dead while he attempted to escape.

The judge demanded that the police, Kanyotu's Special Branch, which was then a branch of the Kenya Police, produce his body.

What followed was a grisly exercise as the police exhumed 19 bodies at the Eldoret municipal council cemetery in search of the victim's body.

An angry Mr. Justice Schofield described the episode as callous and demanded an explanation from the Commissioner of Police and the Director of the Criminal Investigation Department (CID).

Instead, he was swiftly removed from the case and transferred to an up-country station by Chief Justice Cecil Miller. But the judge rejected the transfer and opted to quit, later leaving the country to take up office as the Chief Justice of Gibraltar.

It was not until much later that it emerged that Mr. Karanja had been shot dead and his body cremated in a forest near Eldoret Town.

Mr. Karanja was just one of the many Kenyans in the mid 1980s who were victims of the dreaded Special Branch, which was the lead security agency operating in total disregard of the law and fundamental human rights in pursuit of perceived dissidents.

Mr. Karanja had been arrested in connection with a clandestine dissident movement called *Mwakenya.*

Kenyans first heard about the group in 1986. It was said to be the offshoot of another clandestine group called the *December 12 Movement.* The latter sprang from the blues in 1983, soon after the abortive military coup in 1982.

186

Both were supposed to publish seditious leaflets named Mwakenya, *Mpatanishi* and *Pambana*, respectively.

It was later revealed that both Mwakenya and its seditious pamphlets were creations of Kanyotu's intelligence system, while the December 12 Movement and Pambana were creations of a parallel intelligence system run by Internal Security Permanent Secretary, Hezekiah Oyugi.

The two men were bitter rivals competing to impress Moi on who was more effective in keeping dissent at bay.

The retired Intelligence officer traces the birth of the December 12 Movement and Mwakenya to the early 1979 when the Government grew increasingly worried about growing radicalization of staff and students at the University of Nairobi.

In 1982, former President Moi re-introduced detention without trial and locked up three lecturers; Mukaru Ng'ang'a, Edward Oyugi and Kamonji Wachira.

But dissent in institutions of higher learning went on unabated, and Intelligence came up with Pambana. Many of the University students, in fact, were keen to get their hands on the seditious publications and distribute them to like-minded friends unaware that they were only spreading the net of those to be arrested.

The net had by then spread from academia to include lawyers, journalists, politicians and businessmen. The targets would be held incommunicado for two to four weeks and tortured at Nyayo House.

On being brought to court, they were ready to confess to anything. The court appearances were invariably early in the morning or late in the evening, outside normal working hours.

The unrepresented suspects would always be dragged before a succession of Nairobi chief magistrates who would soon be made judges. The prosecution would be conducted by deputy public prosecutor; Bernard Chunga, later to become Chief Justice, while always hovering in the background would be the dreaded Intelligence officer; James Opiyo of the Nyayo House torture chambers.

1983 was marked by lawless and brutal elections, more so in *Kitutu Chache* constituency, and political controversies in the Kenyan Government such as the accusation of Charles Mugane Njonjo — as a traitor.

The Kitutu Chache election was marked by the death of Mr. Uhuru Ndege who was allegedly gunned down by the then local Member of Parliament. The circumstances behind the man's death had political complications of such high level magnitudes that in the end, the victim's family never saw any justice served or indemnity of any form awarded to them by the Government of the day, or the accused.

Truly, for a society such as Kitutu Chache to be orderly and its crime-rates lessened, first, inequality in the eyes of justice unserved in violent crimes is an evident lens in the social and psychological impact of partiality on societies.

188

Egalitarian societies are less individualistic and more likely to take into account the interests of society as a group, rather than that of individuals within it. They are less anxiety-ridden, less prone to unhappiness and are less exposed to an unhealthier community life, ingredients which curtail safety in society.

The renewed interest in inequality rather than economic growth as an end in itself comes at a time when the economic environment, such as that in Kitutu Chache, is in turmoil due to past injustices and history of unprecedented weights and where individualism and unfettered capitalism are coming under increasing scrutiny by those who have, in living memory, been subjected to social atrocities and inequalities resulting from personal greed and selfishness instead of justly serving the very people who have assigned power to the oppressor.

And rightly so, unequal societies, just like families, do not prosper either socially or economically. Inequalities create social and political fractures within society that can develop into unrest and subsequent murders, genocide, suicides and, or homicides. These vices, in turn, reduce incentives and a conducive environment for investment and force governments to devote more spending toward internal security.

Historical poverty, as that of Kitutu Chache constituency and Kenya in general, has little impact on violence levels, but when pervasive indigence occurs in an environment

189

of extreme inequality, the results can be shocking and devastating.

Then on January 7, of 1984, shortly before I joined St. Mary's Mosocho, I was naturally forced to accept the reality of death by witnessing the untimely death of my paternal grandfather—Joseph Simba Morangi.

He was one of the sons of Morangi, a grandson of Obare and a great grandson of Nyaborigo. Some of his brothers included: Zebedeo Nyambegera, Asango, Apenda and Kebarabara Morangi, and had a sister named Nyasuguta.

He got married to Paustina Moraa in 1927. They were blessed with 10 children—5 sons and 5 daughters but only 6 of their children lived to adulthood.

They, both, were blessed with an extended family which includes three daughters in-law: Rufina Kerubo, Jane Kidesi, and Teresia Mocheche; four sons in-law: Agoti Magara, Francis Nyakundi, Oyunge Morira and Ernest Oonge Manyara.

They were also blessed with 47 grandchildren (*abachokoro*—in my native language) namely: Robina Mooti, Lawrence Nyamari, Mark Agoti, Agnes Nyaundi, Machwara, Manani, and Susan Agoti; Mary Orina, Florence Nyasuguta, Gloria Susan, Eileen Kwamboka, Josephine Moraa, Oliver Morangi, Julius Morara, and Donysius Nyamweya; Clare Kemuma, Lilian Zipporrah, Tom Morangi,

George Kidesi, Gloria Penina, and Maurice Mochoge; William Nyakundi, Mama Moraa, and Jane Kemunto; John Morangi, Charles Fidelis, Thomas Mirimba, Judith Matoke, Elizabeth Kwamboka, Philip Omenge, Marcella Omenge and Mary Nyanduko; Jackline Nyangweso, Judy Bina, Nyagechanga, Osoro, Winfridah Moraa, Morira, Jane Kerubo; Perista Nyaboke, Sarah Kerubo, Patrick Onsomu, David Maeba, Evangeline Moraa, Benta Kerubo, William Ondieki, and Lilian Barongo.

Paustina Moraa was born in 1907 to Mzee Ondinya and Mama Kerubo Ondinya of Ibacho, Nyaribari Masaba, was the first-born in a family of three girls and two boys; of whom only three survived to adulthood. They were: Penina Masese, Atura Ondinya and herself.

Until November 30, 2008 when my grandmother went to be with the Lord, she had lived to see 102 great grandchildren, (*abachokororia*), and 8 great-great-grandchildren, (*ebichembene*). It is unclear if she ever saw any great-great-great grandchild (*ekerochi*).

Mama Moraa cared for her children just as well and carefully as all mothers do, and as a testimony, our memories are reverted back to 1936, when my father was born, and how he was occasionally kept in the famous "box," soon after his birth, following the demise of several siblings in the family. As we grew up into maturity, this story was time and again narrated to us by Mama Bonareri Mochoge, and, whenever she had cleared her throat with some liquor or busaa, she sang about the "boy of the box," or "Mr. Tome's Machine."

After the death of her husband, Mzee Joseph Simba Morangi, on January 7, 1984, she remained under the care of her eldest son, Mzee Peter Omosa Simba, in whose care she remained for about 24 years.

She died on Sunday, November 30, 2008, and her final farewell ceremony was conducted by Bishop Joseph Mairura Okemwa on Thursday, December 11, 2008.

Bishop Mairura

They both left behind one son and four daughters, at least by December of 2008, and several grand children, great-grand-children, and great-great-grand-children.

192

Joseph Simba Morangi   Paustina Moraa Simba

Mr. Simba was also married to two other wives: Kerubo and Philomena Simba—who is the mother to Agnes, Gilbert, Tom, Dennis, Jacqueline and Stella.

Philomena Simba

From left, Peter Omosa Simba, and his 4 surviving
immediate sisters: Paulina Kemunto Agoti (Nyatichi),
Maria Oinga Nyakundi (Morere), (front row), Phylisila
Nyamokami Oyunge, (far right), and Patricia Mokeira
Oonge (far back)

Mr. Omosa's family is large too, and is made up of two
wives—Rufina and Jane—and fourteen children.

Mr. Peter Omosa Simba   Mrs. Rufina Kerubo Omosa

Rufina's children: 5 daughters; from left; Professor. Mary
Bonareri, Dr. Florence Nyasuguta, Dr. Gloria Susan,
Eileen Kwamboka, and Josephine Moraa.

3 sons, (from right); Oliver Morangi, Donysius Nyamweya
and Julius Morara

Mrs. Jane Kidesi Omosa

Jane's 6 Children: Gloria Penina (above left), Lilian
Zipporrah (front left), Clare Kemuma (above center), Tom
Morangi (front center), George Kidesi (front right), and
Maurice Mochoge (right)

197

CHAPTER NINE

ST. MARY'S MOSOCHO

This then became my first time to spend many days, weeks and months outside my home, although I often made weekend visitations—after the ceremonial celebration of the day my grandfather went to be with the Lord in the holy place. I then became a brand-new *mono*; who had to serve others' interests while in school in return for protection and orientation, at St. Mary's Mosocho, and any related ordeals incisively became evident on each "opening day" in the institution.

Opening Day

The road to St. Mary's was always straight on opening day. Our future came a day at a time. We lived as if death was imminent the following day but learned as if we were to live forever, irrespective of any frightful occurrences whenever we took our eyes off the goal. It was time to be aggressive and vigorous when it came to letting go of the past and press forward to the abundant life God had in store for us. It was time to rise up and audaciously go after our victory, the time to develop a warrior mentality and proactively pursue the humor, health, and peace that God had promised in His word. We always had the opportunities to move forward in life. We wanted to grow and reach our full potential. Anytime we took a step forward, the adversary would try to bring opposition and adversity against us.

We may have had brilliant ideas, but if we couldn't get them across, our ideas wouldn't get us anywhere. This we knew, and when we stood out in faith and opposition, we stood our ground and kept doing what we knew to do. We proceeded in prayer, read the Bible, went to the local chapel in Cardinal Otunga High School, and walked in both ethos and agape love and forgiveness. We kept our hearts tender and spoke words of hope and triumph over our lives. We realized that, when the enemy saw we were more determined than he was, he backed down; and we advanced forward to new levels of victory. We, all along, stayed focused and overjoyed no matter what came against us and overcame opposition and marched through the door the Lord had opened to us. Because we did our part to have a restoration mentality, God took every obstacle that came into our lives and turned it into a stepping-stone that would take us to a place of higher nobility and greater blessing.

Success—if defined as failure turned inside out, was inevitable since persistence repeatedly broke down resistance. Each day, we were increased, and our visions enlarged into new levels of victory. Wisdom had been manifested in us that, prior to success, we had to see ourselves being successful. Before our dreams came to pass, we had to look through our eyes of faith and see them come to pass.

St. Mary's Mosocho traditionally stood unbeatable in the annual national examinations whenever they were held. Before I coupled myself up with the institution, I many a time envied its students and their outstanding success unlike other neighboring schools whose members, despite their abject poverty, were incomparable. Their uniforms too were mere pieces of cloth of many colors threaded together so as to distinguish them from members of the public. Here, I learned that success is surely a choice and not a chance, and luck was when good planning met opportunity.

In the course of years, whenever I passed by the school, its students always looked complacent, comfortable, and their ways of life prestigious. I wondered why they referred to all their teachers as "sir" when, in the eyes of the common man all men were created equal. I was not the only one though because many other boys from the neighboring schools hoped they would one day end up being scholars in the institution so that they would also be envied by the less privileged. The most astonishing was the English language they spoke. All other students from the neighboring schools never understood why and how the boys managed to communicate in that foreign language.

The local boys, as they were commonly known, were educated in their own native languages. Then a question arose as to why the contrast, that *St. Marians* spoke English. They probably boasted because the majority of them lived in Nairobi. This seemed to be the obstinate belief in the minds of those who had not been blessed to become "St. Marians," within the Mosocho community, because, to them, speaking English was shameful!

The English language consequently became a tradition in St. Mary's Mosocho, and communication in native languages was a taboo which could have a student suspended from school. This separated St. Marians from other schools during inter school gatherings due to their communication difference, and in the end, their uniqueness generated reasonable distances by foreign schools in order to cover up embarrassments.

This was not the case in surrounding schools where you could find a fifth-grade student who had never practiced how to write his own name.

Opening day was one of the most surprising days of the year as we welcomed the dawn of a new beginning; with renewed faces. These obsessions take my memories back to the days when parents, from various walks of life, revisited the school with authority and recognition, confirming their parenthood. It was also a day of rare opportunity when the neighborhood was filled with vehicles of all sorts. Opulence and indigence were exposed simultaneously on this day while those of us whose homes stood next to the school compound sneaked in after dark. As a matter of fact, there was not enough reason of going home for holidays since the school was always conspicuous from all possible corners of our homes.

Nairobi boys, who traveled overnight, arrived in the early-morning hours of the day. Brother Lambert Nissik, who was the then-outgoing headmaster, was fixedly present on this day—endlessly patrolling the school compound while he restored any aggravating situation for town boys, whom he favored with proneness.

Shortly before and after lunch hours, common boys started arriving. These were individuals whose domiciles were at least outside Kisii District.

203

Anytime between four o'clock and the following morning, a special group of boys, known as *bushboys*, arrived without most people's realization.

The presence of bushboys was usually felt the following day but no one could explain how and when they got into the school compound, and never missed dinner on their day of arrival. So that no one could recognize their arrival pattern, they delivered most of their paraphernalia at cockcrow morning hours of the day and only escaped into the compound shortly before darkness, with light belongings, straight into the dormitories. Whenever they formed illegal gatherings in the institution, in the course of their stay, the incumbent headmaster referred to them as the "local community" or a bunch of grandmothers who never had anything new to offer to society, just because they originated from the bushy surrounding.

As it was his order of the day, on opening day, Lambert overtly expressed his brotherhood by aimlessly lingering from one point to the next. He was, in many occasions, the night school-guard, an untrained typist, the repairer of most obliterated school equipment, and the entertainment head. The man, on such occasions, as well, bellowed obscenities disrespectfully at students such as: "*zoot*, forget it, bushboys, local community, *fak-a-tomato,*," and, when in a cursing mood, promised that heads would roll in the course of the school term. Mostly, when the school reopened, he ranted some of his slang and would never give a welcoming hand

204

to bushboys since he saw no reason of them going home for holidays because he saw them each day after the school closed—a reminder of how bitter and hopeless life was for those less-privileged boys because none of them requested God to create them as permanent Mosocho residents.

Older boys like Minyega and the *Elder* told of legendary, analogous stories of how this man acquired his nickname. That, because the Dutch native smoked a pipe, he was consequently nicknamed *Kebwesi*, bringing about a tradition of nicknaming in the institution, which saw his counterpart, Vincent Simmonis, nobly acquire his. Vincent had replaced Joss, the owner of a small inchoate puppy named *Pache*, a dog that was also nicknamed Maragia J. —who happened to be a student that followed the devoted religious servant wherever he went within the institution.

Brother Vincent seemed the most powerful because he hovered all over the compound at a much faster pace and shouted louder than Kebwesi. The school then, being grateful of his loyalty, awarded him the onus of running and supervising the school kitchen, authority over school pigs, hygiene maintenance in the institution, issuance and collection of pastime equipment, and ensuring that the boys slept and got up at the expected time. He had, at the time, just emigrated from the Netherlands and, for this reason, had little or no knowledge of the English language. Due to this fact, his nickname sounded more disturbing than that of Lambert. The boys chose to call him *V-vait*.

St. Mary's Mosocho is a missionary-sponsored school of the Catholic Church and therefore prayer before and after meals was compulsory. He then acquired his nickname because he saw some boys imbibe food before prayer. "*Hey*! *V-vait*," he burst in upon their eating amid ponderous laughter. Since then he became V-vait.

Brother Vincent Simmonis

In 1984, the then-incoming headmaster, Peter Nyambasora, collaboratively trained with his assistant, Charles K. Mugambe, on the school criteria and trends of welcoming the boys back to school, as well as the admission of *monos*—the brand-new, jocund, novices of the institution.

Monos were traditionally hosted by the older members of the institution from whom they learned new rules and skills and, sometimes, acquired immediate partners on the first day whom they would persistently serve and nurse in return for protection. The power behind it would always be lesser than the task ahead.

Most of us had never visited Nairobi at the time. We only heard about the city which they sometimes called a "city in the sun." This was therefore enough reason to be scared of and honor Nairobi boys because they knew and understood both our bushy origins and Nairobi. We had nothing to defend. Whenever they discussed movies they had watched at the Kenya Cinema, Fox Drive In, or Nairobi Cinema, they made us wonder why we were born unfortunate and betrayed! They described films only known to them such as *In Place of Older Women*, *Scarface*, *Commando* and *Rambo II*. At times, they would also tell us about the film stars in Hollywood such as Chuck Norris, Arnold Schwarzenegger, Clint Eastwood, among others.

They were always special in everyone's eyes, knew our ignorance, and had experienced and enjoyed luxuries beyond our dreams. They discussed trips to and from school and visitations to tall buildings in the city with electric doors that opened at the touch of a button. Eventually, we learned that these machines were also called elevators. It was surely not possible, at the time, to imagine or envision their revelations.

207

209

210

211

Meals

Serious studies commenced on the first day of the term, and this was surely a day to venerate because all aspects of school life looked new and the boys much more esteemed than ever. At least everyone appeared neat and clean regardless of their origins, and some will have grown taller, some thinner, and others fatter. Added weight was, however, attributed to town boys who originated from well-off families unlike bushboys who toiled vigorously over the holidays. To this effect, it was also factual that since the surrounding was poor there was no possible way bushboys could get dietary and abundant food to help them gain weight.

It was wise to comprehend that perspective was a great quality as the vulture flies over the animal kingdom, focusing its energy on death. If we looked for the negative, that is exactly what we found and vice versa.

A quote from Sidney J. Harris reads: "When I hear somebody sigh that 'life is hard,' I'm always enticed to question, 'Compared to what?'" Yes, life has its challenges, but it is as well filled with beatitude and endless possibilities. It all depends on your perspective. Look for the positive, and you will realize that a setback is a bend in the long road and not the end of the road.

However little sustenance we had to eat down at St. Mary's, it still kept us moving compared to many hungry stomachs one can envision around the world.

For the first few days, every boy's box contained edibles, and such reality brought about financial anomalies to both the school administration and the local vendors. The administration complained of feeding school pigs with so much school-food discarded by students while the women vendors yelled across the school fence, complaining that there was low or no demand for their *mandazi*—a donut baked from corn flour. At this point, the town boys eminently engulfed luscious delicacies such as cookies, squash, Blue Band, bread, cereal, and jelly, among others, while the gawky-regarded bushboys gleefully feasted on their local harvests. This included boiled potatoes, maize, sour cow milk, sugarcane, and *chinkara*—fried, dried corn flour grains used as the main ingredient in brewing traditional African beer (busaa).

After the first month of creating rivalry among themselves because of these rare viands, the only direction the entire student population faced was the market place, which was just along the fence. Here they spent the few coins judiciously conferred to them by their parents.

Ondigo, the then-local insanity-stricken activist roamed about the place, occasionally snatching away the women's merchandise. Those who resisted had their breasts felt or

214

their posteriors lashed mercilessly. He would then be seen commanding through the tiny path which separated St. Mary's and Cardinal Otunga High School. This man was often the reason why quite a number of boys like Muigai and *JP* made themselves available at the market place so as to witness his barbaric actions, and because he also smoked cigarettes through his nostrils. He had numerous stabs all over his body which many had misconceived to be a symptom of the deadly foot-and-mouth cattle ailment. Perhaps this also helped some boys to withstand their boredom in school. They loved spending most of their leisure time along the school fence, meandering back and forth, in search of the capricious man so they could listen to his frequent, erratic utterances.

At this stage of events, the boys started *bangarafting* each other—a term that referred to befriending another when he had some reasonable money left so as to spend it together malignantly. This ill will usually took place when one was visited by his parent and given some extra coins as pocket money. But there was sharp discrepancy here as no bushboys would dare *bangaraft* town boys because they were known to be venal. Such ominous malice and division consequently developed everlasting animosities which could clearly be singled out by a keen onlooker. This profligacy was one of the senseless barriers that ravaged the uncompromising relationships between bushboys and town boys.

Time told, and it was later learned that real life in the institution commenced as soon as the entire student population indiscriminately embarked on the insipid school food.

On Mondays, we ate porridge for breakfast, *mixture* for lunch, and *posho* and *veggies* for supper.

Mixture was a term used to describe a combination of corn and beans while posho was a form of traditional bread cooked out of white corn flour.

Porridge for breakfast on Tuesdays, as it was the order of the week, bananas and porridge for lunch, and beans and posho for supper. Mixture was once again served on Wednesdays for lunch, with hot, viscous porridge and a piece of pork or beef with ugali in the evening. This was the day for "pieces," as meat was commonly known, patronized by Saturday's dinner when beef or pork was provided, depending on what *Matumbo*, the cook, thought fit or dietary for the boys. It was basically a sensitive day for everyone because V-vait lavished those indispensable "extra pieces" or "fats" in turns, depending on where you sat in dormitory order and position. Bananas were once again served on Thursday lunch with hot porridge, veggies for supper with ugali, while mixture was served on Fridays for lunch with porridge, and beans with posho for the day's supper. Mixture was availed on Saturdays for lunch, again, veggies on Sunday lunch, and beans with posho for the day's supper.

All these meals were prepared by the five hardworking cooks—Doyle, Matumbo, James, *Ndugu*, and *Amka-Tuende*, who tirelessly cared for the boys' nutrition in the institution.

Weekly *dividers* and *cleaners* too, were of essence since each of the weekly meals, which were surely meant to beat poverty, were determined by them. Because the most significant thing on earth was not as much where we stood but the direction we faced, V-vait consoled those who were regularly *punished*—meaning those who got food that was insufficient, about a hopeful and better next time! This also meant that they were expected to be optimistic and increase their hope and faith of more food on the next round.

Most, if not all, of these meals were insipid. But this is what kept us enlightened, perhaps the dead weevils which we expected in our daily meals before we even ate. These were all setbacks but we focused our energies because our imagination was the only limit to what we could hope to attain in the future. We never focused on the problem but on the solution. There was no sure reason to take our eyes off the goal and instead focus on the challenges that fenced around the goal.

217

Contemporary St. Marians had no time spent on worrying about the problem but looked for solutions whenever problems arose. We in place thought of the good that was ahead of our lives rather than what we went through in the institution. Each time we stood for an ideal, we sent forth a tiny ripple of hope in the visible and invisible challenges that we faced and those that were imminent and unknown since a powerful, true, and realistic ego is the most appropriate readiness for success in life.

Reminiscences

One of the main keys to overcoming disappointments in life is learning to let go of the past. You let go of the past by choosing to forgive those who have hurt or wronged you by believing that God will restore to you anything that was taken. When you receive Christ's forgiveness in your own life, you are released from the pressure to make up for past mistakes or failures. You begin to experience the bright future our Father has in store for you.

"I have come that you might have and enjoy life and have it to the full—until it overflows!" said Christ.

A major key to enjoying life is that we live to give.

True happiness and true fulfillment come when you give your life in some way to others. God promises to multiply back to you what you give. When you step out in faith, you open a door for God's hand of blessing to move on your behalf—a simple principle of sowing and reaping.

God has a specific plan for every one, of our lives. His plan involves reaching out and touching other people with His love, mercy, and compassion. Ask Him how you can share His love with others by giving your time, your talents, and your resources today.

Due to our few teachers' collaboration and mutual understanding, St. Mary's unceasingly neared the tops in the country after yearly national examinations. The students' perseverance and hard work also counted as one of the contributions that facilitated that customary success. In 1984, there were only four teachers who worked toward that positive end, and although by that time Kebwesi was about to leave, he was still one of the teachers, Peter Nyambasora, Charles K. Mugambe, Peter Omayo and Otiambo Obare.

This was the year of our newness to the institution and its episodes. As a result of our consistent ignorance, in the institution, as monos, in that particular year, Kebwesi gave us a tedious time in class; and this was because most of us barely understood the English language which we viewed as foreign, and so he seemed to have taken the very weakness for granted. A number of bushboys occasionally complained of his headstrong, malicious utterances and native Dutch spells.

I recall one instance when he asked me to mentally calculate a sum: "17+15-8+431, Omosa!" he croaked. And within the next two seconds, he had already dastardly revealed to me that I was a dunderhead and hurled numerous insults at me, reminding others that I was a bushboy whose home was most conspicuous from the school compound. *"Bushboy eee . . . , only thinking of bananas and guavas."* Another irrational evidence to support his bigotry for bushboys is the fact that he never believed that a bushboy could be sick for more than two days, and that is why he once penitently assured Morangi that his body had a built-up mechanism to resist malaria. "*Mogangi*, you should have adopted to the local weather by now because you are a bushboy, and I therefore don't see any reason why you should be ill for more than two days!" he advised him relentlessly. In exasperation, he many a time vowed never to let any bushboy sleep in bed in false pretense of sickness while others studied. But such painful experiences by the bushboy community never ended there, and only became a routine lifestyle which in the end improved their resistance in the institution.

Irrelevantly, when the man asked a town boy to solve a mathematical problem, it was always the simplest imaginable: "Maurice, what is 10+3-6?" This time, he grinned, a laugh of derision enabling his *cousin*—as town boys were sometimes referred to, to find the answer with ease.

He had very bad teeth blackened by his pipe. One was missing on the left side, and when he laughed, the gap looked like a vacant plot in a slum area. He claimed to have smoked the pipe since he was 13 years old, to the very moments he coughed like a prolonged roll of thunder.

The only fact he ignored by doing so was that he was loosening his cousins' minds thus increasing their degree of imbecility while, on the other hand, he made bushboys propitious in the long-term. In other cases, while one of his cousins timorously worked out the solution of a mathematical problem he remembered beauty in the Netherlands, explaining how the sea was moved to create productive land.

If we hadn't discovered the values and dignity that we would die for, then we did not indeed deserve to live!

We were great because we stood in such a position so that others could dispense pain and death on us and confine us at their own felicity without anyone asking questions. Although the discrimination was to our detriment, we never despaired shaping our destinies and only viewed that as extended colonial days of bondage and buttressing of war and uprising. This ultimately unified the victims as they frequently clustered, trying to find a solution to the man's bias as his cousins rivaled against one another with selfish ambitions of trying to be more of a cousin to him than the other.

As it was "every cousin for Kebwesi and Kebwesi for all cousins," all bushboys worked in the gardens during his regime—getting rid of unwanted tall grass and ensuring that places where others urinated and tested their bowel movements, were hygienic. His cousins worked in teachers' compounds, swept the school office and staff room, and any other petty duties necessary during manual work assignments.

Even if we did not slander anyone, we had to make an earnest effort to avoid becoming judgmental. Christ himself condemned such a spirit when he said, "Stop judging that you may not be judged; for with what judgment you are judging, you will be judged; and with the measure that you are measuring out, they will measure out to you. Why, then, do you look at the straw in your brother's eye, but do not consider the rafter in your own eye?"

Simply destroying the good people and saving the wicked was not enough to resolve the problem of servitude and hatred once and for all. Such hatred was often the result of improper training of people's hearts and minds. However, that is where God's government excelled. Practical instruction and education would be provided in order to train people so that they would love righteousness. The changes in people who may once have had animal-like characteristics are well illustrated in the scriptures pictorially.

Viewed as nature that was an epitome of Mosocho, the school regime stood a fit chance to be defined as ailing, stringent, and supportive of commotion, oppression and exacerbation. . It excluded bushboys and the poor from the social code, acceptable ideas, opulence, and the position of ascendancy over others.

The student rebellion symbolized itself in numerous ways; the latter thrust being the one which more directly

223

demanded and gained by effort of the bush-boy emancipation, by freely agreeing to endure physical and psychological agony. The former thrust of the student rebellion commenced in early 1984 with bushboys such as Morangi who played a central and indispensable role in the struggle for their human rights. Essentially, the rebellion sought to break down the hindrances of social segregation in the institution, attain equality and justice for bushboys, and unionize them into an egoistic, conscious force capable of defining, protecting, and advancing their fundamental interests.

Gilbert Morangi Simba

One of the most essential thoughts in the whole bush-boy resistance, which waged the tussle for their freedom from disparity and mutability, was the thought of relevance—a concept that had both academic and social lengths. Relevance, as a fundamental category, was inevitably referred to as emanating from education's addition to liberation and a higher level of life for bushboys. Basically, the social affairs of students centered around the propositions, subjects of exclusion, chagrin, brutal treatment in school, academic conversions and production of a live, committed, and capable group of intellectual people, and on what all this signified for the bushboy community. Consequently, some of us, myself especially, boycotted, discarded, discredited the entire academic system in the institution, secretly, and declined to comprehend any of the so-called academic theories put across to us. The sad event of my life in the institution did not lie on not reaching my goal, but it never occurred to me that I never had a goal to reach.

An academic and refinement of intellectual and artistic taste confined to a region of this sort can only lack faith in the school's claim of inclusiveness, objectivity, and the quality of being inflexible or unyielding for its curriculum. It also reflects a fictitious image in Mosocho where bushboys have now stepped back on the dais of human chronological record of significant events with an explanation of their causes in both dramatic and unavoidably significant ways and roles and must be on the educational manifesto.

This inquiry into the bushboys' past has openly shown its relevance as an addition to the rescue and restructuring of the their history and humanity. This structure is both an expression of assent and negative academic and social scheme; the bushboy analysis affirms the truth of our history and humanity and negates the discriminative myths assembled to deny and misshape us. By refusing to respond to trivial, apartheid-like contentions, it rises to halt and demand the countersign of traditional and modern town boys and the sponsor of that regime, which have augmented their ingenious partiality, omissions, and obliteration. It makes actual the link between history and the quality or state of being human and is aware of the mere open fact that Kebwesi denied and ravaged our history in order to deny and dwindle our humanity. The bushboys' study and consequent analysis then commences firstly in this book with severe research and crucial intellectual production in the most important social study—history—which lays the foundation in favor of and announces overtly and without fear to the rest and which will strengthen the reality of their reminiscences in the sensitive stage of childhood and deny the existence or truth of the partial myths which have surrounded it.

The bushboy, town boy clarification is generally a crucial addition to a modern social study which will not only benefit traditional bushboys, but also current ones, town boys, and the world population in general.

If this is viewed as an additional study involving man in general; his sources, background, development, and customs, the bushboy, town boy reflection, which is interdisciplinary, grows into a model for the many-length approach to social and historic revelations. It is a role model for a graceful study involving an epitome society, not only simply focusing on bushboys, but also critically involving town boys and other circumstantial members of the Mosocho community at large in suitable absolute socio-historical eras and places of interaction with the so-called superb, divine Brothers and telling everyone about its significance.

For whatever reason, the subjugating town boy group refused to interact freely with the bushboy overcome element and directed its domination on this absolute domination. But the opposition was essentially on class distinction and would shockingly be resolved, in old and modern history, by merely instigating others to commit suicide.

When the plot of eliminating the bushboy existing population was in its making, a feeling of collective guilt and self-hatred, which was difficult to keep from being unknown, captured the conscience of the White mercenaries. These people who had settled in the area under the cover of religious offerings gave rise to an expiatory image to be seen and felt today in the figure of legends of the founding of the institution. Here the bushboys were charged with all the ravaged states of human nature in which the self is

227

estranged from God. Kebwesi and his cousin gang, in this way, recuperated and regained a savage spirit, an inchoate purity in some cases, at times, expiatory rites recall the acts of violence through which the conditions of this sort were developed.

We are in rhythm with a situation whose realities exactly concur with those of the school. The institution was not knowingly created to isolate and subjugate one group of the entire student population rightly or wrongly regarded to be distinct as a result of origin, tribe, or domicile from the town boy gang. They were, so to speak, for internal school consumption and, consequently, present a less-sudden aspect. For this purpose, they were prone to engender a more or less-imparted social stratification admitted by the people so long as the regime earnestly renounced outright abuses.

Such inequalities were not imposed overnight by that group of exotic invaders coming from the outside after thorough unification. They were the effect of on-the-spot growth of internal contradictions in the school regime; therefore, they were habitually seen through the extenuating optical instrument of custom—a tradition that blended with the initial foundations of the school. This, we can say, concocted to an understanding and appreciation of the bushboys' definition.

The bushboys' definition only deserves the definition of St. Mary's itself and then using that definition to define the bushboys and its relevance.

St. Mary's, then, is the struggle and record of bushboys, town boys, teachers, and the vicinity, withstanding foreign invaders called Brothers, in the process of humanizing the earth. That is, molding it in their own image and interests. To mold the earth into a human image is to give it a human form, and to conduct and to shape it in human interests is to make it serve humans rather than threaten, deform, or ravage them. In a more simpler term, molding the earth into human image and interests is to make it a context which reflects and ensures human defense, growth, and ultimate self-realization.

The then-incoming headmaster handled official duties with a heavy hand and, unlike most other schools, he was not an exception in the teaching profession. He was a respected, feared, and quiet teacher whose sole ambition seemed to be to shape up citizens of moral character and authenticity. Commonly known as *Zida*, he condoned no balderdash and was difficult to understand especially when not in his office. If it was serious class time then that meant the same and failure to comply with his wishes led to hard knocks on the head supplemented with hot whips on the culprit's hind end.

229

During Zida's reign, the notion of favoritism and *cousinship* ceased and was discredited and abandoned, now that the pioneer of the regime had handed over that pompous office to him. In his eyes and Mugambe's, all boys were created equal and this is what subsequently led to his achievements, reverence, and success as a headmaster in the institution—enabling him maintain the good standards of the school, and through this, town boys began the capitulation of their discriminatory ancient trends of imaginary superiority.

Peter Nyambasora Okari

Mugambe believed that anyone who had never made mistakes had never tried anything new. So he introduced the *Eight's Times*—which was a school magazine, as means of improving our English understanding and communication ability. Artists; such as Syayi, Mwangi, Nagila, and *Odhis,* were responsible for the title: Eight's Times, while the rest of us wrote articles to be posted on the magazine each Monday morning. Those who excelled in the English language scrutinized the articles to be posted and handed them over to the inventor for final analysis before being compiled and stuck on a large piece of plain paper.

Mugambe, understood as a benevolent teacher with distinguishing physical characteristics, made himself a teacher of urbane, unique character whose qualities many learned from, mimicked, and venerated. No one missed his classes without an appropriate cause. Not even *Peke-Yake*—unless the teacher himself forcefully threw him out; because this was a man who, at times, created comedic entertainment in the course of his teaching which is still pertinent in our minds today.

Whenever one was inattentive in the classroom, he pounced on such a boy and asked him to perform obnoxious activities such as jogging several times around the "First Field," balance a container full of trash on the head and laugh continuously, among others. He was the English language teacher, and his success was seen and heard of in the neighborhood and beyond because St. Mary's produced some of the best English language candidates each year. This goes as far back as 1985 when he received awards for training some of the best candidates in the English language—countrywide. His theory was simple and precise as such success inevitably became a tradition each year, ascending to subsequent years, because as a good teacher, he ensured that whatever he taught was satisfactorily comprehended. He thus used the students' interests as a weapon to make them understand what he put across, for instance, using the boys' nicknames as characters in a passage in question. He was fond of mental sums too whenever he taught mathematics, and I shall never forget the quizzical Ugandan song he conferred to us in 1986, when he was the music teacher:

Ntunze, ntunze,
Omunyolo atunze nandere

Ntunze, ntunze,
Omunyolo antunze nandere

Kano kekebiri,
Omunyolo antunze nabiri

Kano kekesatu
Omunyolo atunze nabiri

232

Charles K. Mugambe

If we had our nerves filled with traditional humor at any given moment related to Mugambe's Ugandan songs, we convened in the refectory to describe Otiso; son of Manyange, who was said to have jeopardized his two testicles on a bicycle seat before he got married:

Otiso o'minto, Otiso akagora enyange; eee!
Otiso o'minto, Otiso akagora enyange; eee!

Akagora enyange, eee, ekero ataranywoma; aaa!
Akagora enyange, ekero ataranywoma; aaa!

Omwana o'Manyange, eee; baba o'mwana o'Manyange,
eee, baba!

Omwana o'Manyange, eee; baba o'mwana o'Manyange,
eee, baba!

Akagora enyange, ekero ataranywoma; aaa!
Akagora enyange, ekero ataranywoma; aaa!

Omayo was a fairly old man who, by then, looked in his early sixties although he time and again made pronouncements suggesting that his age decreased each year, and could not be easily moved by any event thus stood by his principles. He loved recognition as an old teacher who had taught many successful people, including Zida himself, and repeatedly claimed to have been a one-time renowned boxer. He was a force to reckon more especially when he punched tables in the classroom, expressing tactics shown to him by his German trainer as every nerve and muscle stood out on his arms. He was an ancient man who lived in the contemporary present, and it again and again, appeared to be a shock to him that he was teaching boys whose parents he had taught many years before. He had various sinister ways of foretelling someone's future by pointing fingers at him in different styles, explaining what stage each finger stood for before the actual incident occurred—for instance an expulsion from school. This became evident in 1984 when he completed his final finger-pointing stage on James Keya and Gervas Nyamwaya who, consequently, faced an expulsion that year. For petty disruptions like laughing at him or failure to complete his assignments, he merely stood by the wrongdoer and reminded him that he was once a prominent boxer.

Obare was an extremely fast teacher both in writing and talking, a man who believed in speed and accuracy. He was eventually transferred to a different school due to private disputes between him and his spouse, Josephine, contrary to his wishes, only to be replaced by Andrew Gitene, Philip Nyamwega, James Bosire, Vindonye Onyando, Samuel Obae, John Momanyi (*Mwandawiro*), and Peter Ogeto.

Vindonye Onyando

235

Out of all the seven teachers who replaced Obare, Nyamwega was more fascinating as he loved the *Vitimbi* television comedies which he in turn reminiscently mimicked during his Geography and Science classes. He also, at times, in an attempt to socialize himself with the student category, took part along with them in athletic, sprinting events.

Philip Nyamwega

Ogeto loved the African culture without fear or regret. He often explained why he preferred to have just one native African name and whenever the students gardened he reminded them not to discard any trapped rodents, such as moles, which constituted his most favorite delicacy.

236

Peter Ogeto

On each weekday, classes commenced at nine o'clock. Each memorable morning looked calm and peaceful. More so on Tuesdays, when the local people marched to Nyakoe Market with various goods balanced on women's heads. Donkeys headed for the market from the neighboring Luoland, President Obama's ancestral home area, plodded and kicked the air, expelling mud from their crooked hooves, as they kowtowed uphill resisting their masters' prodding.

These donkeys walked every Tuesday from the direction of *Nyang'oma*, Kogelo Village, miles away from the shores of Lake Victoria where hearsay had cropped up of legendary tales told by great-grandmothers and grandfathers of the lake.

In Kogelo Village, those whose donkeys had been killed by the hyenas, or those who could not afford the dear domestic animals, ferried their goods to and from the local markets balanced on women's heads, or, in rare cases, on men's backs.

The people near Lake Victoria always told stories to their children, grand children, and great-grand children.

My great-great-great grandfather; Nyaborigo, told a story to his son, Obare, who also told the same story to his

238

son, Morangi—whose sister was married to the neighboring Luoland, who also told the story to my grandfather, Simba, and, who, in hierarchical turn, narrated the same to my father; Omosa, about reasons "Why Bats only Come Out At Night." This is one of the numerous East African "Why" stories.

That, a long time ago, the impala and the bat were very good friends. But one day, they were involved in a domestic quarrel.

The bat asked the impala to pay her little babies a visit.

"I'm very excited to see your babies," said the impala. "They are very lovely babies. But why didn't you show me your eggs before they hatched?"

"Bats don't lay eggs," answered the bat. "Your babies grow inside your body. Mine grow in my body too. I'm not a bird."

"But you are a bird," said the impala, "and all birds lay eggs. Then the babies peck a hole in the egg. When the hole is big enough, they come out. Everybody knows that."

"I just told you that I'm not a bird," said the bat. She was almost getting cross.

"Don't be silly," said impala. "I can see your wings. I know you can fly very well. Only birds have wings and can fly. So you are a bird."

239

"I'm not a bird!" shouted the bat. This was her third reminder to the impala, and she was now running out of patience.

They both argued for quite some time; consequently, they developed a consensual scheme for achieving the objective

The impala suggested, "If you lay any eggs, you must hand them over to me. And if you grow babies inside your body, you will keep them."

The bat concurred. "If I grow babies inside my body, I'll keep them. And if I lay eggs, you must give me your babies."

The impala agreed.

Every day, the impala visited the bat in her house. She looked for eggs every day. But she never found any. Then one day, the bat had two babies. The impala wasn't there, so the bat sent her husband to the impala's house.

"Come and witness the birth of our new babies," he requested. He saw that the impala had new babies too.

So the impala ran quickly to the bat's house.

"Look! Here are my babies," said the bat. "I did not lay any eggs, did I?"

"No," said the impala, sadly. "You didn't lay any eggs. I confirmed every day."

"So you must give me your babies, mustn't you?" asked the bat. "You consensually contracted."

"Oh dear," said the impala. She was saddened. "Yes, I agreed. But please don't take away my babies. If I don't care for them, they'll meet their demise. You don't know how to look after my babies."

"But we came up with a contractual plan," said the bat. "We both agreed."

"Well, I'll bring them tomorrow," said the impala. The bat was, however, empathetic for her. So she said, "You must give me your babies, but you can visit them once in a while."

The next day, the impala brought her two children to the bat's house.

"Please care for them cautiously well," she pleaded. "I look after my own children extremely well," answered the bat. "And I will nurse yours well too."

The impala returned home. She was maddened by the reality she had engaged herself in.

Later, the bat went out to hunt and gather some food for the children.

"Children, I'll bring you some delicious food upon my return," she promised.

She caught some little insects and brought them home. But the impala's children did not like insects for their nutrition. Impalas feed on grass and particularly wild leaves not insects.

So she went hunting again. This time, she brought home some butterflies.

The bat's children liked them and gluttonously ate them all very fast. The impala's children did not eat any of them since impalas don't eat butterflies.

Oh dear, thought the bat. *What can I get for them? I know! Impalas like grass.*

So she went out again to get some grass. When she returned, she was astonished to learn that the impala's children had eaten her babies. Because of anger on the fact that her babies had been eaten up by the young impalas, she flew over them, scratched, and bit them repeatedly. In the end, they died of injuries sustained. The bat had killed them.

The following morning, the impala came to visit her young ones to see how well they were doing. When she approached the bat's house, she pensively began to listen. But she couldn't hear any children. She peeped into the house but couldn't see any children.

"Where are my babies?" she asked the bat. The bat bowed her head in shame, guilt, and exasperation. "Where are my babies?" exclaimed the impala in disbelief.

"They are dead," the bat revealed.

"Dead?" shouted the impala.

"Yes, dead," said the bat. "This is how they met their death: Your babies ate my babies, so I revenged by killing them."

"But why did they eat your babies? Impalas don't eat bats, we are herbivores not carnivores. Is it because you failed to feed my babies. Recall that I warned that you couldn't be able to feed my children, but you insisted that we had a binding contract to give up my own poor babies to you if it occurred that bats don't lay eggs."

"It was a verbal agreement, but it is legally binding," said the bat. "And remember, you called me a bird!"

A quarrel matured once again. The impala got mad and started chasing the bat around the living room. She was trying to catch the bat by her sharp horns. At last, the bat flew up inside the roof of her house for safety.

"If you come out, I'll kill you!" warned the mad impala. "Whenever and wherever I see you, I'll kill you—you little ugly bastard!"

So since then, bats only come out at night when impalas are asleep and can't see them; as they are not nocturnal.

My great-grandparents heard more and more stories emanating from the shores of Lake Victoria and beyond into Obama's village. A man named Obama Opiyo, President Obama's great-grandfather, was also said to have told "Why the Hippo Has No Hair," "Why the Crocodile Lives

243

In Water," "Why the Baby Chickens Follow their Mothers," and "Why the Hyena Laughs Like Human Beings."

The Impala was trying to catch the bat on her sharp horn

We, according to routine got up at exactly six-thirty each morning. Once *Graham, the Bell* had fulfilled his obligation, V-vait, as if running, emerged from nowhere with a powerful flashlight firmly shouting jargon all around the dormitories: "*Hey! who is he the boy? Now, come on, vake up!*" he called; his eyes glowering in the darkness. If he saw no signs of getting up, then he normally promised stern measures forthwith. "*Yeah! I see you at nine o'clock, the*

whole day in the 's"amba,' and I give severe 'punis"ment.' I
tell Mr. Peter of your behavior, and I don't see you for table!"
he would bellow, hurriedly walking to besiege everyone as
he gnashed his teeth, allowing a deep murmur of suppressed
anger to sweep through the dormitories. After his attacks,
he would then change from himself to a fairly joyful man,
making announcements in connection with manual work
and breakfast: *"During manual 'vork,' I don't see any boy*
not 'vorking.' 'Othervise,' I don't see you for table." Table
was his alternative word for mealtime.

Shortly before breakfast, the boys were expected to
show up for their respective duties, as manual work, and
this is when it also became very easy to identify bushboys
and town boys.

Bushboys, such as Victor Mose, Peke-Yake, Sakwa
Nyaata and *Jigger*, had been specifically elected to feed
pigs, each morning, due to their physical looks and origin
factor and only to complain later, to V-vait, that they wish to
resign because the swine had eating disorders—every day!

At exactly nine o'clock, everyone resumed their studies
as usual while V-vait prepared a list of those to be pummeled
in the realm. Teachers also entered classrooms at this time
and proceeded from where they had stopped, since the
institution's academic standard was based on hard work and
collaboration of all concerned parties.

In between lessons, necessary breaks were permitted to enable the boys to feed themselves with snacks of various sorts including *red basin, nyambegera, oily,* and *parrot* mandazi.

After, these normal activities resumed until four thirty-five; when extracurricular activities commenced so that we could see things as they really were and not as we imagined they were.

Pastime

Pastime officially commenced at four thirty-five, after classes. Once again V-vait dawdled around the three dormitories, forcing the lazy ones out. At this particular time, one boy representing each dormitory queued outside the lout's office for games equipment to be used either in the First, Second, Third, or Fourth field.

Not anyone could play in any of the four fields, however. There were specific members of each field constituting a team of players who competed every day.

First Field was an area specifically meant for the most aged members of the institution, and the majority of these boys formed the school's soccer team.

Second Field was used by those considered to be the following year's members of the school team. In 1984, its members were made up of several mavericks such as Isoe, Swao, Ongoto, and *Mojengo*.

In the Third Field, very old and half-inflated balls were kicked. This field was next to the eighth grade classroom and south of Zida's school domicile, and was the only field with imaginary boundaries of an ordinary soccer field. Most of its members were a special group of boys who could decide to interfere with the proper growth of each other's limbs in the course of their play. One could intentionally abandon the ball and choose to interrupt the natural development of

247

nearby bushes and later blame it on his opponent. They sometimes turned to physical confrontations if injuries from the bushes were severe or, at times, if English, as a language of communication, proved timorous and it occured that there was a teacher nearby—barring them from exchanging obscene words in their own vernacular. Participants here included lads such as Peke-Yake, *Whisky*, and Kizito Oundo Akuloba; who giggled and chuckled as they chased the ball. As a matter of fact, Whisky's titters could be heard and felt as far as the *Brandsma* dormitory, disrupting coordination of more serious events in the institution.

And then, there was the Fourth Field where a game known as rounders was played—by those who considered bathing to be a rite of passage because not much running took place here.

During our era in the institution, the creation of eloquence and slang in the soccer history of the institution was seen which brought about bewilderment if, at all, one was a spectator whenever matches were held. Dialects were created, describing certain styles of either kicking or catching a ball. These were used during inter-school competitions to astonish and ridicule members of opponent schools who were as well, on such occasions, reminded that their bare feet had jiggers and were also trailed by a pungent stench wherever they went. Whenever alien schools attempted to cheer up their teams, they were, in return, jeered by St.

Marians because they cheered in foreign languages, not in English—such as *Nyakome Chinkobii*!

If you silently kicked a ball with your toes, that was *ondole*. Goalkeepers many a time heard aggravating cheers from spectators if the technique was properly applied during competitions. If a goalkeeper caught a hard shot aimed at him, that was *kausharing* and the ball was therefore *kaushwad*. *Kaukarance* was an embarrassing or shameful situation when one missed a target. "Anunda was 'giving them badly,' but the goalie *kaushad* all of them"—such were common dictions from supporters as soon as particular matches ended.

Talented players, in 1984 and beyond, came and went. Reuben Mong'are was one of them. This was an older boy who would kick the ball very far away and chase it and if he accidentally reached it before either his opponent or teammate, the school administration had to replace broken windows the following day. Philip Morara, nicknamed *Peugeot*, and George Morara, *Gecko*, as well made up that era's strong group of individuals who were considered gifted in terms of soccer.

Antecedent times in the history of the school soccer regimes was legendarily crowned by a true story of one fine soccer player, long before we were admitted in the institution, who baffled the entire Mosocho community by altering the true meaning of English words. The guy, one day, revealed to Kebwesi how a certain group of boys had "killed" him on various parts of his body simply because he was a mono at the time. "They kill me here, here, and here, and they call me *omosiki* (homesick) boy!"

Toward the end of 1986 and early 1987, we had become old enough to start adopting new trends and relationships and had gotten familiar with most idioms and cant in the institution.

Although a unique clique of dubious individuals like *Black Beauty,* Owino, *MB* and *Mosquito* merely played to portray their emotional and questionable physical characteristics—so that others would fetish them, Monyenye was a boy filled with credence, who played to develop his physical features and social image. He was a fairly young slender lad who had little light brown legs; invaded by dilated fur. His legs looked naturally flexible; enabling him to dodge others during soccer matches. He was later appointed a prefect in the Brandsma dormitory—succeeding Mwangi.

Subsequently, Marita emerged with outstanding dexterity in soccer in the early days of 1987. He played a better game when barefooted and often stipulated a team of powerful boys to equal his energy. He was a tall, skinny teenager and an adolescent, at the time, with light brown-scarlet, scary eyes from which he derived his nickname—*Macho*. The cause of his vigorous game and hard shots was said to be his gluttony. When in sound health, he could munch a whole basin of simmered beans and several plates of posho—a tendency that led to frequent recriminations and insults from V-vait and the entire student population. For this very reason, JP consequently called him a *knocker*.

Macho was truly not a person to intimidate or look down upon. He once depicted his physical ingenuity on Peke-Yake by striking his bushy eyebrow so that it swelled. Peke-Yake then had a black eye because he made revelations to him that his eyes were red as a result of being a knocker.

Evidently, boys who imbibed too much of school food eventually developed marasmic eating abnormalities, occasionally growing thinner as they ate more and more and, in the end would be seen vanishing into lavatories, in turns, to empty their guts for a reasonable length of time. Eyes could also turn scarlet as a result of prolonged periods of emptying a constipated paunch—or rather *blocking*.

Life immediately took the shape of an onion in the eyes of Peke-Yake and the other St. Marians —with many layers and sometimes made them cry.

At this point, he was then convinced that there were people specifically sent by the devil with the sole mission of ensuring that he was prematurely packaged in that wooden crate, called a casket, ready for export from this competitive world to the unknown next. Everyday, he was hounded by the supreme sinner through his elected agents using a variety of methods so that it came as a shock when, anytime, he managed to complete a full day without a practical problem. The nightmare for the boy usually started early in the morning when, if he successfully slipped through V-vait's fingertips, Mugambe chased him out of the classroom unceremoniously through the window or asked him to remain standing all throughout his class lessons. The result was that the boy could no longer recall what it felt to be seated in the classroom despite the many a time he unwillingly forewent his school meals due to V-vait's bold and final decisions. It was not, however, the fact that he permanently attended his class lessons poised in the manner of a javelin thrower that really worried him, but the fact that now Macho had deformed his eyebrow into an incomprehensible swelling. In the course of that particular day, he had as well been heard regretting aloud by asking himself why he crossed Macho's lines so that he found himself in the hands of a fellow who could easily scare imps away by merely fixing them with a stare of those extra-red eyes. Of course, the eyes were not red as a result of dust and bright lights but rather due to hereditary possessions exorcised, as if by solemn command, from his ancestors, over past generations, who smoked other things besides cigarettes, and whose sources were some of those dimly lit alleyways in *Manga*—his homeland.

Peke-Yake, henceforth, never laid any claims to bravery, so he endured all manners of indignities because he knew that Macho could easily set about rearranging his ribs at the slightest provocation. Later he revealed to some of his most trusted confidants, whom he strongly believed would not pass over the information to his then-brand-new adversary, that he had compared him with the erratic Ondigo. But this comparison seemed extreme and way off limits because, on the contrary, Ondigo, the local schizophrenic, nursed his mind with *chang'aa*—a form of illicit liquor, and dried leaves of unknown origins. This then left a big question to be answered by Peke-Yake himself; it was a self-imposed assignment! Might it have been a possibility that his immediate, brand-new foe also attempted to erase his daily pain and frustrations with dried leaves of unknown origins and their effect crowned by chang'aa? This question disturbed him for his entire stay in the institution that he almost turned wildly impractical.

Peke-Yake's life seemed more and more impractical now that his social problems arose from both possible and impossible perspectives. He felt like returning to his home, *Bigego*, which happened to be adjacent to *Bombo,* but upon recalling the various sufferings undergone to arrive in the area, he ignored that obnoxious paradox in his mind.

It was not surprising though that he had, in the preceding past, been shopping around for a gas mask, occasionally

253

bugging Nairobi boys to contribute to his effort because it was then obvious that he could unexpectedly die of gas poisoning as he traveled from school to Bigego.

While chances of anyone, in the incredibly packed mammy wagons he boarded to his home, letting loose a nerve gas was rather remote, he was packed in such a manner that more often than not his nose ended up in an armpit, which emitted virulent fumes and which could easily knock out a hippopotamus. He more often boarded a lorry called "Voice of Bigego—Original," if by any chance he missed the other two named "Dirty by Nature" and "Up to You." And when he was not forced into crazy angles to ensure that he inhaled a mixture of gases, which could not be described as perfumes by any definition, he was placed in such awkward positions so that he lived a very embarrassed life for the next few months. Such positions included being plodded persistently until he was squeezed between people who, among others, included the age-mates of his mother. The trouble here was that he dared not to do as much as fidget for the obvious hazard of being misunderstood.

On one remarkable school opening day, he boarded a *matatu* that happened to be a favorite mode of transport for meat retailers who normally hopped into the packed vehicles with blood still dripping from their clothes. After being sandwiched between such two fellows, he smelled like a mobile butchery by the time he got in the school compound.

Although it was not every opening day that he smelt like the local abattoir, his clothes were, on such occasions, cramped to the extent that he found it rather tricky convincing colleagues that he did not sleep in them prior to the poignant excursion.

Perhaps life would also not be so disgusting if he did not have to sometimes ride together with sots so drunk that all they could do was throw obscenities all over the place, and things got really sophisticated whenever he was in the company of his mother or father. In such an eventuality, he had two alternatives: either he pretended he was asleep or that language being used was a combination of Chinese and Arabic—which his father and mother could not understand. His entire life was filled up with undefined episodes.

Voice of Bigego—Original

Up to You

Basketball, a game mainly dominated by town boys, was equally an important and recognized pastime in the institution. The pitch was located a few feet away from the market place where Ondigo operated back and forth without regard to ongoing events.

The strongest team in 1985 comprised of various mavericks including Morangi, Ngare, Oburu, Bisonga, Mageria, and Ogolla. But the most deputized team was that of 1987 when classmates such as *Makanyaga, Mo, Wacko-Jacko,* Syayi, *Robo,* JP, Odhis, and Ndubi made up that physical year's school team.

Makanyaga was a short, viable, agreeable boy who played the game to emotionally stimulate his partners, and utilized his knacks of the past in order to have others fetish

256

his ways. He had many peers, apt stayed, and stood by them and that is why he ended up being as dexterous, adroit, handy, and heartrending as he was.

Mo, Wacko-Jacko's long-time, paradoxical pal, mostly seemed determined to improve his basketball skills. This brings about old memories of that material night when the two exchanged fists outside the standard 6 classroom— subsequently each of them revealing their past, privately secluded involvement to the greater student population.

"Don't think I have been *put* as many times; go to hell! Even now *puters* are waiting too long—bitch!" Mo announced, as a reasonable group of boys clustered nearby with arms folded on their chests.

Wacko-Jacko was verily a fellow who scratched faces of his immediate adversaries whenever he was engaged in physical confrontations. This he also did to MB's pretty face in 1987, at exactly nine o'clock in the night, merely because MB called him a girl disguising himself as a boy. But on the other hand, he had a hard time convincing others that he was not of the opposite sex due to his distasteful physical and emotional characteristics. This misconception was, nevertheless, corrected as soon as he started developing a beard and taking showers in the open although many still insisted on having a closer look at his genitals. Despite the boy's constant benevolent smiles and uncalled-for grins, he henceforth had a reason to remain embarrassed

257

with occasional awe related to the one Macho permanently planted on Peke-Yake.

Syayi was a skinny, tall light skin hooligan, probably in his late teens by then, who had a horrendous rough voice and a spot of dark mutated beard below his chin, confined into a horde of untimely beard. His general description was not any different from the kind of game he flaunted at the basketball pitch—every nerve and muscle piteously stood out on his arms and skinny legs as he heavily bounced the ball as if he was about to bury it into the hard ground. His eyes were sharp and sunken and, occasionally, portrayed bare, pensive stares. Nevertheless, the boy later proved to be one of the finest basketball players both in St. Mary's Mosocho and Cardinal Otunga High School.

Robo played exactly the same way he walked; carelessly swinging his hands to all possible directions, as far as he could, and then let them converge right above his elevated buttocks while his head swayed right and left each time he took a stride. When he bounced the ball, an opponent could easily snatch it from him because he bounced it about three feet away from his main body. He was a little taller and darker than one other boy from his Luhya tribe nicknamed *Paw-Paw*.

Odhis played the game in a naturally talented manner, cunningly shifting the ball from one hand to the other so as to maneuver through opponents easily. This particular boy was dynamic. He not only played basketball but his versatility also equipped him with an extra skill in blowing a flute, an instrument which left him a frightful sobriquet. His lips consequently enlarged only to be nicknamed *Big-Lips*.

JP was a paranoid, rustic boy who was, time and again, guided by personally adjusted principles. He could be recruited as one of the players in a match but instead choose to trap grasshoppers in the course of the game; making his team lose. He loved tearing away insects into tiny pieces whenever he saw them or, at times, disabled them so as to cause laughter to himself. His nickname was *Yellow-Man*— due to his skin color.

Putting aside the fact that the game was dominated by town boys, unlike soccer where both categories featured, it also stood factual that those town boys, more often than not, looked healthier than bushboys probably because they habitually wolfed down large quantities of food juxtaposed in refrigerators in their homes. This then remained a contrast to bushboys who fed on mass carbohydrate-rich foods in order to regain vigor, which would be applied on their farms during planting seasons. Such contributed, supportively, to the graceful physical emaciation among the bushboy category in spite of the many other tribulations in the institution, occasionally giving rise to eating disorders so that a victim of such a circumstance devoured incredible quantities of carbohydrates then disappeared into the toilet. Weight loss and bloodshot eyes of a boy coming out of the toilet were suitable clues that he was a victim. Prevention did not seem easy in St. Mary's Mosocho in those days when students were stacked to hate obesity—which was viewed as a personal failing rather than a genetic consequence.

This particular game which was officially meant for and left to town boys, as no bushboy could ever attempt to bounce a basketball whatsoever, was a clear testimony that town boys had a better understanding of the game since they watched Americans play it on television when they went home for holidays. The only time bushboys witnessed the idea behind the game and what a basketball looked like was when they were in school and, sometimes, learned some new terms and rules applicable to the game. Town boys therefore had something to defend, making the bushboy community accustom itself into the sordid, sobriety situation that they would always be savage.

It was a distant relationship between the two groups of boys, and each of them was clearly irrelevant to the other since body lotion or Vaseline was not even familiar to bushboys—only soap to maintain a healthy skin. Town boys used deodorants, perfumes, and various body lotions so that they could smell good and appear exotic and distinct from the indigent community. They had mostly brown, smooth, and attractive skins that had been treated with soothing ingredients to help prevent and temporarily protect dry, red, and sore skin. The unique, fast absorbing, non-greasy lotions they used provided quick relief to skin dried out by weather and harsh detergents. As a result, most bushboys admired some of those town boys so that new, distinct, bizarre relations developed, leading to personal, one-to-one agreements which in the end, augmented favorably to evident mutual togetherness and concomitant concupiscence between the two categories of boys. Resultantly, due to such indefatigable tendencies, comely town boys were in the long-term viewed as lasses and, occasionally, benefited from others in numerous ways. They made their friends suffer from excessive regression and fetishism, leading to exhibitionism and sexual deviation at night when they were expected to be asleep.

On the other hand, town boys used all derogatory, disparaging terms that they knew on bushboys and felt like the bushboy community was betraying them simply by not knowing how to bounce a basketball. Our English was also very embarrassing. They had a belief that bushboys lacked the prospect of success by not following Kebwesi's footsteps on their way to a hilarious, boisterous, and exuberant advancement and were, in this sense, delaying their effort to deviate from African savagery. They wondered why bushboys had to stick to the debris of their ancient, outmoded, and unmannerly African ways of life where a basketball was viewed as nothing but a pumpkin. They seemed to believe that this tendency pulled them back from the already partially attained element of Western civilization comprised of trickery, death, and communal misdemeanor.

This was one of the many unanswered questions by then but remained in record to be visually answered today when, time and history has to reveal it all to ascertain if those victims of circumstance can persist that engagement efficaciously—in respect with the various exotic facilities they inherently hounded themselves in, or not. Here is surely where and when larceny takes a back-seat!

Those who were ignorant of barbarism and evil found themselves in a rather resplendently gorgeous situation of innocence unlike the aggressive, contemptuous ones who were blindly befuddled in the mercenaries' foreign, inapplicable culture; ultimately licking the toes of those mercenaries.

That eccentricity did not stop there but remained to conquer us with massive regression as a multifarious psychological defect—which is actually a matter of common experience that, when one reaches that stage of adulthood and old age, they are often reminded of their childhood and adolescent days.

Those were days in which we were left free of care and responsibility to engage in happy play like *putting*. Remembering in this manner today, we, for a short time, forget current difficulties and bitterness that life has filled us. There is no harm whatsoever in such activity, since memories of bygone days give us contentment, and buoy us with hope and courage to face the present and the future.

This routine then saw us through Friday when we assembled in the school hall and awaited to be reanimated by the headmaster. He commented on the ending week, and indignantly punished those who had dejected the school administration in the course of a specific week.

Laundry

Faith is the substance of things hoped for. One definition of hope is confident expectancy. You cannot have faith if you do not have hope.

Our expectations set the limits for our daily routine on Fridays at St. Mary's Mosocho; meaning that, if V-vait never expected anything fruitful we would never receive anything good. If we never expected anything to get better then nothing would get better. V-vait therefore promised to meet us at our level of expectancy.

We expected to overcome every challenge of washing our clothes on Fridays. We lived these difficult times filled with anticipation that V-vait could, by any rare chance, suspend this seemingly unnecessary school law above and beyond our wildest dreams.

The number of clothes to be washed was restricted. So V-vait alternated around the three dormitories announcing the number and type of clothes to be washed. He either started his belligerent announcements in *Stam* or Brandsma dormitories, since *Doyle* was in the middle of the two: "*Eeeh . . . , pullovers, pillowcase, socks, shirts, shorts, and the elephants.*" According to him, an underwear was sometimes known as "elephant."

Friday was also a day known for spinning basins. This was a common habit particularly in the early years of our stay in the institution; times when Owino, Makanyaga, Ogolla, Mosquito, MB, *Chicken Style* and *Kuku*, among others, were more agreeable than ever, especially when they lay face-up on their beds. This they did as soon as the issue of washing clothes was done away with. More of the spinning was carried out on weekends when there was not much to be done.

Spinners had to be watchful of others with agendas or eagerness to lie on top of them in order to satisfy their egoistic desires. Such boys were the then kings of our hearts. And one moment, you may have been leading a normal, seemingly uneventful life; and the next, you may have found yourself exchanging glances with someone who makes you feel bewildered, excited, and charged with nervous energy. Moments such as these never failed to catch us unaware, and their force and suddenness changed the whole course of our lives. To an onlooker, the phenomenon of attraction often resembled nothing so much as madness.

Attraction was often instant, and because of this, it seemed involuntary and was therefore often put down to superhuman agency such as luck or destiny. Mythology would have us believe that attraction was directed by the gods, and that it hit out of the blue in the form of Cupid's fatal dart. The magic potion on the tip of the dart suspended consciousness, will, and judgment and left its victims in a state of hopeless intoxication.

The ardor or warmth or coolness of any St. Marian relationship depended on the individuals within it and not on any of the arbitrary specifications which might have been imposed by society. For this reason, any infinite permutations and the confusion that resulted from them could not be accommodated by society, which needed order to function. Order meant ignoring varying colorless shades and distinguishing only between black and white; it meant putting labels on things. And since society is never stronger than when it is united against a common evil, labeling things also meant defining society's outcasts. Engagement in such habits was part of growing up and learning—the ability to listen and do almost anything without losing emotional conditions or predisposition of any particular kind or our self-confidence.

Bathing

Mystery created wonder, and wonder was definitely the basis that created the desire to understand. Nudity was guaranteed and witnessed. Each class had thirty-five minutes on Wednesdays and Fridays set aside for bathing— and this was a general rule to us all because we were only required to bath twice a week. Not vituperation nor revile could separate us or deter us from staying together even at moments when peers exposed their maturing genitals in the bathrooms.

Many, being adolescents at the time, got aroused and stimulated any moment they took a glance at their nude comrades in bathrooms. Fear also created arousal, but so did many other emotions including joy, curiosity, or anger. But we could also be over-aroused by semiconscious thoughts or low levels of excitement that created no obvious emotion. Often, we were not aware of what was arousing us such as the newness of a situation, physical change, noise, or the many things our eyes were seeing.

Actually, there were several ways to be aroused and still other ways to feel aroused by other boys, and they differed from time to time and from person to person. Arousal may have appeared as blushing, trembling, heart pounding, hands shaking, stomach churning, or other parts of the body perspiring. Often, boys in such situations were never aware of some or all of these reactions as they occurred but recognized them as soon as there was a practical response either on them or by them—in form of *injector*.

We had already focused that destiny presented us with situations which were predetermined and to which we were guided. They were inevitable and belonged to the pole of necessity. But if we inquire today into what caused these life situations, we shall always find the answer in ourselves, in the deeds of our ego in one or more past lives on earth. If it was then objected that this left little room for freedom, it should be remembered that we ourselves created a situation in which we find ourselves today. By the nature of our response, which lay within our freedom, we in turn created future conditions, possibly endowing this personality with quite remarkable capacities to serve mankind out of mature insight. What we decided to undertake in the way of spiritual development or self-education must never be the result of outer compulsion for it was in the intimate resolve that we made to ourselves that true freedom really began.

It also lay within the freedom of an individual to overcome blemishes in one's character such as envy or untruthfulness. If we paid no heed to these blemishes and allowed them to become rampant, the results would undoubtedly show in one's present life on earth. There was nothing better than the encouragement of a true friend. Nowadays, immoral failings have become physical weaknesses or disabilities because we tend to shy off whenever we interact and recollect our past.

These will be the inevitable result of not having striven to transform such failings in our lifetime. These further helped us to comprehend that free initiative would, in time, break the bonds of necessity; and on the way to that ultimate aim, St. Marians must learn to live with necessity and freedom.

The question of the nature and interaction of this polarity between necessity and freedom, to be viewed and examined unclad, stood to remain as one of the most profound questions relating to our existence and continuously occupied the minds of retrospective St. Marians. This then brought about the issue of secret unions and aberrant nuptials, between partners, which culminated into daily enervations as a result of sleepless nights.

Boys who looked sturdy were swept off their foundations and their faith, and their identities ripped to shreds. As monster confusion hit large areas around the institution, the quality and durability of countless unions were put to the ultimate test. A storm of another nature, however, wreaked havoc on the foundation and structure of the age-old institution of marriage. For better or worse, marriage had been displaced from its pivotal position in personal and social life.

While those in attraction were expected to pair up for at least the period they spent in the institution, the majority spent most of their time searching out potential long-term partners in what would then only be described as hunting. Recent observations indicate that this hunting is still in the making even with those who united then.

Most boys, back then, preferred libido-enhancing foods more especially Mixture; which they referred to as "Mixture for Power." Ways in which they engaged themselves in injector related habits, though not as intricate as those of peacocks, started with the provision of many favors, which among others included the sharing of dear foodstuffs such as Jelly, Blue Band, bread, cookies, squash, and sometimes chinkara—on the part of bushboys.

Being bipedal mammals, they would then advance toward other activities like playing together, and later advanced to conspicuous friendships of spending their leisure time inseparably in perfect agreement.

At the very moments when initial friendships were in the making, it also became a clandestine period when those who had extra skill in seduction snatched away friendships from others; which usually culminated into unseen innuendos, which in time developed to subsequent years.

Yet, there were those more skilled, but beneficiaries in this case, for their youthful attractiveness. This was and is not a new phenomenon both in St. Mary's Mosocho of our times or in the modern world. In the modern world, it has become commonplace for youthful faces to directly declare that they want financial favors in return for bodily services. In more hidden and intellectual mannerisms, sign and body languages, and codes of dressing alone are enough to communicate to those in need, of readiness, willingness to perform.

In the modern world, when you see youthful boys and girls shamelessly advertising their most private body parts in the open, it is sanely not a manner of taking pride in fashion and modernity, but a call to others to worship their looks of attractiveness—as was anciently prophesied that in the end times, "men will worship boys, and boys will worship medals." They are therefore, simply boys and girls of bargain-able affection.

As a confirmation that men are worshiping boys and girls, they are constantly in pursuit of those that are calling them, by the ways in which they are dressed, while the rate and age at which younger boys and girls are falling in love with medals is an indication that it is a prophesy in fulfillment.

It is supposed to be the oldest trade in the world but has proven to be the most modern. It is surely the only business one can engage in without a capital formation.

Nowadays, it is never difficult to find the kind of friendships or partner of your choice. Back in the days, it was all about trial and error; which would, sometimes, land you in embarrassment if not physical confrontations. It is easier today to distinguish between a happy and sad teenager by merely checking the point at which they have fastened their over-sized pants; by monitoring their contemptuous posterior movements, some which appear like they have accidentally soiled themselves.

Such dress-codes often correspond with an individual's age, style and language of communication. Those in anticipation of ever staying younger tend to maintain the latest terms of slang, however offensive or disrespecting as we always witness young-stars popping sinister words out of their mouths in the presence of people who among them include the age mates of their mothers, fathers and at times grand-parents.

But the blame is not theirs but rather the very parents whom they are disrespecting since they learn the same from their seniors, and mostly, some of them cannot even write or spell the sorts of profanities they use to describe themselves.

In an attempt to depict sophistication, the modern youth do not realize how much of hoodlums they prove to be, to the public, more especially to foreigners—depending on the country in question. This happens when they try to show their level of imbecility and ignorance by engaging themselves in pronouncements, which may otherwise fit the definition of childishness or derangement in a manner suggesting ignorance and resultant effects of illiteracy.

In societies where parental responsibility and cultural practices have taken root in nurturing children into socially acceptable conducts, it is rare to find children who engage in, for instance, exhibitionism, in the name of fashioning; but with hidden reasons only known to them and their cliques. To the "old school" gang, it appears just like the newest rhythm or dance move, which is uniquely difficult to understand why young people dress or dance like they do today. One wonders where they get the time to invent such styles, which may as well be interpreted as old wonders like explaining the origin of a butterfly.

Then, mysteriously, such styles give birth to dress and dance clubs or associations which portray maturity, focus, determination and seriousness. However when critically analyzed, it is found that these associations are nothing short of a continuation and advancement of the same conduct, which society views as the root of the training of future deviants and criminals.

On today's streets and schools, the sight of the so-called modern teenagers is enraging.

In St. Mary's of medieval times, for example, exhibitionism and the accidental opportunity to view the private organs of your nude comrade only took place at

273

the hour of bathing, in bathrooms, and not intentionally or publicly advertised in a manner suggesting defeat!

Those who were blessed to be born, at least, in the early eighties and before, are longing for the good old days when children were to be seen and not heard in a voiceless way of speaking—such as the kind of war they have now waged against their elders in order to make them look prehistoric.

To find the best of those old boys of St. Mary's Mosocho, in today's world, is as good as somnambulism. If you walk on today's streets, and watch school boys and girls, instead of seeing boys and girls who are destined for a particular destination in order to build a prosperous world, all you perceive is teenagers, who should be at home either doing their home work or helping in family affairs, wondering the same about you!

Recreation

On Saturdays, each of us got up at our own discretion but before seven o'clock although the majority found it favorable to get up earlier in order to arrange for the "Weekly Tests" which commenced at nine o'clock. These tests were introduced by the school administration as one way of improving the students' academic performance as well as to enhance their proficiency. Supervision during these tests was carried out by one of the scheduled teachers or V-vait.

Once the issue of Weekly Tests was resolved, V-vait rushed to his office to display a list of that particular week's culprits and also indicated on paper was how each of them was to be pummeled. While some got punished, others gathered outside his office for games equipment; younger ones being plodded by the older boys and, thus, subjected to injector, enabling Muigai and Machuka to enjoy themselves with stretches of giggles.

A school regulation stated that students were free to take an afternoon walk outside the compound immediately after their lunch. This, once again, became a joyous moment for the bushboy community since they would abscond to their respective homes. They gathered certain food types such as boiled corn and potatoes, sour domestic cow milk, and chinkara, so that they became kings of the institution upon their return late in the evenings. But this, surprisingly, became the only moment for the rise of the bushboy existence; if only Zida did not catch them with such edibles—which portrayed nothing short of incisive sorcery.

Those who remained in the school compound on Saturday afternoons sometimes played with marbles. They gathered under the huge tree between Stam and Doyle dormitories and made up teams to compete against each other. In this game of marbles, you forcefully indemnified your opponent if you accidentally or intentionally broke his marble in order to avoid unnecessary physical confrontations. But if you warned that you were not liable for any damages before releasing your marble, then you were expected to say *crackies-no-payees* before you played. *Double-doubles* gained you more points if you accidentally struck other opponents' marbles concurrently but there had to be concordance and consensus between all players in the on-going game. If you unintentionally slipped off a marble through your fingers in the course of your turn to play, you were required to say *ponyoks* which was a symbol of remorse. That was one activity engaged in on Saturday afternoons.

Others read about the *Hardy Boys* or *The Last of the Mohicans*—by James Fenimore Cooper. But before they got books, they had to pensively listen to Kebwesi's song-like warnings: *"Don't take them out eee . . . Don't take them out eee . . ."* meaning that the boys were only required to view the books as they stood in their respective shelves and not pull them out.

Once he gave out the books, those who read them gathered under mosocho trees as he lit his pipe and marched off toward the *Brother House*—coughing like a long roll of thunder.

The Last of the Mohicans still lingers in my mind as it was set during the French and Indian War. It is an unforgettable portrait of fierce individualism, deep moral courage, and profound friendship. It is the classic story of a man who, after severing all connection with a society he could no longer accept, found himself irresistibly drawn back into that world. Despite his chosen exile, *Hawkeye*, a frontier scout, risked his life to guide two sisters through Indian country. For this dangerous journey, he enlisted the aid of the *Mohican Chingachgook.*

Their story was fast paced, tragic, and filled with all the elements of great frontier adventure—renegade Indians, innocent settlers, hardened soldiers, and a doomed love affair. The Last of the Mohicans is a deeply American book with insight into their national character and consciousness.

James Fenimore Cooper was born in Burlington, New Jersey, in 1789 and grew up on his father's estate near Lake Otsego in upstate New York. After an unsuccessful stay at Yale, he spent five years at sea as a naval midshipman. He began writing at the age of thirty when his wife challenged him to make good on his claim that he could write a better novel than the one he was reading.

> The chief extended his arm, and taking the other by the wrist, they once more exchanged friendly salutations. Then the Delaware invited his guest to enter his own lodge, and share his morning meal. The invitation was accepted, and the two warriors, attended by three or four of the old men, walked calmly away, leaving the rest of the tribe devoured by a desire to understand the reasons of so unusual a visit, and yet not betraying the least impatience, by sign or word.

This is a summary of the facts from The Last of the Mohicans.

Toward the end of each Saturday, everyone appeared overjoyed since history made St. Mary's Mosocho what it was, and due to the fact that the time for watching a movie was near at this point—moments when boys *sounded* others ceased at least for the next one or two days.

The Elder, who was also our class monitor and whose duties included elimination of disorderly conducts in the course of serious studies, was one boy who deserved his respect and honor because he had seen many years come and go, and had knowledge of ancient catastrophic eras and times; and his experiences therefore made him well-informed. In rare cases, he outlined accounts of many years before when a historical harbinger of locusts invaded the local people's crops, and was one of the bushboys who looked more serious when in the refectory and never revealed their age. Not only had Kebwesi sworn before him that he would imminently suffer from enlarged legs, but also cast a spell on him against prosperity. Whenever he made a slight movement, old age and wisdom were automatically expressed in his face with a broadly wrinkled forehead allergic to public awareness such that he was more frequently forced to gaze steadily onto the ground as he walked. Being keenly aware of most of his betraying physical features, not to mention the slight stoop and his heavy legs, he habitually walked while placing his left hand palm on the forehead— as if protecting his eyes from bright lights, even when in darkness. And whenever this fellow walked in a hurry, his right hand was always stretched straight down to ensure that he scratched his knee.

A boy, nicknamed *Lizard*, once made fun of him by stating that a loaf of bread could easily balance on his shoulders, whenever he walked in rain, without an umbrella, due to ordinary, simple reasons.

His freedom was not indivisible. Any St. Marian of his time can freely testify that the boy was an oppressor beyond any reasonable doubt and required to be liberated just as

279

much as those that he oppressed. He had failed to know that a man who deprives another of his freedom is a slave of hatred locked behind the bars of prejudice and narrow-mindedness. How free was he if he took away other students' freedoms just as surely as he would not be at liberty when his freedom was taken from him? Were the elderly powers imposed on him by the school administration, because of his simple maturity, an appropriate cover to beat others up? He, forever, robbed himself of his humanity.

He also knew the true history of coffee in Kisii District and could substantiate K-47 and *Ruiru* II, citing how well the two varieties featured under tepid and wet conditions. No one, however, was supposed to question him how he arrived at such legendary realities as that could easily lead to physical battles. However, he voluntarily revealed such when in his own unverified moods and apt appeared totally deprived of ordinary knowledge about life.

We are perhaps not predestined victims although some people appear to have more than their share of good or bad luck. There are those who, often, seem to be attracted to the wrong jobs or wrong partners although such people are not naturally oriented to the spiritual world. If one's life is a piece of muddle or one is not getting, complacently, enough from it, then it might help to study one's character —with the Elder's being one good sample as revealed by some symbols. One will then recognize some extremely helpful hints about the sort of person one is and one's basic psychological model.

Having a clean and tidy mind about your own nature is invaluable when it comes to making the correct moves. If one is gentle and pliant in nature, then they are not likely to make a good leader. One may also be good at making decisions but not good at implementing them. It might also help to know this if one is trying to quit smoking or drinking. Here, one is made aware of certain challenges to face, and this must be thoroughly arranged for.

Background, parental influence, education, and the general environment—all play their positions. One's own personality and conduct dictate an essential deal; that is why some people achieve great things while others constantly mourn and never get beyond the starting point. Fortunately or unfortunately, many of us do not like this to be revealed to us. They would rather leave the making of their lives to earthly forces and blame them when life does not turn out the way they expect it to.

We all have choices, prospects, and wishes; and we commonly advance toward these choices in a silent and subconscious manner because a thing inside our physical flesh is forcing us in a particular direction. Following one's hunches is a spiritual truth. According to me, self-realization is not easy to condone as we have to face every sole part of our being. We can all cheaply admit the lovely elements of our personalities.

Once one is in command of their behavior and personality, they begin to trust themselves, and that is the very point where self-assurance commences. An individual can henceforth build faith in oneself and one's abilities and be confident. Confidence is the ability to do what one has to and trust oneself to do it without backup from others. This is when one begins to know who they really are and what one wants to do and, ultimately, turn fate to one's advantage.

It has also been evident that life constitutes of some incidents that may seem frivolous moment by moment, and it is the moment when one acts that makes the difference between success and failure.

The Elder was also known to have, toward the end of 1981, on one cherished day in his village, bade farewell to the bachelors' club by doing what other real men of the land had done and were expected to do when they came of age but, subsequently, separated from his dame because he had to resume his studies.

This then became the villagers' time to celebrate the courage of their son and daughter-in-law in carrying the clan's mantle proudly across *Nyabondo*—his homeland.

Once the long-due news spread that the village boy had tied the knot and brought home a damsel, the home became a

282

hive of activities as young and old sent their congratulations and wished the couple a promising marriage.

The day the bride arrived home, she was welcomed in the most ceremonious way the Nyabondo villagers could afford as they attempted to show her that she had chosen wisely. Local meals, meant for beating poverty, took a backseat as the bride was treated to sumptuous delicacies. A modern music system and a fully recharged car battery were as well borrowed from the nearby radio mechanic for the occasion.

As the story was keenly narrated to us, a time came, in the course of that day's late hours, when the newly married villager had to plead with his kinsmen to leave so the couple could have a time together as it was late in the night and the girl seemed tired. Then that was the moment the married villager discovered that the notion of privacy was still foreign to some of his kinsmen. As early as six in the morning, when the couple was still feeling the warmth of the blankets and in rhythm with their honeymoon, a villager knocked on their half-complete door and, before it was opened, pushed his way in like a commuter taxi tout, seeking fare from passengers.

"Son of my uncle, I saw it fit to come and greet my sister-in-law as early as this before going to the farm because I have not been able to see you since you brought the visitor home," he announced, shoving aside the curtain that divided his cousin's living room from his bedroom.

First, the couple was embarrassed to utter the least and, nevertheless, could not say a single word because they did not want to appear to insist on the total privacy of their shelter. The only way out for the newly married villager was to play it down by yawning, stretching, and saying politely: "Sure, today I'm really late in getting up."

All this time, while he was placed in a tight position of keen scrutiny, the bride too was in the spotlight. As it was customary—for most, if not all communities, the bride was regarded as the brittle, brand-new member of the village who had to be carefully handled.

During their few days' honeymoon, clansmen and villagers of goodwill ensured that, each morning, the newly weds received porridge or related food. The bride's meals automatically excluded fibers and junk food that would stir or disturb her abdomen, causing her loud, nonstop, prolonged flow of diarrhea and weakness. The older men and women of the village knew this and would supervise matters of the young couple's diet with stern and rare keenness.

In most cases, fowl eggs, meat, fish, and chicken were preferred; but the proud, aggressive bride knew it was time to pretend that some of these foods were too filling or that she was simply allergic to them. The villagers had no choice but to prepare things to her taste and complacence to avoid admitting inadequate hospitality.

Work and walking distances had also to be minimized for the Elder's sweetheart because it was not easy for villagers to know of some hidden medical difficulties that could floor her down when she was still brand-new in the area. She was, therefore, treated as carefully as an egg. However, we were never vividly told of the further aftermath following that auspicious matrimony but people gossiped that she, in the eventuality, escaped to her origin—a place called *Bonyama*, and named after meat, upon discovering her man's actual age as well as his unmannerly, impossible, and savage tendencies.

The Elder's father crowning the bride in Nyabondo.

Film time, the only moment for late-night succor, then came about with Kebwesi's assurance to bushboys that movies were foreign and could, at times, turn scary. So he, in this regard, commanded those of us who wet our beds at night as well as the few who encountered nightmares and hallucinated in their sleep to voluntarily go to bed. V-vait too, at this moment, searched out his "friends" who had made his day a thing not to contemplate and ensured that they accompanied the *urinators* and locked them up in the dormitories so they would get some advance sleep.

After Kebwesi unleashed some little belittlement and insults, aimed at bushboys, he then started the projector; and all eyes turned onto the white surface on the wall in open-mouthed bewilderment. The school watchman, as well, appeared from unfounded corners of the school compound and gazed steadily onto the movie actions, through the window, laughing at very serious matters of derangement. Film time was also a time of profound gatherings—moments when cooks like Matumbo and Doyle assembled in the refectory, augmenting the number of intruders from the bushy neighborhood.

Between the long remarkable years (1984 and 1987) our scheme for the reparation of the genuine classification of St. Marians and the submission of bushboys' civilization with history was interpreted. The ravaged view, brought into being by the blinders of neocolonialism, had pretty much intensely falsified the ingenuity of the bushboys' past. We had the most conspicuous hindrance, even among general St. Marians, in attaining acknowledgment for concepts that are today becoming ordinary. No one can rationally fantasize the extent of estrangement of the contemporaneous bushboys. Therefore for us, it seems and irrelevantly, without thinking that even a 1920 man was modern to himself and claim to be modern in this earthly existence; the essential truth is less to have revealed that the entire St. Mary's community was a bushboy gathering; as one of my material, as opposed to mental or spiritual, sources, the old observers, like me, already did, than to have added to designing this concept into a live historical disclosure for bushboys. And more so to making it a concept of psychological slaughter, which it factually is. This is the very point where the predecessors or mercenaries did not come out triumphant.

There will often be some form of upbringing performance, and it is evident now that the unprincipled battle is practically won, that even some town boys are strutting and swaggering around on this achieved ground while passing over to us some confined irritations and never-ascertained hypothesis in an imaginary objectivity. Town boy analysis and image does not exist! Nevertheless, we are aware that Nairobi is at the uppermost populated by Kenyans, Kisii by the *Abagusii* and other Kenyan-naturalized aliens who are all answerable for the advancements and failures of their respective homelands and must not fool around that they originated from Nairobi. The student condition of the ancient St. Mary's, in the eyes of the law or of others, alone must remarkably remain a mystery that is repugnant to justice and morality.

Some also claimed that they had never perceived a cow with their own two eyes before coming to Mosocho, sickening us further by saying that fowl eggs were locally manufactured in Nairobi by the East Africa Industries.

The Saturday movies, for instance, can only be defined as foreign cultures forcefully and painfully imposed on us. By having Kebwesi partially give first priority of such to town boys, it was only a plain fact that he was denying them access to their own ancestral values and heritage and, conversely, strengthening the bushboys' awareness of their own traditions where guns and grenades still remained a panoramic illusion. He was, in other terms, introducing them to a Western lifestyle which was nonexistent and inapplicable in Kenya—hence current fantasy and larceny. This was another ill-treatment in the school marked by arbitrary, often ruthless, disregard of individual differences or special circumstances.

Sunday Mass and Dance

On Sundays, V-vait liberally dissipated sweet bananas for breakfast—moments which resulted to mealtime laudations and nicknames such as *Abbas*.

Those with high fidelity later hurried to church in preparation for the Sunday Mass at the nearby Cardinal Otunga High School chapel.

V-vait, on this day, appeared extremely clean in neatly ironed clothes, and his pants elevated and fastened up below his chest.

Back then, in 1984, outgoing Father Simba Kipara, an American citizen, led the Sunday services. Father Chris, a Scottish priest, succeeded him, and then he was succeeded by Father Julian Wild from England.

> The Holy Mass, which was left to us by our Lord at the
> last supper as the special pledge of his love, should have
> a very special, mostly essential place in our lives, and we
> should not be content with a mere superficial knowledge
> of what Mass is. Mass is the action of Jesus Christ. The
> grace of our Lord, Jesus Christ and the love of God and
> the fellowship of the Holy Spirit be with you all.

These were the priest's usual words as he began the service at exactly nine o'clock.

289

In St. Mary's Mosocho of medieval times, things of serious concern and Christianity were subjects that were dignified and consequential not trivial or petty. They included concerns about our Christian ministry, the critical times in which we lived, and the need for us to maintain fine conduct.

When we discussed such serious matters, we reinforced our determination to keep awake spiritually, maintain our integrity, and never forget to preach the good news of love and hope. Indeed, interesting experiences in our mission, institution, and the then-current events, which reminded us that we were living in the last days, provided a variety of material for stimulating conversations.

The word *righteous* meant being right in God's eyes— meeting his standards. *Chaste* conveyed the idea of purity in thought and conduct. Slander, obscene jokes, or sexual innuendoes had no place in our conversations.

Back in the days, at school or home, bushboys and town boys wisely withdrew when issues took on this tone.

Father Wild repeatedly asked us to pay attention to the heart because, in cultivating the habit of engaging in uplifting conversations, we first had to recognize that our speech reflected what was in our hearts. Jesus said, "Out of the abundance of the heart the mouth speaks." Simply put, we like to talk about the things that matter to us. We need, then, to ask ourselves. What do my conversations reveal

290

about my heart condition? When I'm with my family or fellow believers, does my conversation center on spiritual matters or does it invariably gravitate to sports, clothes, movies, food, sex, or some trivialities? Perhaps unwittingly, our lives and our thoughts have come to revolve around secondary issues. Adjusting our priorities will improve our conversations as well as our lives.

Purposeful meditation is another way to improve the quality of what we say. If we consciously make an effort to think about spiritual issues, we will find that spiritual conversation comes naturally. A heart and mind deeply concerned about the realities of God's Word will naturally overflow with praiseworthy speech. Jeremiah could not hold back from speaking about the things that God had taught him. So it can be with us if we regularly ponder on spiritual issues.

Having a good spiritual routine provides us with plenty of topics for uplifting conversations. Assemblies, conventions, congregation meetings, publications, and the daily scripture text and printed comments—all furnish us with spiritual gems we can share.

That which is true involves more than information which is correct and not false. It refers to something that is upright and trustworthy such as the truth of God's word. Hence, when we talk to others about the truths of the Bible that impressed us, discourses or talks that uplifted us, or

291

scriptural counsel that aided us, we are considering things that are true.

On the other hand, we reject "the falsely called 'knowledge," which gives only an appearance of truthfulness. And we avoid passing on gossip or relating dubious experiences that cannot be verified.

"Let a decomposed saying not proceed out of your mouth," counseled Paul, "but whatever saying is good for building up as the need may be, that it may impart what is favorable to the hearers." It may take effort to steer conversations in the right direction, but the harvests are numerous. Spiritual conversations enable us to share our faith with others and to build up our brotherhood.

Let us, then, use the gift of speech to uplift others and praise God. Such conversations will be a source of complacence to us and of encouragement to others. Above all, they will make God's heart glad because He pays attention to our conversations, and He rejoices when we use our tongue in the right way. When our conversations are spiritual, we can be sure that God will not forget us. Referring to those serving God in our day, the Holy Bible states: "At that time those in fear of God spoke with one another, each one with his companion, and God kept paying attention and listening. And a book of remembrance began to be written up before Him for those in fear of God and for those thinking upon His name." How vital is it that our conversations be spiritually uplifting?

"Through Him, with Him, in Him, in the unity of the Holy Spirit, all glory and honor is yours, almighty Father, forever and ever, let it be!" Father Wild continued, "Peace be with you."

"And also with you," was then a response from the congregation..

"Let us offer one another a sign of peace," continued Father Wild.

After this doxology and upon asking God to have mercy on us—recalling that happy are those who are called to His supper and that we were not worthy to receive Him but only asked Him to say one healing word, in haste, V-vait, with the help of his counterparts (Brother Sixtus and Macarius) climbed up the altar with an expectation of distributing the "body of Jesus Christ."

Brother Sixtus was one of the earliest missionaries who settled in the Diocese of Kisii in the mid-1950s, together with Father Widen and Brother Innocent DeKok. He moved at a very slow pace, possibly due to age, and was solely responsible for the operation of chapel windows.

As they stood along the first step leading up to the altar, Brother Joseph routinely led their way forward, closely followed by Kebwesi, Patrick, Joss, Louis, Julius,

Linus, Anthony, Sato, and finally Morimbocho, and only to be followed by students from both St. Mary's Mosocho and Cardinal Otunga High School—and, lastly, the local community.

Brother Linus

Appropriate moments for private prayer present themselves many times each day as we face difficulties, encounter temptations, and make decisions. When we seek God's guidance in all aspects of life, our friendship with Him is certain to grow. If two friends face problems together, does not the bond of friendship between them

294

become stronger? The same is true with God when we lean on Him and experience His help.

Jesus made a brief prayer to the almighty God when He requested that God give Him the power to resurrect Lazarus.

For our prayers to be favorably heard, we must not reject the counsel of God's Word. "Whatever we ask we receive from Him," wrote apostle John, "because we are observing His commandments and are doing the things that are pleasing in His eyes."

Some of us might feel unworthy to pray because of spiritual weakness or because we have lapsed into wrongdoing. But this is precisely when we need to take full advantage of the provision of prayer.

Pressures and problems are multiplying in these last days marked by critical times that are hard to deal with. And trials can easily occupy our minds. Our incessant prayers, however, will help keep our lives on a spiritual course despite persistent problems, temptations, and discouragement.

"A son is wise where there is a father's discipline, but the ridiculer is one that has not heard rebuke," declares the holy book. Discipline from a father can be mild or severe. It can come in the form of training first, and if that turns inapplicable, then eventually as chastise. A son is wise when he accepts his father's castigation.

295

"Whom God loves He disciplines," states the holy book, "and he scourges everyone whom he receives as a son."

Discipline can also come to us as a correction from a fellow believer who is interested in our spiritual welfare. Any helpful advice that is in harmony with God's word can be viewed, not as originating with that person, but as coming from the great source of truth.

Our utterances as well count a great deal in our day-to-day Christian living. A ruined reputation, hurt feelings, strained relations, and even physical harm are all possible results of thoughtless, foolish speech. Lips wide open can also bring divine disapproval for God holds everyone accountable for his words. Indeed, keeping tight control over our mouth will save us from ruin. How, though, can we learn to guard our mouth?

One simple way to do this is to avoid excessive talk. "In the abundance of words there does not fail to be transgression," says the holy book. Another way is to think before speaking.

When no forethought is given to what is being said, both the speaker and his audience can be hurt.

Neither a false display on one hand nor a concealment on the other is appropriate. If our material resources are low, spending money on luxuries just to appear well-off can rob us and our families of the necessities of life. And pretending to be poor, though he has riches, may make a person a miser, depriving him of due dignity and the happiness that comes from being generous. To live honestly is to lead a better life.

There are pros of being opulent, but having riches is not an unqualified blessing. In the troublesome times that we live in, the rich often find themselves and their families in danger of being kidnapped and held for ransom. At times, a rich man can pay a ransom to buy back his life or that of a family member. But often, the kidnapped one is murdered. Such a threat is always hanging over the head of the rich.

The man of little means has no such worry. While he may not have the many conveniences and material things that the rich enjoy, he is less likely to become the target of kidnappers. This is one benefit of keeping our wants simple and not expending our time and energy in the pursuit of wealth.

Money can serve a useful purpose. Having adequate finances is better than having to live in an austere way or in indigence. To live without the law of the all-wise God is to be deprived of the guidance that can help us lead a better and longer life.

We are all God's special handiwork—equipped and anointed to be the persons He has called us to be! God knew who we were before we were formed in our mothers' wombs. Then and now, we had and have unique gifts, abilities, and talents; and God had and still has special plans for our lives.

297

The enemy may have tried to make us think we had to conform to the opinions of others, but we were secure in who God made us and resisted those outside demands and pressures that tried to mold us into something we were not.

In the Sunday afternoon hours also, bushboys furtively absconded to their respective homes and ensured the availability of bananas, boiled maize and potatoes, chinkara, and curdled cow milk, upon their return.

Each Sunday was popularly known to be a day for illustrious solace. There was a dance late in the evening hosted by Mugambe—who contemporarily featured fashionable *Azaro* shirts and stonewashed jeans.

Town boys, at this time, impended around the school compound either borrowing attires for the occasion, such as moccasins, or practiced newly introduced movements which they may have seen on television. Kidesi, Sir. Henry Otiende, Paw-Paw, George Mageria, David Swao, Steve Olang and Mark Onyach appeared at the evening show in platform-soled shoes and moccasins.

Sir Henry, to this day, has all along maintained his position—which many considered to be some form of exotically acquired pride. He has proven to be on the correct path toward his ambitions in fulfillment of his desired destiny.

298

His high, self-ranking stature, since his childhood days at St. Mary's Mosocho, raised him from desperation to attainment of some of his goals. He climbed up the ladder, within a short span, solely by hard work, focus and self-drive.

Convinced that it does not take one to be successful before venturing into the sorts of businesses that financially successful people such as Donald Trump and or Bill Gates invested in, he discovered an opportunity—cashing in on renovating and then renting or selling run-down houses.

Today, Sir Henry is the proud partner of a shopping center building in Wembley, London, has several houses in Nairobi, and also a co-owner of *Homeboyz* Radio Broadcasting Station, in Kenya.

Sir. Henry Otiende

299

When the very hour came about, *break-dancers* separated themselves from those who danced as *robots*. On the other hand, malignant cultural dancers made no obvious preparations but only uncovered their bellies by stripping off their shirts, and reacted accordingly.

When the show commenced, music was played in turns including legends such as: "Eye of the Tiger," "Party Animal," "Red-Red-Wine," "Gloria," "Ain't Nobody," "Holiday," "Upside Down," "Off the Wall," "Thriller," "Ghost busters," "Ring My Bell," "Disco-*Chaka-cha*," "Buffalo Soldier," and *Sokoro*.

Marley's "Buffalo Soldier" mostly dominated the show since both bushboys and town boys shared the dance floor whenever it was played.

Marley was the man rumored, in ancient St. Mary's Mosocho, to have seen sound and heard colors and whose reggae songs captured the souls of many boys in the institution. Throughout St. Mary's, Bob Marley was viewed as a modern redeemer who had literal and figurative options to emancipate from the bondage of sin. As an injection into the chronological sequence of events in a literary or theatrical work of an event of earlier occurrence, he had claimed to be a *duppy conqueror*. This incidentally transformed some of his enthusiastic followers in the school such as Morangi, Oburu, Peke-Yake, Ekisa, Sakwa Nyaata, Mwangi, Richard Orora and Syayi, into duppy conquerors.

300

These boys, at such moments, shocked the entire school population by stridently hissing the same statements that Bob Marley had boomed in Zimbabwe shortly before he made his freedom from disturbing thoughts and emotions with life, and flew away home to his heavenly recompense in Zion.

Rasta no abide amputation. I and I, me and my brethren don't allow a mon ta be dismantled. Jah, de living God, His Imperial Majesty Haile Selassie I, Ras Tafari, conquering Lion of the tribe of Judah, two hundred twenty-fifth ruler of the t'ree-t'ousand year-old Ethiopian Empire, Lord of Lords, King of Kings, Heir to the throne of Solomon, He will heal me wit de' meditations of me ganja chalice, me catchie—clay hookah pipe—or he will tek me as a son inta His Kingdom. No scalpel shall crease me flesh! Dem cyan't kill Jah, cyan't kill Rasta. Rastamon live out.

Peke-Yake, Makori, Sakwa Nyaata, *Cockroach*, Jigger, and their associates, danced to Sokoro in tune, rhythm, and style. They would enter the dance floor shifting their shoulders in harmony as their hips twisted and raised up and down so that they could majestically swing onto the dance floor in pattern. Because Peke-Yake acted with supremacy as their team leader, he would then whirl several times—making a complete three-hundred-and-sixty-degree

301

turn. They lifted their arms high up in the air in ululation, whined, and whistled, so that they made the situation look more cultural than ever. At the climax, they bent backward, face up, and meandered sideways to ensure that they licked a little dust on the dance floor—signaling reality, devotion, and entirety to their tribal values and cultural affiliations. At times they hopped forward, in unison, into the center, uttered the musician's words concordantly, and when they tired, hopped backwards so that another bunch of traditional dancers took their place.

Interhouse

In life, it is the trivial things that make us miserable. Elephants do not bite people but mosquitoes do, and we should therefore be realistic in our expectations. It is awkward to have sight but lack vision.

Because of the pressures of life, we all grow weary at times. But we must bear in mind that God never promised that we would have a problem-free life in this old regime. People have, since time in living memory, faced adversities including persecution, indigence, depression, and sickness. Today we too have our share of problems and challenges. If, at times, our own problems seem overwhelming and we are tempted to quit, we do well to remind ourselves that the devil has challenged the rightfulness of the Almighty's sovereignty. The deceiver has as well questioned the devotion and integrity of God's worshipers.

Because we were all the time achievers, we did not let anyone or anything make us feel bad about ourselves during interhouse competitions. The early-morning Lionel Richie's "Louder Than Words" and "Truly" love songs— including "Hello," "Say You Say Me," and "Penny Lover," which still hallucinate in my mind, reminded us that it was dawn once again for epic occurrences and we did nothing to sabotage or destruct our success. Attitude as well—being a combination of our thinking, emotions, perspective, our

303

way of viewing events and circumstances around us—was a determining factor in our success or failure. It was a critical ingredient in the results that we produced at interhouse competitions. It was the key that started our magnificent machinery and put it into action in the fields.

To be great, therefore, it is necessary to think the extraordinary thoughts, to do the uncommon things, and to go after extraordinary dreams and goals.

Because a goal is a dream with a deadline, even the most impecunious competitors became eager to be the best on this annual occasion. The most thrilling events were the *funny games*; which traditionally crowned interhouse days. Competitors started with the sack race, followed by the tying of two fellows' opposite legs and have them run to a specified point, and ultimately finished with the *sweet searching event*. This was done by a splash of water on the participants' faces and then had them search a candy from a container filled with white flour without the use of their hands.

Conformity is people acting like everyone else without knowing where they are going and why, and that is exactly what interhouse competitions at St. Mary's during our times was. We dissolved into the mainstream rather than choosing to be distinct. The opposite of courage was not cowardice but, rather, conformity. We tended to go with the flow rather

304

than direct the flow. We chose not to be common boys, but it was our right anyway to be uncommon if we could. We looked for opportunity not security. We did not wish to be kept as students humbled and dulled by having the institution look after us. We wanted to take the calculated risk, to dream and to build, to fail and to succeed. We refused to live from hand to mouth. We preferred the challenges of life to the guaranteed existence—the thrill of fulfillment to the stale calm of utopia. We were never to cower before any master nor blend to any friend. It was our heritage to stand erect, proud, and unafraid, to think and act for ourselves, and to face the world audaciously and acknowledge what we had done and undone. We forgave past hurts, bitterness, indignation, wrath, resentment, quarrels, and slander. We knew that provision with no margin for mistakes, bitterness, and resentment block the flow of blessings in life.

Holding on to the hurts of our past can poison our present and limit our future. But as we let go of these emotional wounds during the interhouse events, we opened the doors to the life of victory that God had planned for us.

The enemy tried to use our past to influence our actions and responses. He would try to paralyze us with fear and shame. But we chose to forgive those who had wronged us and released our past to our heavenly Father's loving care and walked in freedom. We traded our sorrow for God's joy and peace and switched our insecurities for His love and triumph.

We were never defined by our past. We were defined by God's plans for our lives, and He saw us as conquerors and winners in life.

We were made aware that we would never rise above the image we had for ourselves. If we saw ourselves as indigent and defeated, then we were going to live poor and defeated lives.

In order to alter our lives, we had to change our focus. We had to change what we were looking at and believing for. We believed that God was for us and desired good things for our lives. If we chose to stay focused on the things that were negative in our lives, then, by our own choices, we were agreeing with the enemy. We cast the deciding vote. If we believed his lies, it opened a door to destruction in our lives.

During interhouse competitions, we had dreams and desires in our hearts—things we hoped for, prayed about, and believed in. The dreams we had in our hearts were never struggles that we forced to happen. We did not worry ourselves or get frustrated, wondering if it was ever going to pass. Because we lived within the promises of God deep in our hearts, we recurrently had a place of total trust; a place where we knew, beyond a shadow of a doubt, that we would sail through both in extracurricular activities at our rendezvous, retrospectively and academically. It was a place and moment of faith, where God was in complete control, and at the exact, right time. He would bring our dreams to reality and make us proud of what we became once we achieved our goals as opposed to achieving the goals.

At the end of the occasion, the best competitors received gifts from the school administration including soccer boots, track-suits, various sorts of exotic caricatures and toys, and indoor games.

Closing Day

The biggest problem that kept us away from failure was persistence. Even those who took the last position on their quarterly report cards did not falter from their dreams. We all recognized the fact that we were among the best and competed with the best. If fifty geniuses compete amongst themselves, there will always be the first and the fiftieth but that does not necessarily imply that the last of them is not classified as self-regulating. Taking the first position was not everything that crowned one's success but the effort made to determine our destiny was victory unseen by many within the institution. Ultimate failures proved to be by those who did not realize their closeness to success when they despaired.

For every disciplined effort, there is a multiple reward. This is all we knew, and the boys who attained excellence followed a consistent path to their success. They first knew their outcome; that is precisely what they yearned for. They then took action, otherwise, their desires would always be dreams. They had to take the type of actions that they believed would create the greatest probability of producing the results they desired. They then developed the sensory acuity that recognized the kinds of responses and results they were getting from their actions and jotted down as fast as they could to see if they were getting closer to their goals or farther away.

In each of our daily living experiences, there came a time of ultimate challenge—a time when every resource we had was tested, a time when life seemed unfair, and a time when our faith, our values, our patience, our compassion, and our ability to persist were all pushed to our ability and beyond.

We lived in the world that we chose to live in both consciously and unconsciously. Whether we chose bliss or misery, that is exactly what we got in return. Belief was our foundation of achievement and excellence. We chose to do what we loved, and we would never have to toil without bitterness and regret in our retrospective lives. Our beliefs were specific, consistent organizational approaches to perception. They were the fundamental choices we made about perceiving our lives and how to live them. So in achieving excellence, we found the beliefs that guided us toward the outcomes that we desired.

Footprints to our success comprised of knowledge of the outcome, followed by action, awareness of the effect of the same, and the ability to have the flexibility to change until we succeeded.

We had elements of three forms—Stam, Doyle, and Brandsma—but most individuals had one system that dominated. When we learned about other people's strategies to comprehend how they made their own decisions, we as well need to know their major representational system so we could represent their message in a way that gets through.

My life experience tells me of the least-effective ways to assist St. Marians with their daily problems. If I ask them, today, to go back and re-experience some trauma, for instance injector or putting, I will be putting them into the most painful, least-resourceful state they can be in. If I put them in a state that is not resourceful, their chances of producing new resourceful tendencies and results will be greatly diminished. Truly, this approach may reinforce the painful or least-resourceful pattern.

By continually accessing neurological states of limitation and pain, it becomes much easier to trigger these states in the future. The more you relive an experience, the more likely you are to use it again.

Town boys and bushboys kowtowed to their respective homes with promising ideas and newly acquired lessons depicted on their report cards. Failure is part of success, and every successful student had some failure. But they used the failure and, thus, exorcised wisdom and understanding from the failure. They made their deficits their teacher not their undertaker. Of all the qualities that made a difference in the quest for success, persistence was definitely the key to achieving our goals. We learned that what we could and could not achieve solely depended on our determination.

Then the question of faith arose, on closing day, more especially to those who, despite what was depicted on their report cards, kept in mind what they had to severely endure on their journeys home. An instance being Peke-Yake!

To us, faith was the substance of things hoped for—the evidence of things not seen. The evidence of things hoped for meant the essence of things we dreamed and desired and the evidence, the assurance, the confidence, and the proof of those things unseen. In other words, faith, to us, was trusting in things we could not see; yet those we could see the positive effect of. Just like electricity which we cannot see coming into our homes; but we can see the results when we turn on the light, radio, and television! Faith, to a St. Marian of our times, was therefore the substance of those things we hoped for and the evidence, the proof, of the unseen.

V-vait too had faith and persistence in himself, and this is what made that son of the Netherlands a success in his daily endeavors. On closing day, he, all the time, knew that all bedbugs had to be killed before any of us made our way home: *"Ve' don't leave the school 'compount' before killing all the 'betbugs.' The situation of the dormitories is 'veeery' terrible, I tell you!"* These announcements he made absentmindedly while he scratched the back of his right hand. He further warned that whoever displayed

311

impertinence to him, because it was closing day, would be his new "friend" as soon as the school reopened.

It was true that we could not determine what happened to us—the problems and circumstances that consistently hounded us. But we could determine how we reacted and responded to those situations. The results we got were a matter of the choices we made. And the choices we made were up to us, and we had to ultimately take responsibility for them. What we were and where we are today is a direct result of our choices. Success is for this reason a choice and not a chance!

Nevertheless, we developed a vision of victory and expectancy for our lives. God's plans for us were all good; despite what had taken place in our past, he turned our setbacks around, took our tragedy, and turned it into triumph! So we let go of the preceding past and searched our Father's plan and developed that vision of victory for our lives.

In order to fulfill our destinies, we had to make a plan according to purpose and stay focused to fulfill that plan. We woke up every day knowing where we were headed, which direction we took, and what we wished to accomplish—and then stuck with it. We never allowed distractions and busyness of life to get us off course because, however hard essentials appeared, we would never let them get diminished by mere words.

Because we lived triumphant lives, we spoke positive words of faith and declared what God said concerning our situation. Each of us was positive when events went well, but the way we responded when adversity came our way made or broke us! What we said in the midst of our difficulties had a direct impact on the outcome.

St. Marians of our times faced educative challenges and difficult times. God did not send these storms, but it was in times of difficulty that we grew and became stronger. It was an opportunity to let others do what they did, for us, and not to us. This meant that if one wronged us they did something to strengthen and improve us rather than harm us, and therefore, obstacles were simply opportunities for advancement. We couldn't run from everything difficult in our lives and expect the Almighty to deliver us instantly. Instead, these challenges stretched us and enlarged our vision. We remained faithful during times of adversity and made up our minds to serve our heavenly Father irrespective of what came against us; and God honored us, then and today—because fools are sometimes right!

Bends and corners to our various homes were many, and still even for those of us who walked to our homes, across the school fence, bends were many.

On closing day Nairobi boys left at cockcrow hours of the day in order to catch buses destined for the city. Common boys caught local commuter buses or vans to various towns

313

within Kenya while bushboys either walked home with luggage balanced on their heads or, if some were lucky, they received help from their relatives or sympathizers. Since bushboys originated from the locality, chances were high that relatives or friends were in the vicinity from local markets or may have just accomplished their early-morning harvests.

V-vait on Closing Day

CHAPTER TEN

HIGH SCHOOL FLASHBACK

Before 1988, it had time and again appeared to me that most, if not all, people in my community seemed to have made their emancipation from disturbing notions, thoughts and emotions with life toward the end of the year. But on my first year of high school the local Member of Parliament's father, Masega "Onego" Oeri, incidentally passed away in the early morning hours of late January 1988.

Evidently, in Kitutu Chache constituency, surrounding communities and many other parts of Kenya, chang'aa, although it in the old days helped many families meet academic expenses for their children through the sale of this illicit brew to raise tuition fee, became a hindrance to the people's awareness of their social challenges, responsibilities, and a barrier to economic growth both then and in the long run.

Despite the fact that such tendencies and alcoholic habits have lessened in recent times, it is clear, in retrospect, to a keen observer's eye that this was one tactic used by Kenyan politicians, who obviously owed responsibility and service to the very people they were in the process of ravaging, to distract attention of more serious concerns so as to greedily and selfishly amass wealth.

Also, due to illiteracy, poverty and certain primitive beliefs, many despaired in life's struggles, as a result, and never either stood up for their political, social ideals and human rights or simply developed ideas that situations and, or conditions in which they found themselves in were destined by supernatural forces. Today, because of histories of those who took advantage of the society's shortcomings, which they were supposed to eradicate, our African communities are still being hounded by the same problems which we should have gotten rid of by this day and era.

I have many a time heard Africans blame the West for their failures or current status but given an epitome setting of onuses and performance, it arises that Africans cannot just manage the least of projects at village-level, or may end up becoming self-manufactured slaves of transparency and accountability and later expect to be bailed out by the White man whom they have all along blamed for their failures. In the end, they have become lazy slaves and beggars who expect and rely on donations by sympathizers and well wishers. This is evident with African governments too, who, despite the world history, expect the IMF, World Bank and struggling tax payers of prosperous nations to sort out their economic and even social difficulties such as alcoholism; which have their solutions right at their doorsteps.

People in developed countries face economic and social difficulties too, and work excessively hard, a fact unknown to most Africans. In fact, challenges arising as a result of civilization and development such as crime, drug-use, alcoholism and domestic violence are higher in the developed world than in the less developed countries, but seem to be better managed in the West than the few prevailing in Africa.

Myself, used as a model, I was born and brought up in the above criticized social settings but I have come to believe and trust that we all serve a purpose for our earthly births. We must accept our social positions, responsibilities and, every day, try to advance in the smallest magnitude possible.

Giving in to little failures and weaknesses such as chang'aa and or drug addictions is the smallest and most unintelligent of despair as witnessed in many parts of the world and among the youth of today.

317

There will always be more and less successful people than each of us in all aspects of life, more so materially, but as long as we do our best, God will always bring the best out of us. Success is not necessarily living in the most comfortable way possible but the attainment of happiness and goals desired, however negligible. We have heard of and witnessed people in our earthly existence who were not blessed with abundant monetary wealth but managed to be successful in achieving their goals and desires and living their destinies to the fullest of their potential. It is surely credible to be a successful and happier maintenance-man, window cleaner or gardener, and still be happier than millionaires—depending on your desires, limitations and level of happiness.

Most great achievers were not wealthy people, in the sense of money or material wealth, but they in the end achieved their goals successfully. Such people are regarded as greater than those with abundant material possessions because they lived their destinies with a goal and purpose. They may be defined as prophets or men of more purpose and remarkable success for they changed the lives of God's people for the greater future and well being on the world histories; to be reminisced more than monetarily famous individuals.

Excessive wealth may not be ideal for us, as well, as it may lead us into discomfort, stressful lives and can

318

also eventually cause us anomie suicide. Just as much as the indigent do not comprehend the discomfort or cons of material possessions or wealth, the rich do not, on their part, know the full pain of poverty as much as those who feel its actual consequence. The most ideal living, then, is the moderate one in which one has access to the basic human needs and a little extra luxuries characterized by occasional deficits. This way, their lives are balanced so that they may at times have a portion of what they don't need and often engage themselves in endless struggles.

Considering my own life, I can testify that I have been to both ends in life because I have been to the least imaginable desperate ends of human-life-experiences, and also witnessed the mountain-top. To the mountain-top, is not an implication that I have been wealthy but lived among the opulent and have tangibly felt from a distance what it means to be in such a position. But the opposite is not imaginable or exaggerated as I have, in most cases, lived very embarrassing life-styles, not because I unintentionally find myself there but, because I want to share the suffering and pain felt by the least fortunate—but often more blessed. Blessed not with poverty but because they are less of slaves of self-imposition and transgression.

The poor may never recognize how wealthy they are until the day they lose their poverty positions, in society, and vice-versa. The rich will simply be intimidated because of lack of experience with poverty while the poor will only enhance their happiness if they are blessed with some riches — above their poverty lines.

Nevertheless, these arguments must never be misconceived by anyone since it is not offensive to acquire rightful wealth. It is wise to be rich if you have been blessed with such earthly blessings but monetary gifts must all the time be carefully handled as this is the only known easier path to evil and mortal sin.

So, that very Tuesday morning my late paternal cousin, William Morere, arrived at my home in one of the Gusii County Council Land-Rovers to deliver me over to a distant high school located in the Gusii settlements. I was surely nervous because, to me, the name of the institution sounded so sinister that I was skeptical of my survival there for at least one full semester. But because I strongly believed that God himself had anointed me to make a prolonged historic visitation in the school, I proceeded there and persevered to endure the kind of hardships which I experienced in the course of my one year stay there.

Despite the many other struggles we went through, such as hunger, I always liked to be the last one of them all to bath because it was sort of awkward to expose my maturing genitals to fellow school-mates—since we, without choice, bathed ourselves in the river.

I cannot, however, complain because this was only the beginning of my numerous episodes which only became unexpectedly evident in that particular year, into subsequent years, as I involuntarily found myself constantly in conflict with virtue, family and society.

As I later learned, realms can be helpful or detrimental more especially during the delicate adolescent, teenage years of an individual—characterized by ignorance and group psychology. And this is when understanding and social studies are crucial since these stages are fundamentally applicable to each one of us, at some point in our lives, rather than unjustifiable blame and judgment!

If children are left free of parental care in the crucial, delicate stages, of adolescence and teenage, they end up taking natural courses in their lives which may chance to be positive or negative in the eyes of society. This is sadly not the stage where the mother's care is essential and mandatory but necessarily the father's involvement. If I developed without an initial fatherly presence in my early childhood care, then chances were higher that I may have, more especially as a son, ended up in a socially unacceptable livelihood, which seemed to be my case, due to differences in our tolerance levels and judgment within my family unit. My personal anger, deficits, comparisons and, or as a means of retribution, may have played a role in my social behaviors, and later decision, to be whom nature had shaped

321

or destined me to be. Still, I do not want or expect anyone to be judgmental as none of us can explain the causes and consequence of our daily lives and concomitant episodes, such as those that conquered my painful reminiscences between 1988 through 1996, and perhaps beyond into this day.

We have all been molded to be ourselves today not by circumstance, but by true justice, injustices, vices, virtues and all actions by others, whether it be strangers and, or family members. Moment by moment, just like water droplets which in the end fill an empty container, or innocent babies who are born into this world without notions of evils like racism, tribalism, hate, prejudice or stereotypes, but end up growing into complete supporters of such cheap human-manufactured evils. Should they then be judged or blamed for the very evils that were created and developed by their predecessors on an earth which its main role seems to be an instigation of fresh, innocent souls into sinister tendencies which are at the same time defined by the exact evil-inventors?

If we deduct our socially acceptable values from humanity itself, the result will be that each of us is right in their own little world. Then who is wrong? Or, if each of us views the other as crazy, if we do not agree or are not alike, then the consequence will be that we are all crazy and only differentiated by the degree and style of craziness.

Therefore, if we critically and frivolously analyze the causes of my past so-called social mistakes, I may be right and society can be held accountable for false accusations!

Then came about 1989, and, Mr. Tom Mokua, nicknamed *Sensible*, the then headmaster of Cardinal Otunga High School, freely accepted to rescue me from the 1988 agony by admitting me into the school, of which he was now in charge, after succeeding Brother Anthony Konning.

Little did I know about the true definition of phi las love until that material day I managed to join my former school-mates from St. Mary's Mosocho and other strange students in Cardinal Otunga High School, in 1989. Then, I discovered that there is three solid types of love—ethos, phi las and agape love but the only one that rescued me from hate, prejudice and abrupt death was agape love, in the mid 1989, before I lost my maternal grand-father to the holy place and beyond.

In this particular year, as people-loving as I have always been, I consequently developed friendships in the institution because, as an adolescent, I wished to explore and learn practically as opposed to hearsay or speculation. Occasionally, I sneaked out of school to social places in Kisii Town with friends, a tendency, which if compared to what I know today and in spite of being a student then, should never have been treated as seriously as Mr. Joseph Bosire, Evans Gesicho and Cleophas Ondieki did.

Considering my experiences in the United States of America in contrast to the status quo at Cardinal Otunga, then, I can only conclude that Africans must seriously engage themselves in the civilization and exposure process. They must do it not just for their own individual good, but for the well being and relevance of the world in general.

However remorseful I may be of my misdeeds and extortion of Anthony Ayatta, back in 1989, frivolous misconduct at an age when we were free of care and as delicate as fowl-eggs, must never be conceived by society to be a sort of homicide simply because it chanced that Julius Omosa was the suspect in question. Perhaps such occurrences were meaningful and of essence in society so as to awaken us, as well as caution, against social enmity, fury and inordinate envy due to failure on the part of others. We may have climbed the highest mountain, swum in the deepest sea, but in the ultimate end we inevitably found our destined prescripts!

Each frivolous occurrence in our daily lives must never be misconstrued to be meaningless; but part of the long paths through which we are treading toward our recompense.

It was however unfortunate that the forces of ill-will within the student population, the extremely corrupt, the people on the opposite side of morality, monopolized on misbehaviors of fellow students more effectively than those who meant good—by physically assaulting others.

We lived in hazardous times down in Cardinal Otunga High School, back in 1989, considering the cliques of haters who existed within the institution made up of sinister attitudes arising from various backgrounds and envy, where those who had no moral reason to hold leadership status had more determination than those set out to stop them. We lived in an institution where school prefects and captains harassed crusaders of justice and humanity. We were in an institution that rewarded evil and shunned those who were obstacles to the vices in the institution, but were in the end consumed by their hatred and bigotry.

A genuine leader is not a searcher for consensus, but a molder of consensus. It simply implied that those of us who were never prefects or captains in school liked expediency, since we were cowards, and so that expediency encouraged us to search for popularity.

In life, there arises a time when we must take the position that is neither safe nor popular, but we ought to do it because conscience urges us to do it. Conscience is of essence to people who claim goodwill.

The kind of student leadership which was portrayed by those who were in charge of our freedoms, in Cardinal Otunga High School, at the time, assured me that we had difficult days ahead in the quest for justice and integrity.

325

Some of my former school-mates at Cardinal Otunga High
School in 1989, among them: Enoch Obwaka, Thomas
Bisonga, Kennedy Maranga, Castro, Michael Masongo,
Tom Openda, Graham Omasire, Leopold Nanyuki,
Anthony Okara, Mogaka Simba, Geoffrey Manyara,
Kiki Onyonka, and Peter Kamau.

While in the midst of my struggles at Cardinal Otunga
High School, in mid-1989, I was informed that my maternal
grandfather, Paul Isaboke Onyiego, had passed on to be with
the Lord.

He was the son of Siro and Bonareri. He got married to
Elizabeth Kemunto in the mid 1920s, following a desperate
attempt by his family to ensure that Mzee Siro's lineage
was not brought to extinction by the colonial masters. This
was because my grandfather and his brother, Marita, had

326

been arrested for demanding that the colonialists leave Gusiiland, and their relatives feared that the small family of three children would be prematurely exterminated, with just a bachelor son left.

My grandmother, Kemunto, because of her long trademarking teeth, became the bride for Onyiego's family. She was also known as Nyarigoti.

Nyarigoti was the first born in a family of six made up of three boys and three girls. She was born in 1903, about the same period of Northcorte's arrival in Gusiiland—a White settler to Mzee Nyamote and her mother, Kerubo, of *Nyaribari, Mwamonda*.

Nyarigoti was adoring and charming—a devoted wife; selfless co-wife; a loving mother; a sacrificial neighbor, a special and doting mother. She was the pillar of support, encouragement and inspiration both to her immediate family and the extended family. Her unending love, care and wisdom were benevolently bestowed to all those who were blessed with her company.

As was then demanded by tradition, she helped her husband to identify co-wives, which she did selflessly to the limits of ensuring that they stayed on. A staunch Catholic, she was baptized in 1955 and attended mass on a regular basis at Kisii Parish; the very reason why she chose to give one of her daughters, Sr. Carmel, to the church which was in retrospect against the prevailing wisdom and the back

327

drop of the fact that her mother-in-law was actively engaged in *Enyamumbo*—a resistance movement against British colonialists.

They were blessed with several children but in the end only eight survived infancy, namely: Prisca Manoti Nyamora, Maria Boisabi Manyi, Sr. Carmel, Rufina Kerubo Omosa, John Onyiego Ogwora, Margaret Bigingi Nyabuto, Karara Moige and Tigi Siro. They were blessed with 29 grand-children, 78 great-grand-children and 48 great-great grand-children.

She went to be with the Lord on Sunday, October 19, 2008, and laid to rest on Friday, October 31, 2008; at the age of 106 years old.

Paul Isaboke Onyiego

Elizabeth Kemunto Onyiego

From left: Prisca Manoti Nyamora, Maria Boisabi Manyi,
Sr. Carmel, Rufina Kerubo Omosa, John Onyiego Ogwora,
Margaret Bigingi Nyabuto and Karara Moige.

329

For the sake of purgatorial ecstasy of extortions on Anthony Ayatta, in 1989, my father and Mr. Charles Barongo (*Kasarani*), the then headmaster at Kisii High School, came up with a consensual notion that I would be better off transferring from Cardinal Otunga High School.

Since by 1990 it had then become evident to society that I was getting admission into a new school each year, I seemed to live under the benign specter of death either through natural means or in the hands of a senseless satanic messenger who had succeeded, twice, in his sinister determination to hinder my future. So I was forced to draw wills of resistance just in case the whistle-call beckoned when I was unawares.

The first student to welcome me in Kisii High School, in 1990, was Whisky, who had been a fellow classmate at St. Mary's Mosocho. This he did by whistling supportively out through the window as soon as he saw me, and I later learned that there was quite a number of boys whom I personally knew before this day such as: Tom Mirimba, Darius Nyamiaka, Kircra Bosire, Steve Njoroge, Musa Oiruria, George Miruka, Sam Mohochi, Lemmi Aswan, Francis Ayatta, Ondicho Keana, Mutavi Kioko, Fred Omurwa, among others.

The way I quickly caught up with the school routine and regulations was so drastic that it was as if I had been there the preceding year because I happened to be recruited as a member of the *Green-Land* crew, the following day.

There was a special clique of boys in the institution who happened to spend most of their time deep in the school forest, which was also known as Green-Land, a place which had such numerous smoking sites, so that it had the capacity of housing wild animals. It had various sites, which were used by those students regarded by the school's administration as social deviants; who had the least respect for rules and who had therefore chosen their destiny which no authority or law could hinder. The only two sites I knew were *Trench-Town* and *King-Stone,* from which exhaled cannabis smoke issued and would sometimes be smelled from areas which were regarded as places governed by the rule of law.

Close to King-Stone, which was simply made up of three gigantic stones on which members placed their posteriors while they erased their daily pain and frustrations in school, was a small hut in which lived a short, dark-skin man named Tanzo. He had been rumored in the area to have given a hand in the construction of the East Africa Railway line back in the early 1900s, when, while Indians were coerced by British settlers into the construction process and consequently eaten up by lions, he heroically wrestled and killed Sir. Thomas Wolde Michael because he allegedly attempted to rape his first wife.

331

The most astonishing claim I heard, on my first week at Kisii High School, about Tanzo was his ability to stir up controversy wherever he had attempted to settle; and he and his family were constantly on the run because of what he proclaimed himself to be. I was also momentarily shocked at the revelation of this man's claims, in 1990, that I almost thought I was hearing voices, until the very day I visited him in his hut, at *Omoremi*, and personally witnessed that his claims must have been as a consequence of hallucinations incurred from excessive consumption of marijuana.

Tanzo believed he was the deity and the father of Jesus Christ. For this reason, he claimed to have escaped countless attempts on his life.

It was surely easy to dismiss him as an insane man suffering from illusions and senile dementia but for the confidence he exuded when asserting that there was no other god but he. He claimed not to be human and came to the world just like his "son" did more than 2000 years ago. He therefore vowed not to die as humans do.

In his homestead, were two small thatched huts. At the center, stood a red flag and a wooden stool on which he placed his sword. He boasted ten wives and more than fifty children, who labored on peoples' farms in order to earn a living and feed the aged man whose advanced age did not enable him to work.

The sword and the flag were a symbol that the world's end was nearing; and he would use the weapon to pummel the evil people of the world.

One of his wives, named "holy spirit," approached me and cried out that she hoped I had brought some special gift for "Jah," since he was old and poor and had many wives and children.

So, I bestowed five pounds of sugar to "god" and instantly one of his sons came and knelt before him before he took the sugar to his mother—who was the eldest of the ten wives.

Tanzo was clearly stunned when I asked him if he had been to heaven and when he intended to bring this world, which is filled with madness and vices, to an abrupt end.

"You humans will simply perish because of your imbecility," he replied with a sharp, wrinkled face. "How dare are you ask your father if he knows his home or communicates with his children?"

After his bubbling statement, he silenced himself for about a minute, then looked upwards and requested "Jesus" to pardon me for doubting the "creator." Then a tense moment followed, and as he fingered a stone of spliff into his hookah pipe, I thought he would exercise the end of the world on me, prematurely.

He then sneezed and asked for a handkerchief and his crown, which were delivered by his eldest wife, who knelt before handing them over to him.

"Go tell your people that one of these days, I will stop the sun at midday and it will not proceed to set for three consecutive months. You will all come to me, running, for forgiveness due to lack of faith."

Then he allowed the conversation to proceed from where we had stopped, by confirming that I was not any different from the people who on numerous occasions had attempted to erase him so as to prove if he surely was God.

"I cannot die," he declared. I came to conquer the world. This is just your flesh that I'm wearing but I'm the Lord your God. Those who trust in me will not perish."

I tried to find out from my schoolmate, Mohochi, if we could leave the area because a number of intruders arrived in the home. They bowed and exchanged greetings; as they referred to Tanzo as "Jah." He had a special, three-legged stool, decorated with colorful beads, with "Jah" inscribed on it.

"If there was any other god superior to me, would he allow an impostor to live? He would have eliminated me with lightning for false pretense, and I would do the same to anyone pretending to be me, your god," he explained.

Displaying his arms, he claimed to have created this earth just as it is described in the book of Genesis.

334

"I will end the world in the way as it is written in the holy book. I will turn the sun into fire; resurrect the dead and embark on judgment. I will create twelve doors in heaven through which the righteous will go while fire will be on earth where the sinners will burn for eternity," vowed Tanzo. He also said that he had not fixed abode because wherever he went, non-believers chased him away, accusing him of blasphemy.

"I only settled at Omoremi about 32 years ago and almost instantly, about 400 young men ambushed me and wanted to separate my head from my main body to see if blood would ooze out," he announced.

The men, armed with machetes, demanded that the man come out of his hut to face their weapons and death but he remained inside; so they were terrified to break into the hut to forcefully eject him out.

"I knew they would not slaughter me and did not choose to go out to face them because I did not come to this world to die like my son Jesus Christ," he said mercifully.

In concordance, his wives and a number of neighbors who had gathered in his compound to consult the supreme being, corroborated the story and harmoniously confirmed that indeed young men invaded his home one night. According to them, the men comprised of locals and others who had trailed Tanzo from his previous domicile at *Namanjalala,*

335

Kitale District, from where he was sent running for his dear life.

"I'm sure they had been sent by the supreme sinner to eliminate me but I'm beyond death," he vowed and immediately broke into prolonged laughter.

One of his two thatched huts was his throne. As a result of his large family, food was cooked on 20 fireplaces, constructed outside, which were made up of three stones each.

He also revealed to us that his parents were resting in heaven and continued to insist that when he was born, his parents knew he was god, so they took the greatest care of him possible. He further said that he never attended anyone's school but instead embarked on seeking followers, and continued that his four sisters recognized him as god rather than their brother.

He further said that all his ten wives and more than fifty children would accompany him to heaven so long as they avoided transgressions against him.

"If they sin, they will die here on earth because I have sired them with humans," he declared.

Tanzo regretted that he intended to marry 400 wives but the thought of begetting many children who would succumb to "this sinful world" made him change his mind. He also claimed that none of his ten wives had ever fallen sick and because he was not human, he too never fell ill.

His only regret was that we humans had refused to care for him, and warned that if people failed to do so in five years, they would regret.

Although he had a harem, Tanzo warned that "men will be judged harshly when the world comes to an end because they worship women; the reason why there is so much immorality in the world. Unless men change, they will be severely punished for idolizing women!" he warned.

In conclusion, he cautioned that churches, "will lead many people to hell because they are made up of people who are hypocrites and liars." He had never attended mass in a chapel and said that since he was god, his followers instead came to his home for blessings.

"I have a sizable number of followers and I do not regret that. I'm not after offerings to make me wealthy. I have come to save the world and not to make money. That is why I'm not rich as you would expect.

Do not let church leaders deceive you because they are led by the chief sinner who has as well blocked your eyes and minds to the fact that I'm lord your god. Come to me instead," declared Tanzo.

Tanzo

Since that material evening, I vowed to Mohochi that I would never come close to the man's compound during my subsequent years at Kisii High School. Although I frequented Green-Land with friends such as Norris Oriero, *Abbrix*, Francis Ayatta, George Sawe, Geoffrey Ongwae, Brian Gesicho, Steve Njoroge, *Papray*, George *Wine*, Aroka, among the other many, Tanzo's mystery all along remained obstinate in my mind for my entire stay in the institution and beyond.

Since Mr. Thomas Maengwe, the then deputy headmaster, had no problems with those who consumed other things besides cigarettes; as he repeatedly announced that Kisii High School was a school of its own class, which he never compared to Mangu, Alliance or Cardinal Otunga High School, we remained permanent visitors to the area up to the end of 1991.

In 1991, as our seniority in the institution was coming to an inevitable end, since we were in the middle of the national examinations, in November of that particular year, a situation emerged in which the entire process was halted due to suspicions of an examination leakage—which sent us home indefinitely.

While at home, I lost my paternal uncle—Omenge Simba. Then, more evidence of people passing on toward the end of the year captured my soul.

He was my father's only brother, on their mother's side, since others had died at a young age. It was a disturbing reality to my father, especially, although he still remained with his step-brothers: Gilbert Morangi, Tom Mbuya and Dennis Ombaba Simba.

Omenge's family, however, is a large family of eight children; which is made up of four sons, four daughters and several grand-children.

(from right) John Morangi, Charles Fidelis, Thomas
Mirimba and Philip Omenge, and four daughters: Judith
Matoke, Marcella, Mary Nyanduko, Elizabeth (missing)
and their mother, Teresia Omenge (Above-Center).

CHAPTER ELEVEN

JOURNEY OF A LIFETIME!

If only the amount of work done in the United States of America in a week would be done in the African continent in a year, most of Africa's problems would have been solved within the shortest period imaginable.

Through my many lessons learned from most of the States in which I have lived including the North-West Pacific and the entire East Coast area, I have been tuned into a system of life whereby, work is the most important factor in one's life.

After living in the Washington State, I moved over to New Jersey, in the East Coast, and surely this was the most mind-boggling experience since I was still new in the country, at the time.

Nothing would have truly brought self-responsibility to me like the State of New Jersey did. From the halls of Union County, when I got my first job, through a miserable experience in Jersey City, Hudson County, and Irvington, Essex County, I discovered that America is a place where one can foresightedly succeed and easily fail—at the same time. And everyone stands alone. By the time, being new in the United States, I was still suffering from Kenyan hangovers of socialism and friendly attitudes, and had not, then, learned that a true economic attitude toward material success depends on self strength, determination, discipline and service, and sometimes a self-centered lifestyle and, or selfishness. This was learned on the day I got on a work schedule after which financial responsibilities began reigning upon me.

As an orientation to the Americanization process, Africans go through immeasurable ups and downs in preparation for adjustment but at this point in life, I know that none of them has found it easy in the United States. Each of them has a long story to narrate, but equally, all of us have had good and sometimes bad experiences as a result of the long safari we have traveled through America. Economically speaking, I have learned quite a bit, in the broader sense, which may as well be viewed multi-laterally.

America is a country of which without money, or rather in simpler terms, employment, one cannot survive. The American system of life, which is now a seemingly worldwide way of life, is ideal in the sense that human physical and mental genius is exploited to the maximum in order to bring the best out of an individual. This is what we wish for all governing authorities; worldwide.

However, the West, more especially America, lacks some sort of culture which takes into consideration human weaknesses, deficits or origin factor, before immigrants eventually become Americanized, which can create some form of space for adjustment. If, for instance, an American is visiting one of the African States they are honored and accepted according to their way of life; which is not the case in America. If diversity and eventual mutual togetherness is the key to the many problems affecting worldwide human existence, then there is certain cultural gaps which must be bridged concomitantly with recognition and mutual respect. But before then, there will have to be charity and self-training from home first. The implication here is that, for American children to earn international acceptance and desired respect, they must acknowledge that it is a two way avenue. This involves parental training and diversification of their formal education syllabuses, to include international

343

facts and schooling which touches on other cultures, and the need for responsibility, socialization, commitment, decency, and competitiveness. This way, then, American children can join the rest of the world class into a world of solidarity and mutual togetherness.

There is much in need of revelation if only given attention by the American youth.

Children are of course innocent at birth but the sort of society into which they are born determines their character and destiny. So many a time we have seen Black and White children play together and intermingle, during their initial ages, but as they mature the social gap widens due to what they learn from their seniors.

American children must be taught, for example, that foreigners are not any lesser than them. But just because of the kind of prejudice, hatred and contempt, and propaganda into which they are born, they tend to despise, prejudge other cultures, thinking that they are of more class than other humans, which actually separates them from reality and ultimately leaves them behind global information which can otherwise be of essence to their well-being and survival. No one can stand alone. However poor your next door neighbor may be, they have their role to play in one way or another.

Nevertheless, in the course of my stay in the East Coast, I learned that prosperous people's view of money is distinct. To them, money is not seen as small pieces of paper and coins adorned in pictures, but rather value every denomination as a seed—which when planted, will germinate into monetary trees that can fulfill their desires and long-term dreams.

Each monetary denomination has the capability of growing. It is therefore essential to preserve and protect money. All this depends on how long you allow it to grow and the rate at which the growth is rationed.

In America, it is easy to acquire a source of income, which is commonly a job, because there is a lot of employment opportunities. But it is extremely difficult to save your money as a result of a fast paced economy and lifestyle—which means that the money is quickly acquired and equally spent fast.

Most people in America waste so much money without notice, due to easy availability and fast spending; but difficult to save or invest in sustainable assets.

Joblessness is also not something foreign. Because of the many opportunities to get employment, then that means that most people's employers are not professional but just temporary hiring firms; which can hire and terminate or become liquidated easily. Then the reality is that joblessness can arise as easily as the job was gotten, which puts employment at risk or jeopardizes people's lives in the case of unemployment—which has time and again occurred to me in my American experience.

Since no one can survive in America without a source of income, experiences of unemployment subject people into idleness and hopelessness.

In New Jersey, for instance, most immigrants need to alter their attitudes toward employment opportunities. They require attitude change to enable them see and seize opportunities than just believing that particular job classes, as long as they are rewarding in order to meet their financial obligations, then they are suitable.

It is correctly almost impossible, before Americanization, for an immigrant to make their objectives and expectations candid. They take it that as life unfolds fate will define their expectations but, in the end when it is almost too late, realize that they chose unwisely. Instead of clearly envisioning their requirements and insisting on commensurate performance, most of them decide to settle for what they can get out of the fact of just being in America, and end up sticking to such casual jobs for a lifetime.

This mostly happens in cases where the employers, like Chinese restaurants, want to be populist or accepted by the employees, whom they exploit, remunerate with the lowest possible compensation; but yield the highest profits, regardless of their undermined qualifications or abilities.

And in such cases, these employees help their employers meet the production benefits and profits.

As a lesson over the years, if then we had to maintain a job, in the midst of our dilemma and subsequent orientation, then we had to keep utmost co-operation without lowering standards, instead of finding alternative strategies and ultimate advancement rather than letting others get away with exploitation.

For those of us, during our initial stages in America, who let employers get away with such shady profit-making ambitions by prescribing exploitative mechanisms on those they could find, we eventually paid the price of time-wasting and unyielding results. So this resulted in career stagnation, which meant that there was no movement, development or progress on the part of those who expected change in their financial status.

One of the many reasons why we were stuck in stagnation was lack of adequate skills and acceptable knowledge within the fields in which we engaged ourselves—like the security profession we engaged ourselves in, in New Jersey, for years, as others moved up the career hierarchy. Those who tried to upgrade their skills were "fired," which meant that they would then either seek another similar job or switch careers; and eventually get into confusion of career choice in the process.

Our progress was also hindered by fear of challenging onuses, under the context that we felt secure and comfortable with our then current jobs and never looked into other areas of opportunity and advancement. We therefore never wished to take extra responsibilities that came with promotion and career progression because we felt that promotion came with uncertainty, fear of inadequacy, and so we for these reasons chose to remain in the low-level careers we had taken, and in effect, hindered our own progress.

Others were in fear of exposure, and felt that they would rather stagnate in their positions instead of a gradual advancement into higher levels for fear that their inadequacies, ignorance and weaknesses would be exposed.

This sort of stagnation was also due to failure, on the part of those who aided us upon our arrival in America, in directing and guiding us from their own past experiences, on ways in which we could pursue our dreams and ambitions which would ultimately create advancement and foregoing benefits. Most of those we met here, because they had already made the above financial mistakes, saw no reason of aiding others; as they wanted everyone to undergo similar experiences as theirs in order to learn the hard way!

Back then, between 1997 and 2003, most people ventured into the house-buying and selling business. Most of us would have invested in the same. It was a booming business at the time, but while the history and objective of a mortgage was well intended, it became a gold-mine for banks. The banks made almost twice the value of the houses, which was justified by the compensated time.

For those of us who were venturing into the business for the first time, the interest on the mortgage was compounded. This meant that we would be paying interest based on the principle loan amount and not on the outstanding balance as was the case with many other credit products.

Usually, the banks will tell you it is your house upon signing the mortgage papers but should you default in making payments for just a number of months, then you will prove whose house it actually is.

The risk taker in a mortgage business is not the bank but the client; the risks include inflation, deflation, a recession, interest fluctuation, property devaluation and depreciation. Even if you hit a lottery and wished to pay off the loan in a year instead of 30 years, the bank will demand you pay off the sum-total which you would have paid in 30 years without recalculating the interest.

There is a jackpot in the mortgage business and it is every bank's wish to hit it. 30 years is a long period of time and we all go through financial ups and downs. Some may be able to succeed and some will definitely fail.

For those who fail, the bank quickly repossesses the house and will sell it off at the current market rate. It will not reimburse the profits it made on top of the regular house

349

payments. This is how most people get stuck, and sometimes resort to pulling the trigger or hanging themselves, since they do not get a refund of the money paid in installments.

While loans are appreciating assets, a house is a depreciating asset I strongly believe that we all grow concurrently with wisdom. Some of the opportunities we wish we would have taken advantage of, are those that are today yielding positive results or in the history books.

In this modern science of making and investing, there are two personality attitudes—those who focus on opportunities and those who focus on obstacles. The former realize potential benefits while the latter see great losses and risks in any venture they undertake.

But success or not in making and investing money, it boils down to the age-old question: Are we some of those who see the glass half-full or half-empty?

Because there is lack of a more alternative definition, either on which I might fall, successful people are always among the optimistic, while the poor fall under the pessimistic category.

On one hand, the most successful expect to see positive results irrespective of the challenges they foresee, as they comprehend that the higher the risk, the higher the reward. The indigent, on the other hand, expect failure. Since they never trust in their abilities, they fear losing should they invest. They take a long time to come up with decisions and by the time they are ready, the opportunity may have passed them. If the period spent to make a decision is long, the chances of losing the opportunity are high. In the meantime, the opulent; who are astute investment investigators will have caved in, made their money and moved out. The very reason why success is a choice!

Successful people take informed risks that are based on solid verities and information, and to excel financially, one has to do something, make a purchase or invest in some form of income generating asset. At times, it might be out of luck because luck is defined as when opportunity meets good planning. But thorough initial preparation is of essence so as for opportunity to be possible.

The pessimist poor mostly target what they do not want. Most of those who fail mimic the successful instead of formulating their own ways according to their beliefs and or soul searching — forgetting that life is not necessarily about solving problems, but by spending time, energy and constructive thought in moving boldly towards your goal.

For any kind of goal to be achieved, there must be some form of action taken. Deciding alone, without action will not get you to your desired destiny. The unsuccessful do not believe in their abilities, they would like to know every hindrance before them and how to sort it out before taking action. The successful see the opportunity, take advantage of it and as a result benefit from it.

351

CHAPTER TWELVE

CONCLUSION

In conclusion, I know that I'm not an angel, neither is any of us. I may have erred at some point in the course of this long journey of practical performance of God's duties, of which we shall all be judged for the sole purpose of purification and ultimate graduation into the next level.

I'm strongly remorseful to those I may have offended in this life-adventure of trying to search my soul and talent, and expect the same from each human being whom I have had a chance and opportunity to encounter because none of us is an angel or sin-free. It is the only sure way we can learn and be better representatives of our Creator.

Throughout the years, 1992 through 1996, when some of my life experiences and circumstantial encounters appeared to be sudden magical, incomprehensible flashes of episodes, whether positive or sinister, as may have been perceived by individuals within, it may have chanced that I wouldn't be my full self and fulfiller of my intended good and destiny—were it not for the sort of history and finger-prints which define Julius Morara Omosa.

Each of us has a unique role to play in our arranged existence, without which we couldn't make the expected full circle in life in preparation for the next generation, into the endless future, which is surely beyond our understanding and prediction but within the powers of our Creator.

If we momentarily discard the notion of materialism, all of us are equal in all aspects of Godly and human definition. Whether you are black, white, yellow or red, it only gives us answers as to why we are of different skin-colors.

That, for the scriptures and prophecy to be fulfilled accordingly, we had to be of a difference in a way that will see the rise of racism, tribalism, class-distinction, prejudice and stereotypes, so that conflict can arise, thus fulfillment of the last book of the Bible—Revelation.

Most of us are not blessed well enough to see exactly what and why certain happenings come about, but a well informed and spiritual soul can complacently stand in a perspective to accept life as it is; since we are simply members

353

in the human team and cannot change the consequence of our existence, whatsoever. The very reason why I accept myself to be who God has designed me to be which should be the case with each of us and we must not be judgmental or envious of our brothers and sisters.

Nothing on earth can give or take your destined fortunes or negative consequence, as defined by our heavenly Father. At times, such detail may sound irrelevant or untrue in the ears of material worshipers or non-believers, but those who discredit the reality of who they are, are surely non-believers and for that case do not know their purpose and consequence on our earthly existence.

Materialism has, today, deprived people of their humanity and faith, a good example being some of our brothers and sisters in America where all human values have been taken away from their humanity, and only left them to decide between money and death.

In today's world, humanity is defined by one's degree of opulence and not respect for human values or humanity itself. But without the basic ingredients which give us the human definition, the adoration of material wealth only takes away our Godly definition and humanity itself.

In many cases, I have assured those who have had the opportunity to share some wisdom with me that people who are less gifted with material wealth seem to be happier than the rich, if only they do not raise their level of material greed in order to equal the more opulent in society. What creates resentment and spiritual poverty in us is comparison and greed. If we could only accept the status quo as long as we are happy with the little we are blessed to possess, including basic human needs, we would be the happiest individuals, and this would be a problem-free world.

Truly, happiness lies in our minds and souls. It all depends on one's choices, desires and acceptance of realities in life. If money was the only solution to life's problems why are the rich not problem-free people? If this was the case, then none of us would seek happiness at the poverty level. Money should simply be understood by mankind to be a medium which enables us to achieve our desires, needs and wants in life. But a problem arises when humans fail to measure the degree of their desires, needs and wants!

When we develop endless desires, then a situation arises in which we require police officers, and all other law enforcers, to protect us from ourselves and the kind of problems we have caused ourselves due to greed and dissatisfaction. The solution lies simply within our humanity and choices, and not on the materialistic system of life which we did not invent but find ourselves in. We have the spiritual power of choice, desire and limit.

As African Americanized as I have incidentally become, I stand on a peak where I have the choice of either discarding my initial African heritage or blindly adopting to the new trends. It is not an implication that my Americanization process is detrimental to those who live within it, but I have to tread carefully so as to appreciate and value my roots and concurrently adjust to where I find myself today. This sort of acceptance and understanding is what has created the kind of dilemma and confusion which is evident among most of us, more especially the kind of ignorance that exists among the African American community. It is, however, understandable considering historical facts of American Blacks and the kind of political blindness and propaganda that has been injected into their minds, and resultantly developed over the years—aimed at the partition of the Black race.

There is no human race that has been so grieved and affected by historical injustices like those in the African continent, putting in mind the historical paths through which its people are subjected by inevitable circumstances. Such circumstances have led to a conflict of interest between Africans and African Americans in such a way that prejudice and stereotypic tendencies have cropped up, so that each group views the other as the cause of their everyday failure, pain and hardship in one way or another.

Most African Americans think that Africans have caused their status quo, and therefore possess a hidden feeling of inferiority to Africans, considering their historical paths and truths, without the understanding that on the other hand Africans are crippled due to the fact that African Americans were stolen away from their continent. Irrelevantly, Africans do not lay their blame of the facts on African Americans — but Whites. It only culminates into a game of finger-pointing at each other, and while African Americans blame vigor and reason for their failure from historical injustices, Africans have taken a path of forgiveness and collaboration toward unity and a future which is energized by history and solidarity since divisions will just tear us apart more.

Being of African origin, comprehending and considering historical truths and injustices and the kind of conditions in which my black brothers and sisters find themselves in, at least as of now, nothing stops me from bestowing all the three forms of love available. The only spiritual factor that dismays me is their contemptuous innuendos toward Africans which occasionally augment to the kind of divisions already in place. And the only available solution to such meaningless conflicts, so that we may all think about tomorrow instead of reviving yesterday's pain, is plain commitment to information, literacy, eradication of ignorance and a sense of focus and development. Carrying forward past pain will merely add to more pain, but learning from the past and being innovative in finding modern ways of sorting out differences and obstacles, which may not give

357

rise to conflict and savage tendencies, will prosperously keep us advancing to new levels.

One major cause of misunderstandings among the African American community is the lack of values within the family setting, and lack of parental responsibility in early childhood development—as mentors.

In short, initial parental training is of essence to American children, more especially those of the African American community. As their fellow brothers, it breaks our hearts to witness the kind of destruction which the lack of parental involvement has, and is still continuously, causing the Black race in America.

These are indeed minor solvable hindrances to success and prosperity within this community, rather than raising children who seem to face one straight direction of irresponsibility and disrespect. And, understandably the blame should not necessarily be laid on the American Black race alone. The sort of situation they find themselves in, which is simply a composition of ignorance and brainwashed minds, surely seems to be a consequence of past bold racial conspiracies, by past regimes, which were solely directed at them, and projected to keep them in total darkness—at least after slavery was terminated in the 1860s by Abraham Lincoln. Sometimes it defeats logic, more especially when one is still new in the United States, to see ignorant, uninformed people born and raised in the so-called developed world. For instance, savagery gets its real definition by witnessing the sort of notions and beliefs most Americans have toward the African continent. Some believe that Africans spend their nights on trees or simply give the continent an image that all distasteful, backward realities are owned by the African continent. At no given time, are good images about the African continent featured in America; the very reason why there is high ignorance rates of information and truths about other cultures of the world — among Americans.

This misinformation is not only a deterrent to the county's diversity so that American children may be in a position to compete with children from other parts of the world, but is one reason for the rise of divisions along racial lines. When African Americans reflect on their social status in America, for instance, they tend to lay blame for their failures on Whites or Africans, due to slavery, because of lack of exposure and adequate education, on the part of some, so that histories may be well digested by them without bitterness toward innocent people.

Most, if not all, African communities are generally guided by proverbs. In the Swahili culture, for instance, there are two proverbs which I would like to attribute to the African American community. The first one is: *Asiyefunzwa na mama, ufunzwa na ulimwengu*—meaning that one who fails to be taught by their mother, learns from the world. The second one is: *Ukistaajabu ya Musa, utaona ya filauni*—If you are stunned by Moses's Ten Commandments, you will face the wrath of criminals.

As much as there is equal opportunity for all American citizens, there should be no reason of reverting to historical injustices in order to justify economic failure, which in the end results to envy and crime. I have in the past had African American friends who had obnoxious beliefs that those Africans living in America are secretly favored by the White population, facilitating economic success, while they are left to languish in "projects;" without realizing that those who have attained success have toiled for it, regardless.

It is simply a world of two forces secretly pulling apart. To a critical onlooker, there seems to be two "Americas"— although the commitment of service and the system of life leaves all people, irrespective of their skin-colors, with little or no choice but to live within the existing culture so as to survive. I mean two Americas racing on twin tracks, or in more sophisticated terms, two Americas orbiting in parallel universes, one blackened by time and historical injustices, and the other whitened by historical opportunity and choice.

The whitened universe is one of great promise—on the threshold of a governance and economic breakthrough, and the blackened universe is one of great despair, on the brink of systemic collapse because in this universe, its occupants seem to have only been freed from practical yokes and shackles which were in turn forced into their minds.

Then there is the America of innovative and world class entrepreneurs, comprising of the Asian community who seem not to be at war with no one, and have only accepted the world as it is. They are the non-complaining flock who have never had historical injustices cast upon their lives but seem to get along with both the blackened and whitened universes. These are owners of competitive firms that have consistently reported abnormal profits each year—for decades and past centuries. This is the America of brilliant roadside, primitive entrepreneurs eking out a living by the sweat of their brains

Then there is the America of more burst than boom— where catastrophic loss in personal fortunes is the ordinary. The America of emaciated Africans feeding on wild fruits in a continent littered with livestock carcasses, victims of the cascading tragedies of drought, disease, economic detriment, a stolen culture, famine and starvation.

On the other hand, there is the nation of multi-racial, diligent and hardworking public servants and entertainers— who stand in the middle of a society which values race more than humanity, whose contribution helps the economy moving. This is the nation of high-flying technocrats and intellectuals who can stand their ground in the competitively racial stage.

Finally there is the America of uppity and conceited of partisan political servants and corporate leaders who perceive preening as their most ideal calling and the feathering of racial nests as their second. This is where racial favoritism is a treasured art; where racial elites will enable and defend the continuity of ancient, outmoded racist, partial philosophies, as long as narrow racist interests are met.

Viewing the status quo, and out of all the war-like battles in the "land of opportunity," in anticipation of material success, the poor Africans seem to be getting some glimmers of hope in the very continent that they abandoned to become African Americanized. It has now become a hotly contested space for business investment—putting the East led by China, against the West—led by the United States of America, in a secret yet unseen battle for supremacy.

There is, presently, gloom all over the place with endless tales of rampant insecurity because if the Chinese bring African economies up from shambles, then that signifies danger to the future survival of the West considering the fact that Africa possesses all sorts of natural resources one can envision. Even if there is a general argument that this is a form of modern colonization of Africa, by the Chinese, it seems to be a humble one since there is an indication of quid-pro-quo.

Some of us may have despaired on the fight for justice, fairness and prosperity, bearing in mind that this is probably God's intended direction of human history and status quo, either due to exhaustion, or, as is the case for the more gifted in our societies, succumbed to their base instincts. There is a lot of hunger out there outright, moment by moment answers to the many burdens of political malfeasance and apartheid-like tendencies.

This may sound like Utopian philosophy simply because it is, but let us keep dreaming on as long as we play our parts. Human societies, just like the animal kingdom, are quite complex — sometimes chaotic, disorderly and hazardous. There is simply numerous moving parts, significant variables and multiple dimensions.

From ancient histories, we know that change and human emancipation comes in two ways: either by an evolution or a revolution.

In the end, neither a revolution nor an evolution is the just remedy for human injustices. What is required is a combination. In place of a forceful revolution, a rebellion, time and again may be workable.

As Thomas Jefferson, the third American President said: "I hold it that a little rebellion now and then is a good ideal, and as necessary in the political world as storms in the physical. It is a medicine necessary for the sound health of government."

Indeed, rebellions or serious protests are the tool with which to prod intransigent governments, and if they prove to be the appropriate tool, it starts with recognition that in today's world, it is basically a mindset problem along two dimensions: racial, tribal and social position.

Dominant images and messages in the open arena often design perceptions and consequently reinforce particular mind-sets. Those who are fortunate to possess the biggest portion of the open mind have authority over mind-sets. Therefore, to alter mind-sets, a mind-share formula is mandatory

The duty of designing and implementing a mind-share formula is better left to an independent commission of experts made up of patriotic, non-partisan, and influential people from across racial lines. But is seems more challenging when African Americans discriminate against Africans, not on racial lines, but on particular, unknown, yet to be researched inner, inferior feelings which they find timorous to expose but can still be detected by a keen observer.

These are all elements of resentment which have been accumulated over time, by trivialities and instances of personal failure resulting in a delicate, yet dangerous position of indecision on who to blame for their status in today's world. This then reverts us back to the facts of the kind of social life that has been designed, in the United States, in which children are basically nurtured in their

364

early development years, not by their biological parents or foster parents, but by government authorities. This is surely dangerous in the sense that children grow up comparing themselves to well-off, successful people, without the understanding that those who are successful have over time worked their ways through, the hard way, and have attained their possessions rightfully, and patiently without wishful thinking or short-cuts.

In Africa, for instance, children, in their early development process, of up to about 13 years, are culturally kept away from learning about monetary issues for fear of deviation from socially acceptable behaviors within the community. Surely, this then makes the West an epitome society, as a case study, in viewing some of the cons which are brought about by development and modern ways of life in regard to the negative impacts of the same. All forms and ways of life truly have their pros and cons but some of the cons within systems of life can be revoked or avoided, more especially when the consequence of particular freedoms is continuously abused. But my emphasis is still on early upbringing of the child by parents. That is the root cause of all subsequent positive and negative conducts since, "charity begins at home."

The child's early days are the most crucial as they determine their future in various ways, and these are mostly the times when a child learns from what they perceive as the right behaviors. So if a child grows up in a family where his or her superiors erase their daily pain by the use of illicit drugs or brews, chances are high that that particular child will more likely than not mimic the same behavior in the long run. At the higher levels of growth, authorities must never be blamed for execution of the rule of law; since laws are clearly outlined in a country's constitution—so long as such laws are indiscriminately applicable to all people of that particular land.

In America, for example, there is a tendency of individuals declining to admit their legal mistakes under the cover of racial lines. Although there have been past evidences of racial profiling, America still leads the world on the democratic paths of equality, justice, opportunity, fundamental human freedoms and remuneration for what is rightfully, equitably deserved for services rendered.

Most of the young people, today, however, have many aspects of their lives that need attention. Since the age of maturity and mind development seems to decrease moment-by-moment, the ages between the 13s and 19 present urgent needs, responsibilities and obligations—all with sexual and financial ramifications. When we give our lives a critical analysis in consideration to the kind of obligations that await young men and women of today, they appear overwhelming. They must view life as an elephant to be eaten by them in one sitting, metaphorically speaking, one bite at a time, and this should be the rationale which we should adopt in tackling the sort of obligations that are ahead of us in life.

You can drive cows to the river but you cannot force them to drink. That is a plain fact which relates to today's teenagers, who, despite the many opportunities surrounding them, they have chosen to raise their hands up in surrender, and in place engaged in excessive sexual deviations. In short, they value their beauty and good looks more than they care about their future success and prosperity.

There is nothing wrong with appreciating one's good looks or attractiveness but such a gift must be combined with success—lest good looks without prosperity will only promote ugly impressions. As children of today appear to eat all the elephant at once, therein lies the reason for most failures. They do not take time to comprehend the dynamics of whatever they hound themselves in and master its operations.

True to our human obsession with making social advancements at every opportunity, we must remember that when humans are given too much freedoms they may end up abusing them, and turn them into a platform of absurdity.

It seems that everything that is being done by modern young men and women is often meant to depict an impression of opulence and sophistication. But we could be better people if we cut out the vanity of material intoxication

367

which has stolen away the souls of our youth—the point from where I make my observations and criticism.

It never makes any sense, at society-level, to have young men exposing their most private parts, below the waist area, in public, in the name of fashioning themselves with modern times. Exposing one's posterior to the general public by letting pants drop down and be fastened around the thighs, it only raises so many questions. For instance; this makes one wonder if truly there is any reason of need to privacy to these individuals whenever they are in need of using a bathroom, because the very privacy which forces them into toilets has nowadays become an ordinary thing— by advertising their buttocks in the open.

Most of today's boys appear to be trans-gender in disguise of fashioning with modern times. They are truly not men-enough as it was back in the old days, especially in the African traditional society.

Some of our grandfathers and fathers wish they were born in these modern times when we were. Granted our generation has been ravaged by fashions, materialism, despair, corruption and disrespect without concern for security of our future well-being. The only thing that men of this generation have to smile about is getting a girl for a song and useless prestige.

During the times of our grandfathers, they visited their in-laws with beehives full of live bees. This signified that they could fend for the fair females. And as if that was not enough, they were made to strip to their briefs by their wives so that they could examine their legs prior to making a lifetime commitment to the geezer. This cannot happen in our times considering the sort of arrogance and specialty with which today's suave boys are holding dear their bodies. They may only do what our grandfathers did for their wives at the sight of material possessions and liquid money. In fact, in terms of money, they are ready to perform more than our grandfathers did—and at times more obnoxious, paradoxical gymnastics.

If there is a girl, in modern times, so foolish enough to anticipate marrying a traditional lion-killing man, then she should better give up whatever drugs she is operating on. The days when a slew of life-threatening customs were held in high esteem and respect are long gone, and we only seem to be living in a world governed by self-defined cultures and beliefs which sometimes end up defining practical insanity portrayed by crazy people dressed up like normal people, and yet half-naked. Or legendary times of our grandfathers whose heroic past was defined by revelations of their perseverance as they got circumcised with a piece of broken bottle or a blunt machete.

The youth of today like short-cuts, drastic fixes and get-rich-quick schemes. In other words, everything they want, they want it yesterday and in many circumstances, they are

369

ready to circumvent the process to achieve it. Unfortunately faster does not translate to better in making peace with the fact that some process is a commonplace order of life. Life is full of much tedious process and while some of it requires elimination in order to jump-start effectiveness and efficiency, some of it is essential.

"People don't resent having nothing nearly so much as having too little," declared an English writer, Ivy Compton-Burnett. The sad part of poverty is not to go hungry or poorly clad, but to not have quite enough to keep up with your next-door neighbor, or even do better than them.

Surely, there is nothing wrong with people possessing riches; the irony comes about when riches possess people. If we do not grasp the fortunes of instant, abundant riches, we may end up losing perspective and empathy. And if we do not foresee wealth when it is coming to us, it will not be easier to revert to our previous simpler existence and use our wealth in favor of others who as well need to benefit, not as much as we have benefited but at least to acquire basic human needs by investment, enabling easier access to skill-training or self-sustaining economic projects.

Most people who have been blessed with the gift of wealth, more especially today's youth, lack the sense of responsibility and gratitude that comes along with newly acquired wealth. Wealth and status bring about serious onuses toward the community, such as education, health-care, vocational training, scholarships for eloquent, needy children, help to children who are destitute, as well as to one's own family.

In the modern world, we are only witnessing the development of the new poor, due to lack of special programs, by those who have been fortunate to succeed, which aid those with numerous illusions of a better life and the youth in development of their focus and hope toward their dreams instead of despair. This is the cause of establishment of slums in the developing world, and particular conducts by our youth, today, in the name of fashioning up with modern times, by engaging in extraordinary tendencies such as the advertisement of their most private parts to their parents and the general public. These circumstances only leave our youth in cycles of poverty, semi-illiteracy and ignorance, only to be beaten down by joblessness, the uncertainties and harshness of a life of casual labor, hence casual income, and the resultant atmosphere of insecurity and hopelessness. But the indigent do not have to train on how to be poor—they know how. They only have to be tough and resourceful instead of wasting away time and opportunities, and eventually appreciate what they possess. This is the same philosophy they have hounded themselves in over the years, so that now, due to anger and frustration, they have just chosen to develop queer, don't-care attitudes;

which, because they have no specific blame, result to public misbehaviors, in an effort to portray their troubles.

In modern times, money is a sensitive commodity, more so to the young men and women who are blessed with abundant wealth. It sometimes takes a literal shape of a book of matches or razor blade in the hands of a toddler.

It is also clear in our life-time that if the poor are blessed with the gift of riches or opportunity, they tend to be extravagant due to inexperience with the same, unlike the rich with experience in handling abundant riches. Take for instance someone like Michael Jordan, the famous former basket-baller, or Bill Gates, they do not have expensive rims on their vehicle's wheels or tinted windows. It is close to zero-chance to find them playing loud music in their cars because they know the value of their wealth and are not after advertising their poverty to the public. In fact, most of those who tend to show-off with such luxuries are the poor, defeated, with little means people, who have no experience with management of riches.

In the Swahili language, there is a perfect proverb that affirms this claim: *Masikini akifanikiwa, matako hulia mbwata*—that, if a poor person succeeds, society will recognize their fortune simply by means of show-off.

Equally, in a society which is infested by inequality and upheavals, even the successful cannot live in peace, unless it is in rare occasions when the poor are brandishing a bottle of liquor, a joint of *weed* or a weapon.

Most people today consider the word "poor" offensive without looking back at the causes of indigence to those affected by it. Society treats poor people as if it were their fault or something shameful they have brought on themselves. Poverty is a form of sickness which causes mental disorder. The kind of sicknesses people bring on themselves come from over-indulgence such as liver sclerosis, obesity, and still, not because they wish to fall sick, but out of ignorance or weakness. Poverty or social, financial-status-inequality in life has many causes which include family background, ignorance, despair, abused childhood, extremes of stress, historical traumatic events, addictions, friendships and relationships, racial injustices and inequality, but even with fair ground and opportunity, cases of poverty will occur, and where to draw the line between poor, the comfortable in-betweens and rich is usually difficult. Just imagine some people in places like Africa or Asia who are considered to be poor, by people in the West, but if you approach such victims, you will surely learn that they are some of the happiest people in the world. Healthier and stronger too, as they do not spend sleepless nights searching for money. Happier than some of the wealthiest individuals on earth because they are satisfied with the little they posses, and have no greed for more than they have since they are either not aware of what others define as riches, or are simply comfortable in their small world. Conversely, it is absurd to imagine that people with immense wealth are always happier. The more you have, the more you have to worry about!

In the past, there were no poor people in society; as those who had little benefited from those who had more, and vice-versa. Generally, people lived in a social network of give-and-take or sharing among themselves, unlike today when there is individuality and greed to rule over others because of inequality in material possessions. The word "poverty," in the modern world, in all aspects denotes something beyond the norm, or exceeding reason.

In America, for instance, because of modern ways of life, whereby those short of material possessions, without regard to the world history and the real definition of riches, some people have developed hatred toward those who have not been lucky enough in attaining material wealth. But the senseless part is that they fail to understand that it was never a fair chance for all in the beginning of scrambles for the little that God placed on this earth for us all. There was injustice, imbalance and partiality on the part of acquiring the same at the start of events and this has been inherited over generations into the present day.

I have come across people in America who develop contempt, prejudice or hatred toward others because they originate from a particular part of the world, which in just out of mere hearsay, speculation, propaganda and brainwashing rumors, is viewed as poor. And most of those with such preconceived beliefs are the unlucky poor in America. According to me, poverty exists in peoples' minds and souls. It seems wiser to be poor in the material or monetary sense but be rich with wisdom, mind and soul.

Poverty, just like craziness, only requires definition by the affected persons themselves, or in other words, it has no definition, just as much as each of us believes that we are more normal than our neighbors which then gives craziness no standard definition—but only depends on the degree and style of craziness which in turn may be defined as normal or abnormal just like geniuses and saints who are said to have a streak of craziness. Then this means that they are either more normal or less normal, and yet, more perfect than the majority who consider themselves to be normal.

The money issue is also a disturbing question more especially among the youth of today who are constantly exposed to luxuries and modern fashions, instead of investing it for the good of their uncertain future. It does not matter how much one earns but what they do with their income.

This is useful because poverty levels are determined by how one's money is spent, and since recognizing one's own individual financial personality habits is the determinant cause of financial success or failure so that good habits can be nurtured and discard the bad ones.

There are various types of money personalities. The happy-go-lucky people do what they can with their money until it is all spent, while they actively endeavor to augment their income, but their spending habits shoot up simultaneously.

While they do not often land into serious financial difficulties, major financial needs usually find them unprepared. Their main weakness is that they do not have clearly defined financial goals

Most Americans fall under the happy-go-lucky personalities category, considering that most of them live on credit cards and or live from pay-check to pay-check—and whenever a major financial need arises due to a recession or job loss, they are caught unprepared because they have no nest egg to rescue them from such catastrophes. Of course they set goals, but they are aimed at short-term survival. They think about their rent, mortgage, household expenses and immediate lifestyle requirements. Most Americans in this category ignore or postpone major long-term needs, in anticipation that life might get better. But really, nothing improves, and with time, their needs increase and they find themselves increasingly overburdened.

The second class of personalities is the fear immobilized personalities who often make self-fulfilling prophesies. They often say things such as, "I can't afford it" or "that is for rich people." They are good at avoiding risks and will not invest in their own self-enhancement or risk switching jobs.

As a consequence, their income does not augment as much as it would have over years. Such people tend to spend their leisure-time in their bedrooms with their spouses and as a result, end up increasing their expenses through unplanned pregnancies. Their low income offers little leeway for saving and investment. If they do not save, their ultra-conservative tendencies lead them to low-return investments.

On the opposite end of the spectrum is the lottery player and constant visitor to the casinos in Las Vegas, Nevada. This type of personality wants wealth drastically. Such people are forever putting their money into one scheme or the other that gives them hopes of becoming millionaires overnight or strict believers of luck. Like the daily lottery players or gamblers, it is of utmost faith that it will one day chance that they become millionaires, and as a result, end up spending all their incomes on prospects of chance and luck.

Of course, the mathematical reasoning behind such schemes is equally as convincing as it is attractive.

377

Nevertheless, the sole truth is that pyramid schemes are never any worse than scams, and those who end up empty handed are the majority.

With multi-level marketing enterprises, a large percentage of the would-be players often find themselves puzzled with enormous chunk of difficult-to-market merchandise that they have already wasted all their money on.

Addictions to such is a common disease already in the bloodstream of most Americans, more especially the vast majority of African Americans, who spend their hard-earned incomes on the latest fashions, daily parties, cook-outs and unnecessary fast-foods—instead of substituting such wasteful expenditures with mature conducts and self-responsibilities such as relying on home cooked foods more, so as to invest for their future and that of their children.

This lack of prudence is like keeping lion cubs for pets. They are fun, cuddly and lovable, but as you feed them, they grow bigger and hungrier. If you feed them longer enough, soon or later, they will get bigger and hungrier that you and your family might make up their next meal.

Whenever I try to comprehend the American way of life, it has time and again appeared to me that the system is either inhabited by some of the most emancipated people, from the shackles of self-enslavement, or simply a place of people who have trapped themselves in a crater of self-enslavement, guided by the supreme sinner.

The land's freedoms are those characterized by the ability to do what one believes to do, as defined by the constitution of the land. It is great since no human being can explain life's daily unfolding events and episodes, and surely, none of us can justify right from wrong.

Right and wrong is as good as an item named "spoon" and another named "cup." But imagine that the item branded "cup" was named "spoon," wouldn't we all believe that it is indeed a spoon, and vice-versa?

Yet, these freedoms lack the limitations or extent at which they can be exercised because if freedom has been granted to humans, then they should never be regulated since people have varying levels of exploitation and satisfaction. This therefore means that human spirituality, egos and levels of humor are not part of the freedoms being enjoyed by them so as to avoid abuse or over-exercising them or interference with the law of the land. On the other hand, the legal limitations and consequences on these freedoms is so harsh that it deprives people of the very freedoms which they are supposed to enjoy or leaves no significant sense of the freedoms which they are guaranteed. It feels like an invitation to a football stadium, where people have no requirement to pay for their entertainment and other services but if their ignorance or over-reaction from the same leads

379

them into breaking the rules, the consequence will discourage them and others from such freedoms, henceforth.

Giving people freedom and punishing them for exercising the same freedoms is not freedom itself. This is not an implication that society should be free of rules, regulations and or the rule of law, but apart from Common Law, all other limitations to freedoms and their punishments seem too harsh and unnecessary.

None of us is perfect, including animals, but in my view, animals seem to have more of natural freedoms than human beings, and when man-made laws are constantly broken or excessive freedoms abused, then that alone is an indication that people are living within regulated freedoms and when granted too much freedom they tend to misuse it because they need more emancipation.

Then this brings us to Common Law and the Ten Commandments within which all God's creations lived in the beginning, and by which wild animals are still guided— hence their seemingly extra emancipation.

Humans have only complicated their lives further by re-defining Common Laws and substantiating the Ten Commandments in an attempt to create their own understanding, supremacy, so that they serve their selfish interests and desires.

Due to confusions arising from human definitions of the Ten Commandments, Common Law, which is simply common sense, is at the verge of discrepancy. For instance, the simple common sense of determining where to relieve oneself, of urine, in the time of need!

There must be no man-made law to define a toilet, but places where the need to relieve ourselves of natural, involuntary body excretions should be guided by common sense, and not man-made laws which sometimes result in legal consequences.

Then one wonders how gross men can be when they are given too little or too much freedom. The 21st Century man is not a pretty sight. In fact, the scarce, well-cultured man's image is constantly being tarnished daily by his irresponsible mates.

Cities across the world are filled with men whose looks don't, in the least possible way, correspond with their habits; a case of gentle faces coupled with faded etiquette without bothering to add any adjectives like uncivilized, foul or sometimes tacky however much they may befit them. Women occasionally tap their toes in desperation and distaste at the uncultured crew of men that intermingle with them everyday. This is a good example of used and misused freedoms which require common sense, and not legal consequences!

In the modern world, not only do men engage in shameful behaviors such as public urination, but most, modern youthful boys and girls are practicing inanity and incest.

In the clamor for relevance, young boys and girls are supposed to keep their legs crossed until the day when they are expected to engage in sexual activity. Today, sexual matters have become the most discussed subject both by the media and across family tables, an issue, which in the past was avoided more especially by family members because it was referred to euphemistically—as it appeared to be a shameful subject that would erode our cultural values.

Over the years, aided by our religious beliefs, we have maintained that sex is a sacred act which only involves two people—the giver and the receiver. But in today's world, sex has been confused with love, and we are being misguided by the notion that abundance of sex equals excessive love and little of the former signifies less of the latter.

In rare occasions it has occurred to us that there is many unions lacking love with abundant intercourse due to the powerlessness of one of the partners.

Besides sex being commercialized in modern times, abundant involvement in sexual activities is ideally good, but the giver-receiver approach is responsible for a lot of bad sex that is evident in our societies today—considering that most of the sex is offered not out of willingness but for monetary remuneration.

382

When you see young givers and receivers on today's streets, they appear to be innocent and ignorant of sexual activities, and don't seem to want sex but they are more desperately in need.

Receivers, more especially those still in teenage, more so the bumbling, fumbling ones who are constantly in high libido, have overrated sex and obstinately think they can get their way with givers, who are animal-like, anyway, and whose minds are mostly occupied by sexual deviation so that wherever they hover, they are designing, crafting ways through which they can get some booty.

Incest is not only addictive and dear, but also infectious in numerous ways. After rounds of sexual intercourse with a receiver met on the computer or telephone chat-line, the giver hops to the younger school receiver, who in turn hops to the giver who owns the latest tinted Dodge Charger; who then returns to his live-in partner, who turns to the neighbor, when the giver is at work, who eventually hooks up with the most attractive, ever, giver at the *Paradox* Night Club in Baltimore or a 15 year old at the basketball pitch—who is badly in need of money to purchase a video game or a pair of sneakers.

In this vicious cycle of incest, we fail to observe the cardinal regulation that uncontrollable erections are very costly to the taxpayer because, in due course, Governments

383

will spend millions to control the spread of some pandemic or STD s.

We all have weaknesses, but some weaknesses which are hounding some of those we are sharing a life-time with are avoidable or in some cases reversible. They must not, under any circumstance, be sexual!

On my part, I strongly believe that it is better to have an alcoholic or drug weakness than to have a sexual problem. Maybe they are equally the same but the sexual weakness is worse because, in most cases, it is commercial and does not necessarily pertain to self-desire or complacence—as may be the case with alcoholism or drug addictions.

Commercial sex, also, does not require a capital formation whereas alcoholism and or drug addictions require some money in one way or another, in order to satisfy the need. It is simply about self-discipline and early, concrete, stout parental involvement in early childhood.

In the Swahili language, once again, the same proverb which states that: Asiyefunzwa na mama, ufunzwa na ulimwengu or *Asiyesikia la mkuu, uvunjinka guu*, meaning that; one who fails to be educated by the mother learns from the world or one who fails to listen to their senior will break their leg, is of utmost importance when considering the consequences of such acts.

In America, for instance, despite all the positives about the country, this seems to be the greatest shortcoming which not only hinders the nation's development and future prosperity but becomes a nonsensical barrier to the motivation of immigrants, who may easily end up in the loss of enthusiasm about raising their children in America.

Internationally speaking, it is also an embarrassment to the historically rather good image of the country, being tarnished, apart from the true domestically known image which is only known by those immigrants who have had the opportunity of exposure to the outside world.

Since Africa is guided by proverbs and stories, I'm obliged to explain a story which is related to this argument, which also justifies my argument that today's children are maturing too early.

This story is about a 14 year old boy in an area called *Maili Nne*, in Kenya, whose residents were treated to some sorrowful drama when the boy handed his mother a pack of condoms instead of a book of matches she had asked for.

Though Noba had done it inadvertently, his mother couldn't hide her shock, and screamed her lungs out before she collapsed in a heap and fainted. The incident alarmed neighbors who rushed to the home to find the boy making frantic efforts to simultaneously hide the offending condoms and offer First Aid to his mother.

Earlier in the day, the family house-help had sought permission to go and visit her parents. The woman had readily granted her request unsuspecting that a plot was being crafted between the maid and her son.

The house-help had secretly arranged with the boy to spend the night in his room and leave very early for her home the following morning.

She had left the home casually but surreptitiously made her way back into the compound and hopped through the window. Noba had left the window of his bedroom unlocked to facilitate the plot.

Their plan, carried out with precision, could have perfectly succeeded were it not for a power blackout in the early evening.

The woman, who was caught in darkness, went to the son's room to borrow a book of matches — as she could not trace any in the house.

Noba, engulfed in darkness and throes of passion, accidentally picked up the pack of condoms, and quickly handed it to his mother. He wanted to prove his obedience and willingness to help his mother at all times.

But when she opened the strange looking "book of matches," she couldn't believe what her two eyes were seeing to find herself holding some condoms and immediately collapsed and fainted.

"What is happening?" asked some neighbors when they found the puzzled boy in a life-time dilemma, wondering what his next action should be.

He was too dazed to explain, and it did not take long for them to gather what had happened. They shone a flashlight at the boy demanding an explanation. Some entered the room and flushed out the house-help.

When the woman came back to consciousness, she found Noba and the house-help kneeling before her, remorseful, pleading for mercy and forgiveness.

In shorter terms, today's teenagers don't really have to devise hidden methods like those that Noba had crafted for his mother—were it not for the power outage. They have what, by most definitions, would qualify as the most perfect booties, at their tender ages.

People stop to stare at them; a thing they have become accustomed to. But they have also realized what a potent asset their booties are. Whether at shopping malls, to or from school, in parks, on the streets, on public buses and trains or clubs, they have mastered the art of tantalizing those in constant pursuit of their youthful booties so they drop their guard, if only momentarily. And that is all they need to go for the kill.

To some of the "old school" minds it is often disgusting while to others, they get aroused and enhance their determination to work extra hours in order to treat these

387

young "angels" to sumptuous delicacies of their desires. For those who are disgusted, by the time they are done ogling, the youthful givers would have gotten what they want.

Likewise, others with similar potent assets, would never trade anything to be in their chasers' Dodge Chargers, Range Rovers, BMW s, Cadillacs, and so forth. All they need to do is bat an eyelid, show some leg, cleavage or just swing some fat booty; and they would get their way with most predators.

This may seem manipulative and cheap. But I guess we have all done it at some point in our lives—by leveraging some part of our sexuality so as to get our way through! The theory is known as *quid-pro-quo* or giving something for something in return.

Back in our childhood days, we learned the innocent wide-eyed look works wonders in melting stone hearts. In the modern times, money is the most common manipulative element, but the youth, who mostly do not have dependable sources of money, know cheaper ways like advertising the body-parts you wanna perceive, flattery, flirting, seduction with dress-codes, chat-lines, innuendos and computers. Nowadays, sex has become a bargaining chip while in the ancient days, barter trade was the mode before people realized that they can cheaply engage themselves in bodily trades which do not require any capital formation.

On the other hand, this is a signal of hopelessness, desperation and shortage of advocacy maybe because the youth feel that they have been let down by Government, their parents, or as a result of historical injustices or due to financial frustrations. This is possible because the sexual arena is the only item that they are in complete control of. They can accept or decline and that is why the youth resort to using sex as a tool for manipulation or as a commodity in a barter trade as they realize their power as the access controllers of sexual intimacy due to their youthful attractiveness. They can use sex to their advantage and withdraw it when it is convenient for them.

In most cases, more frequently than not, it is troubling to use sex in a cold-hearted and calculated manner as a tool for trade. Using sex as a tool for exchanging favors demeans both partners, although it is the common denominator between sexes, friendships, economic classes, and can also sometimes be used, by teenagers, as a way of voicing their concerns, frustrations or may just be out of difficult economic times or domestic brutality, mistreatment by parents—so that teenagers find that the only asset they possess and which they can trade to meet their needs is what most people highly yearn for.

Today's fathers don't really care what habits their children engage in. In any case, prostitution and or incest are both conducts which many fathers have contributed to—in their families in one way or another. When children are left without a father's wisdom in the home, it means that they are growing up half-full; considering that their mothers have to play both roles including work to safeguard the financial well being of the children.

A tragedy such as death of a father is quite understandable and different from when a man cannot settle his own domestic disputes with his wife or when he just tries to be a womanizer. Envision a situation whereby mothers also discarded their children just as most fathers do!

Mothers are therefore supreme. You don't have to look very far to see how many grown men and women still seek their mothers' guidance on a host of issues, which might probably explain why mothers seem to be perpetually at loggerheads with their daughters in-law!

Likewise, sons in-law tend to be in a state of permanent war with their mothers in-law because they believe their wives rely too much on their mothers' counsel. Motherhood is eternal; from the moment of conception at pregnancy to the grave. And yet, more especially in the modern world, mothers seem to suffer most as cases of single parenthood are rising over time resulting to unusual habits among their children—like advance sexual misbehaviors.

Contrary to popular belief, there are certain virtues in mothers that fathers no longer hold at a premium. And since most mothers are unaware that fathers have reviewed their expectations, they are left clutching to virtues that have since waned in importance.

On the other hand, there is honorable mothers of the older days who require their due respect and recognition, whereas there is an upcoming group of phony, uncaring females, who are only wearing feminine physical features but do not deserve the definition of mothers.

These are the ones we see, everyday, parading the streets, dis respectively, and whose sole interest is to trade their bodies at any cost for money.

Their endless desire for money only gives them a reason to paint themselves all the colors of the rainbow. Someone also lied to them that they become more marketable by the way they walk—by swinging their booties from North pole to South pole, in an attempt to attract more idlers. Those behaviors are just as temporary as a seasonal river. Within the shortest time, they will be pregnant, and will not be able to walk majestically any more. The catwalks in the making by modern women who feel like they are on top of the world, when their onuses as mothers have become their wildest dreams, cannot stand the test of time.

In America, for instance, African Americans have engaged in such behaviors or certain dress-codes because of their past history, and sometimes feel less privileged. These sorts of behaviors are simply as a result of inferior feelings, and as a mode of compensation for the same, they end up with a "don't care" attitude but their anger is directed at the world instead of looking for solutions of solving their social problems in an amicable manner.

On their part, all their behaviors and problems arise from the blame on racism and historical injustices, in which they did not carry the real burden as their ancestors did. In any case, their forefathers prepared a level ground for them from which they stand today, pointing fingers at people who are as innocent as they are.

There has been and probably still is, a history of racial injustices in America but it now seems like a good excuse used on the part of African Americans to defend their failures and unwillingness to rightfully succeed just like others.

Looking at all the opportunities and rights available to everyone in America, it only defeats logic when you see people blaming slavery and racism for their failed state. It is good to know your history, but that very history should be an ideal tool for encouragement and determination into a better future rather than a hindrance to progress.

On the case of Africans, they too have a historical story to tell about injustices and racist contentions but it is extremely very rare to find an African basing their failure on past injustices such as colonialism and or the loss of their people through slave trade.

In my view, African Americans tend to be bent toward racial lines more than the White people. During my brief stay in the United States, I have never come across a situation whereby someone is deterred or openly protected from advancement or success just because of their skin color. But, yes, on the part of immigration status.

In fact, in modern America, racial contentions are minimal, but what is being misconstrued as racism by the African American community is disregard, annoyance and discrimination on the grounds of ignorance, savagery and illiteracy—by those who are well informed.

It is annoying when one comes across a person who wants to expose the little they know to the general public, under the pretense that they are well informed. It is simply a form of stupidity, ignorantly disguised by racial claims!

In Africa, for instance, it is very difficult to find a situation whereby people are judging each other on the basis of their skin color or viewing someone of a different skin color as the cause of their failure. Yes, people definitely detect their differences in skin colors but may only refer to one as European, American, Indian, Chinese, Japanese, South African, and so forth, but not in the context of historical differences or grudge, but as a way of simplifying identity. In fact there is more contempt and stereotype between Africans themselves than there is toward foreigners or visitors. An African is more welcoming and friendlier to

393

a European, American, Asian, Australian, and so on, than they are to their fellow brothers and sisters.

In the last historical election in which Barack Obama became the first African American President, ever, in the history of the United States of America, if the facts were the other way round, he wouldn't have been successful in his presidential ambitions. The implication here is that, there is no such a thing as divisions along racial lines on the part of Whites when it comes to putting the country first— considering that were it not for their part, Obama's presidency wouldn't have been possible. In other words, they ignored the race-issue and laid their focus on their ideals and put country first.

However, from my own observation, President Barack Obama, "the son of Kogelo Village," might as well be the first and last African American President in the American Presidential history, at least for many, many decades to come, if the African American community cannot wake up to realities of life and stop pointing fingers at Whites for enslaving them, and Africans for "selling" them to the West, as slaves. They will only continue to be self-made mental slaves in America, and engagements in frivolous, stereotypic reactions to innocent people will not be the solution to their many troubles. The answer lies within their social setting.

The remedies to some of their social problems include facts such as parenting.

Variations in parenting techniques that depict group ways of life are essential influences on the intellectual development of children. The parental relationships between African American parents and their children is almost non-existent—in terms of guidance, wisdom giving, advice, how they deal with aftermath of their children's achievements as well as failures, and so forth. In their case, in fact, each one of them tends to deal with their individual difficulties at personal level without the involvement of the either side.

Their children seem to be left free of care from their early stages of growth in such a manner that they choose their own freedoms and ways of life, which in most cases leads them to prisons due to lack of guidance from their parents. The kind of parental care they mostly seem to lack is physical affection toward them by their parents, attention to the child's concerns, and discipline other than physical punishment, self-respect, and for others, engagement in material, relevant aspects of life, real existence and personal responsibility.

Another problem African American families are facing is baseless rebellion toward society, which in the end leaves them the losers in terms of achieving academic success and their goals. They tend to base all their arguments on unending racism in America; which surely becomes a good reason for laziness, even among innocent children who have no knowledge of racism but because they are born into a society which is constantly blaming racism for its failures. The children therefore, have a good reason not to excel in their academic obligations too because they are born into a society which has already defended their failure under the cover of racial inequality. They are made to believe that however much they succeed or qualify in their academic endeavors, it will still not pay off.

I have in the past come across some African American children who are already convinced that educational matters solely belong to the White community, and so, when they see African immigrants pursuing their further education in the United States, they are convinced that Africans are simply betrayers of the Black race. This includes friendships. When they see Africans who get along with Whites, it only becomes more evidence to them that Africans are "double players."

What they fail to understand, and maybe this is the most crucial part that education plays on an individual, is that we cannot get anywhere if we carry past injustices into the present day! We may be aware of our histories, be angry at others, but let us use that history to bridge the gaps and differences, so we may settle old disputes—for a better tomorrow.

They believe that their academic rebellion justifies their racial resistance, but fail to recognize it is to their detriment which gives rise to their social status in America to this very day.

Evidence of American children's lack of discipline, more especially African American children, can be gathered from their conducts in schools. One wonders if schools are set up to train future gangsters or responsible, patriotic citizens, who are solely concerned about the welfare of their nation. Those who have ever watched a film entitled: *Dangerous Minds*, will definitely comprehend this argument.

Charity begins at home, and without proper training of children by their parents, then it is as good as commissioning a blind person to search for a lost needle in a football stadium. No wonder academic solutions have been discarded by the African American majority, so that each of them now believes they can be professional football players, basket ballers or renown Hip-Hop artists; forgetting that each of us is born with differing gifts of nature.

We cannot all be athletes just because we were born black, and then one wonders, if not worries, if there is much credibility and value in education, not only for material success, but also for its application in diverse aspects in life. And then this eventually grows to be a culture, as it is, whereby all Black children follow suit what they have inherited from their seniors and in the end it becomes a society of wasted minds.

For instance, a student who is constantly ranked as an average student is likely to be less hard working than one who is an A student and has at some point slipped to A-. The latter will of course not want to lose his position because it is easier for him or her to detect their weakness and adjust, whereas the former tends to despair. If you research both their ways of life, you might find out that the average student spends more time on Black Entertainment Television (BET) and other unnecessary entertainment, than the better students do. This is truly a fact with most American children. They tend to place fun and entertainment before serious matters of concern which may otherwise determine their future prosperity, and if this is the trend, then it means that America will keep on depending on foreign manpower and outsourcing, which makes it difficult or impossible for them to compete with other children of the world in almost all challenging aspects of life.

Instead of African American children trying to find ways in which they can catch up with the rest of the world's children, they have continuously remained at the same position over time and seemingly given up in the race. But again, not all the blame lies on them. The blame also lies on the ways of life set up to govern them; considering that not really much exposure is granted them about the rest of the world so that they are time and again forced to believe that they are the best in the world, when the truth is unknown to them. All the same, maybe life has become too easy for today's children because it is very rare to find many of them who can work out simple division, addition and or multiplication sums, mentally — without the use of a calculator.

Poverty cannot provide academic benefits. Culture can provide informal education just like it was in the ancient times before the invention of formal education because children who are well nurtured and cultural, know how to respect their seniors, know their respective responsibilities, including self-respect, and so on. Culture, in this context refers to knowledge, enlightenment and sophistication acquired through education and exposure to the arts. Not Hip-Hop madness!

Most African American children have been confused by the Hip-Hop syndicate which has confused the word "culture" for social deviation, and are now engaging in acts that are completely unacceptable in any social setting, such as exhibitionism. These are all effects arising from lack of parental involvement in their children's well being, poverty, frustrations, and urban residence.

These behaviors are detectable at an early stage of the Black child's development—an indication that these conducts are sort of hereditary, and there is something in the lives of these children that is limiting their intellectual growth. The same problem has also been detected among children of African descent who have been raised in African American neighborhoods. They as well tend to blindly adopt similar protocols possibly due to friendships or because they think it is cultural to be socially irrelevant.

On our streets too, it is very rare, if not impossible, to find an African American gathering informative information from books, magazines or simply being informed about the world and current affairs—by reading newspapers. No wonder it has become an ordinary thing to Africans when they are asked maddening questions such as: "Are you from Nigeria, Egypt, Ethiopia or Africa?" "Do you still have Kings in Africa?" "Why is there AIDS in Africa?" And if they must watch excessive television, then watching news on other TV channels would be more helpful than an obsession with BET.

As a consequence, African American children have disciplinary problems throughout their school lives. Although some of them hide under the excuse of racism and historical injustices for their misconduct, there is no convincing verity for that claim.

Excelling in school, just like any other serious obligation in life, requires determination and continuous hard work but most African American children spend most of their time on video games, music and BET; which cannot augment anything fruitful to their school studies—the only known key to success unless they are naturally gifted in other areas such as sports or entertainment. But still, even talented athletes or entertainers still require some extra skill and, or knowledge in their industries for investments and growth.

Just by having an African American President or even a complete Black government is not enough to solve the many social problems the Black race faces in America, and unless a complete overhaul of their ways of life and beliefs is done, they will eternally remain where they are.

Firstly, this must commence with the change of their attitudes, recognition, and respect for other cultures, more especially the Whites and Africans, with whom they should freely interact in order to awaken themselves from that hole of misinformation, ignorance, in which they are hounded, and be ready to face new challenges as well as verities of life. The bigger chunk of pride mixed up with sheer ignorance must be done away with—just like babies who upon weaning, give up their mothers' breasts for good and embark on solid food.

African American academic under-achievement, despite rooted historical injustices, has over time, since the eradication of slavery, in the 1860s and other provisions such as guaranteed freedom to equal civil and human rights, been propped up by repetitive excuses to old injustices and racism so that the loser is the past victims of the historical

401

injustices—because their descendants have not made good of their struggles and enslavement.

In Africa, for instance, there was injustice and denial to basic human rights and opportunities up to as recent as in the early 1990s—in Southern Africa. But Africans chose to let history be history and pressed forward because insistence on the past cannot bring any social, economic development and other positive changes to the lives of the people. This is why diversity, interaction and consequent exposure is of essence to the African American community, so that they may learn new ways in which they can bring fundamental change and solutions to the many social, economic obstacles they currently face. Africans too have their problems; but they do not have as many options and opportunities as African Americans do. In fact, were it not for hard work, dedication and academic achievement, despite the many other hindrances in between, the African continent would not have come this far, within a short period—in all aspects of life.

The only known major problem which the African continent is facing today is the "governance problem" and the management, allocation of national resources—which leads to "Allocative and X-inefficiencies," in proper economic terms. Now that obstacles such as illiteracy, poverty levels, disease and lack of exposure or enlightenment, on the part of Africans, are in their gradual eradication, there is hope of prosperity. Leadership positions are also being taken over by younger, enlightened and educated minds.

On the part of African Americans, the answer is simply within them and at hand but they have obstinately refused to swallow their pride and focus on a better tomorrow. These are some of the strongest words of concern: education, ignorance, self-discipline, racial isolation, fantasy, irrelevance, pride, acting Black, parenting practices, excessive entertainment, responsibility, commitment, dedication, hard work and respect.

The truth, distilled from conventional wisdom is that we all aspire to be wealthy, live in the best suburbs, drive the most expensive vehicles, take a vacation abroad. When the end of our short stories comes about, we expect to be laid in an expensive casket, with dignitaries attending our funeral and obituaries appearing in the press.

Yet, those of us who are lesser than the more privileged tend to envy their achievements and assets. To equal them, most poor people sometimes try to live beyond their means. As a matter of fact, those who drive the most expensive vehicles, in America and elsewhere, are the poor, who want to act as if they are wealthy or just think that success is defined by the kind of car you drive or mostly, for the lucky ones, those who unexpectedly meet fortunes, such as lottery winners, boxers, athletes and entertainers.

By driving cars with expensive rims and a five-thousand dollar music system and or television, they are unaware that they are only enriching the company owners of the very vehicles they are showing off with, while they increase their debt.

However, there is the harsh truth that getting opulent is not easy. The rich rarely explain to us how they ended up becoming wealthy. And even if they had a forum, not all the details would come up in their minds; essential elements to success like patience, commitment, orderliness, can only be experienced as they advance toward their opulence. That is what is sometimes referred to as "tacit knowledge" which cannot be codified.

Poignantly, the rich become successful under varying environments and circumstances, which are endlessly versatile and dynamic.

In an attempt to comprehend how people become successful while in schools and other institutions of higher learning, still the algorithm that guarantees material success remains illusionary. We can of course describe the behaviors and characteristics of the opulent, the process on how to become wealthy is still a panoramic illusion, not at the individual level alone, but at the national level, as well. It is the same philosophy as to why some countries are richer than others, and sometimes seems easy to explain in form of excuses, but at the individual level, given opportunities and resources in order to succeed can also be impossible. Then I think it is wise to say that those who are blessed with abundant wealth may as well be some of the talented few; just like athletes, musicians, poets, writers. There is people who can come across a rare opportunity of, for instance, 100,000,000 dollars, and still due to their inexperience, and other reasons, end up failing.

Others believe that, in order to become materially successful you need to talk to Donald Trump or Bill Gates. That does not work. I strongly believe that these two individuals can only advise you on how to invest and manage your money, and not how to get to their level—which then gives us a reason that most successful people are naturally born talented or destined to succeed in whichever way.

This is why we should all accept our positions and the fact that we are who and what we are destined to be. We must never envy our brothers and sisters but accept that there is a reason why they are rich, keeping in mind that they too, have their share of tribulations which may otherwise be larger than ours.

We have many a time come across people who are extraordinarily wealthy but are barren or impotent. Their money only becomes useless after their earthly lives as they have no descendants to inherit their riches. On the other hand, we have poor men and women who have been blessed with certain things, which the rich cannot afford to buy with their money. Again, there are some of us who are poorer than the poor and yet still happier than the comfortably poor and the excessively rich, as they have nothing to worry about. Within their small world, they have no business with computers, TVs, telephones, fax machines, mail, vehicles, but still happier than those who are constantly hounded by the everyday worries of materialism.

All of us cannot become rich. Just envision a world whereby everyone is rich. The difference will only be the same, and material possessions will be meaningless and will therefore be no growth and development, and possibly, people will stop thinking. So, each of us has a role to play in life. The biggest problem is that people are worshiping material possessions instead of using material assets as a tool to advance to the next level with ease or a medium of exchange between the state of living and poverty, or not having. Everything has its pros and cons, just like one who does not drive has little to worry about vehicle expenses or emotions which arise when a car cannot start or when it breaks down on a rainy day. Conversely, the driver does not have to worry about the consequences of walking on frozen snow or fulfilling many of their obligations within a short time.

As much as opulence has its negative consequences, poverty too has its own; which are definitely not anomie suicide, but when they turn against the rich due to their defeated state, either through attitudes or at times physically through robbery or theft, the insecure rich have to barricade themselves behind walls, electric fences and doors, and big, dear vehicles. The more they protect themselves from the indigent, the more mysterious they become to us, and again the more our tempers flare toward them. Just like the rich countries give financial donations to poor nations, or through programs like welfare, unemployment benefits and others, to the majority poor in America, then they are able to cool the flaring tempers of the poor.

Without such remedies, and if they are left to fend for themselves, like is the case in African countries, they would end up with unexplainable bitterness which would drive them beyond the understanding why someone drives a Range Rover HSE Sport alone, while someone else has involuntarily missed three basic meals.

Then, children must be taught on how to be successful, and not about the beauty of wealth. That is what is ravaging the spirit of American children; as they want to be rich in a day just like all the rich people they see. It becomes difficult for them even to see the significance of education when they imagine cheaper shortcuts towards opulence.

American children are surrounded by so much material wealth, that they sit back and forget their roles as children. Maybe, distant boarding schools, just like the Military men and women, St. Mary's Mosocho, Cardinal Otunga High

School, or Kisii High School, would do them good so that they are kept away from what is not theirs to enable them concentrate on their future—since the rich and the poor rarely meet each other.

Without measures to all these arguments and wisdom-filled analysis, societies will always be raising people endowed by nature, risk takers such as bank robbers and petty thieves, Dependants of the rich and the few who see opportunities others cannot see.